ASCENT®
CENTER FOR TECHNICAL KNOWLEDGE

Autodesk® Civil 3D® 2022
Fundamentals
Part 1

Learning Guide
Imperial Units - 2nd Edition

AUTODESK.
Authorized Publisher

ASCENT - Center for Technical Knowledge®
Autodesk® Civil 3D® 2022
Fundamentals - Part 1
Imperial Units - 2nd Edition

Prepared and produced by:

ASCENT Center for Technical Knowledge
630 Peter Jefferson Parkway, Suite 175
Charlottesville, VA 22911

866-527-2368
www.ASCENTed.com

Lead Contributor: Jeff Morris

ASCENT - Center for Technical Knowledge (a division of Rand Worldwide Inc.) is a leading developer of professional learning materials and knowledge products for engineering software applications. ASCENT specializes in designing targeted content that facilitates application-based learning with hands-on software experience. For over 25 years, ASCENT has helped users become more productive through tailored custom learning solutions.

We welcome any comments you may have regarding this guide, or any of our products. To contact us please email: feedback@ASCENTed.com.

Contents
Part 1

Contents
Part 2

Preface

The *Autodesk® Civil 3D® 2022: Fundamentals* guide is designed for Civil Engineers and Surveyors who want to take advantage of the Autodesk® Civil 3D® software's interactive, dynamic design functionality. The Autodesk Civil 3D software permits the rapid development of alternatives through its model-based design tools. You will learn techniques enabling you to organize project data, work with points, create and analyze surfaces, model road corridors, create parcel layouts, perform grading and volume calculation tasks, and lay out pipe networks.

Topics Covered

- Learn the Autodesk Civil 3D 2022 user interface.

- Create and edit parcels and print parcel reports.

- Create points and point groups and work with survey figures.

- Create and manage styles and label styles.

- Create, edit, view, and analyze surfaces.

- Create and edit alignments.

- Create data shortcuts.

- Create a Civil 3D template drawing.

- Create sites, profiles, and cross-sections.

- Create assemblies, corridors, and intersections.

- Create grading solutions.

- Create gravity fed and pressure pipe networks.

- Perform quantity takeoff and volume calculations.

- Use plan production tools to create plan and profile sheets.

Prerequisites

*   Access to the 2022.0 version of the software, to ensure compatibility with this guide. Future software updates that are released by Autodesk may include changes that are not reflected in this guide. The practices and files included with this guide might not be compatible with prior versions (e.g., 2021).

*   Experience with AutoCAD® or AutoCAD-based products and a sound understanding and knowledge of civil engineering terminology.

Note on Software Setup

This guide assumes a standard installation of the software using the default preferences during installation. Lectures and practices use the standard software templates and default options for the Content Libraries.

Configuration Changes

The following configuration changes need to be made to ensure the practices run smoothly. For more information on making these configuration changes, consult the Civil 3D help menu.

*   Set the *Template* file location to ***C:\Civil 3D Projects\Ascent-Config***, as shown below.

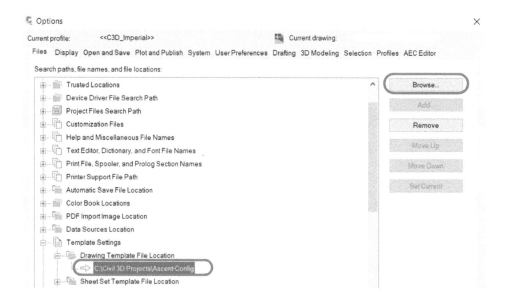

- Set the *Pipe Catalog* location to **C:\Civil 3D Projects\Ascent-Config\Pipes Catalog**, as shown below.

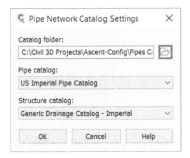

- Set the *Pressure Pipe Catalog* location to **C:\Civil 3D Projects\ Ascent-Config\Pressure Pipes Catalog\Imperial**, as shown below.

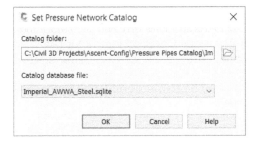

Students and Educators Can Access Free Autodesk Software and Resources

Autodesk challenges you to get started with free educational licenses for professional software and creativity apps used by millions of architects, engineers, designers, and hobbyists today. Bring Autodesk software into your classroom, studio, or workshop to learn, teach, and explore real-world design challenges the way professionals do.

Get started today - register at the Autodesk Education Community and download one of the many Autodesk software applications available.

Visit www.autodesk.com/education/home/

Note: Free products are subject to the terms and conditions of the end-user license and services agreement that accompanies the software. The software is for personal use for education purposes and is not intended for classroom or lab use.

Lead Contributor: Jeff Morris

Specializing in the civil engineering industry, Jeff authors training guides and provides instruction, support, and implementation on all Autodesk infrastructure solutions.

Jeff brings to bear over 20 years of diverse work experience in the civil engineering industry. He has played multiple roles, including Sales, Trainer, Application Specialist, Implementation and Customization Consultant, CAD Coordinator, and CAD/BIM Manager, in civil engineering and architecture firms, and Autodesk reseller organizations. He has worked for government organizations and private firms, small companies and large multinational corporations and in multiple geographies across the globe. Through his extensive experience in Building and Infrastructure design, Jeff has acquired a thorough understanding of CAD Standards and Procedures and an in-depth knowledge of CAD and BIM.

Jeff studied Architecture and a diploma in Systems Analysis and Programming. He is an Autodesk Certified Instructor (ACI) and holds the Autodesk Certified Professional certification for Civil 3D and Revit.

Jeff Morris has been the Lead Contributor for *Autodesk Civil 3D: Fundamentals* since 2019.

In This Guide

The following highlights the key features of this guide.

Feature	Description
Practice Files	The Practice Files page includes a link to the practice files and instructions on how to download and install them. The practice files are required to complete the practices in this guide.
Chapters	A chapter consists of the following - Learning Objectives, Instructional Content, Practices, Chapter Review Questions, and Command Summary.
	• **Learning Objectives** define the skills you can acquire by learning the content provided in the chapter.
	• **Instructional Content**, which begins right after Learning Objectives, refers to the descriptive and procedural information related to various topics. Each main topic introduces a product feature, discusses various aspects of that feature, and provides step-by-step procedures on how to use that feature. Where relevant, examples, figures, helpful hints, and notes are provided.
	• **Practice** for a topic follows the instructional content. Practices enable you to use the software to perform a hands-on review of a topic. It is required that you download the practice files (using the link found on the Practice Files page) prior to starting the first practice.
	• **Chapter Review Questions**, located close to the end of a chapter, enable you to test your knowledge of the key concepts discussed in the chapter.
	• **Command Summary** concludes a chapter. It contains a list of the software commands that are used throughout the chapter and provides information on where the command can be found in the software.
Appendices	Appendices provide additional information to the main course content. It could be in the form of instructional content, practices, tables, projects, or skills assessment.

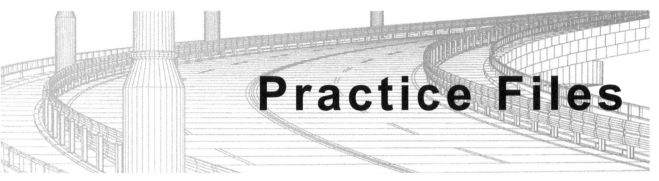

Practice Files

To download the practice files for this guide, use the following steps:

1. Type the URL *exactly as shown below* into the address bar of your Internet browser, to access the Course File Download page.

   Note: If you are using the ebook, you do not have to type the URL. Instead, you can access the page simply by clicking the URL below.

   https://www.ascented.com/getfile/id/ceratocentronPF

   Note: If you are completing the optional practices in Appendix A, you will need to download the point cloud file from the URL below.

   https://www.ascented.com/getfile/id/ceratochilusPF

2. On the Course File Download page, click the **DOWNLOAD NOW** button, as shown below, to download the .ZIP file that contains the practice files.

3. Once the download is complete, unzip the file and extract its contents.

   The recommended practice files folder location is:
   C:\Civil 3D Projects

   Note: It is recommended that you do not change the location of the practice files folder. Doing so may cause errors when completing the practices.

Stay Informed!

To receive information about upcoming events, promotional offers, and complimentary webcasts, visit:

www.ASCENTed.com/updates

The Autodesk Civil 3D Interface

In this chapter, you will learn about the Autodesk® Civil 3D® software interface and terminology. You will learn how to navigate the available workspaces and the Toolspace, and how to work in a dynamic model environment. You will also learn how to change the settings within the program to conform to specific standards.

Learning Objectives in This Chapter

- Switch between the Autodesk Civil 3D tools, 2D drafting and annotation tools, 3D modeling tools, and planning and analysis tools by changing the workspace.
- Locate the basic features and commands of the Autodesk Civil 3D software interface, which include the Ribbon, Drawing Window, Command Line, and Toolspace.
- Access commands by right-clicking on an object or collection of objects in the *Prospector* and *Settings* tabs in the Toolspace.
- Access predefined reports and create custom reports to share useful engineering data about AEC objects in a drawing.

1.1 Product Overview

The Autodesk Civil 3D software supports a wide range of Survey and Civil Engineering tasks. It creates intelligent relationships between objects so that design changes can be updated dynamically.

- The Autodesk Civil 3D software uses dynamic objects for points, alignments, profiles, terrain models, pipe networks, etc. Objects can update when data changes. For example, if an alignment changes, its associated profiles and sections update automatically. Commands can be safely undone in the software without the graphics becoming out-of-date with survey and design data.

- These objects are style-based and dynamic, which streamlines object creation and editing.

- Autodesk Civil 3D objects (surfaces, alignments, etc.) are often stored directly inside drawing files. The exception is when working with the Autodesk Data Management System (Vault), data shortcuts, or a survey database.

- The Autodesk Civil 3D software supports a multiple document interface. This means that more than one drawing file can be open in the same session of the Autodesk Civil 3D software at the same time.

- The Autodesk Civil 3D software can be launched by selecting its icon on the desktop or by accessing the command through the Start menu. The icon indicates Imperial or Metric. Once launched, the software initiates with the standard Autodesk Civil 3D profile. Your BIM Manager can customize the shortcut to have the software launch with project based settings. This is accomplished using a custom profile.

1.2 Autodesk Civil 3D Workspaces

When the Autodesk Civil 3D software is launched for the first time, a *Let's Get Started* window displays, as shown in Figure 1–1. This window is used to verify your Autodesk Civil 3D license. There are three options for communicating your license information:

- Sign In: Use your Autodesk Subscription account information to verify your purchase.

- Enter a Serial Number: Manually type in your software serial number and software key.

- Use a Network License: Point the software to your network license server to find the software license.

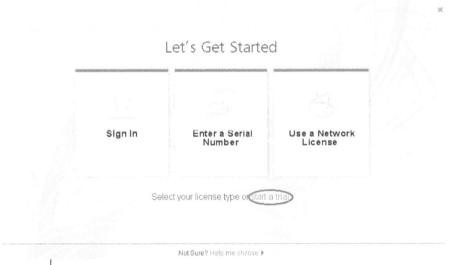

Figure 1–1

Start Tab

By default, the *Start* tab is continually available even when a drawing file is open. It enables you to complete several actions, as shown in Figure 1–2:

- Open existing files (1)

- Create new drawings from template files (2)

- Review and open recent documents (3)

- Browse to Autodesk Docs (4)

- Access Learning Videos and Tips (online) (5)

- Various online tools and support (6)

- File Type (either local or cloud-based) (7)

- Select the search columns to display (8)

- Opens the **Connect** panel to submit feedback to improve the Civil 3D Product (9)

- Pin a drawing to the Start screen to be a permanent display on the Start screen (until it is unpinned) (10)

- Choose to open the drawing as Read Only or not (11)

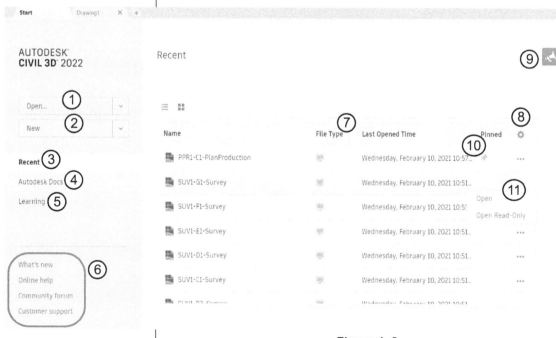

Figure 1–2

Hint: In order to open Autodesk Docs cloud-based drawings, you need to have access to Autodesk Docs.

The *Start* tab is persistent even when other drawings are open. This makes it easier and faster to open or start new drawings. If the *Single Drawing Interface* is enabled (**SDI** System Variable set to **1**), then the Start tab will vanish. The *Single Drawing Interface* only allows one drawing to be opened a a time. When another drawing is opened, the current drawing must close.

The Civil 3D workspace is the default workspace upon initiation of Civil 3D. It is recommended that you stay in the Civil 3D workspace most of the time. As a review, AutoCAD® Workspaces are saved groupings of menus, toolbars, and palettes, which can be customized as required for specific tasks. You can modify the default workspaces supplied with the Autodesk Civil 3D software or create your own. In this material, you work with the Civil 3D workspace, which includes a complete list of Autodesk Civil 3D-specific ribbons, drop-down menus, and tools.

Workspaces can be changed using the Workspaces switching icon in the lower right corner of the Status Bar, as shown in Figure 1–3. They can also be modified using the **CUI** command. **Note:** This task is typically performed by your BIM Manager.

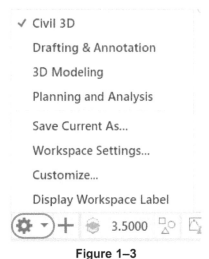

Figure 1–3

Each of the ribbons from the workspaces are shown in order in Figure 1–4 and include the following:

- **Civil 3D workspace:** Contains tools used to create AEC objects, such as surfaces, alignments, profiles, corridors, grading objects, etc.

- **Drafting & Annotation workspace:** Contains tools that are commonly used in the standard AutoCAD software, such as those in the *Home* tab>Draw and Modify panels.

- **3D Modeling workspace:** Contains standard AutoCAD 3D modeling tools for designing 3D solids, mesh surfaces, etc.

- **Planning and Analysis workspace:** Contains tools found in the AutoCAD® Map 3D® software that help you to attach and analyze GIS data for more efficient planning of projects before starting your design.

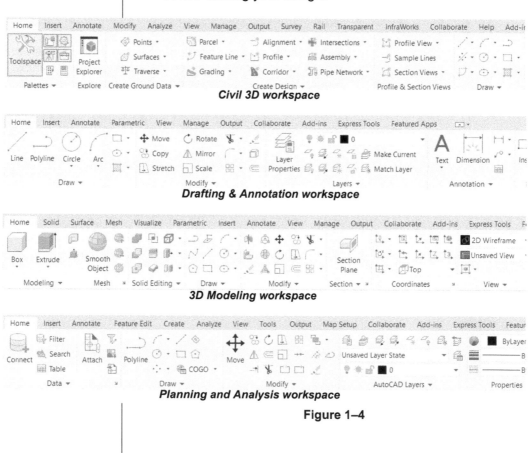

Figure 1–4

1.3 Autodesk Civil 3D User Interface

The Autodesk Civil 3D software user interface is shown in Figure 1–5.

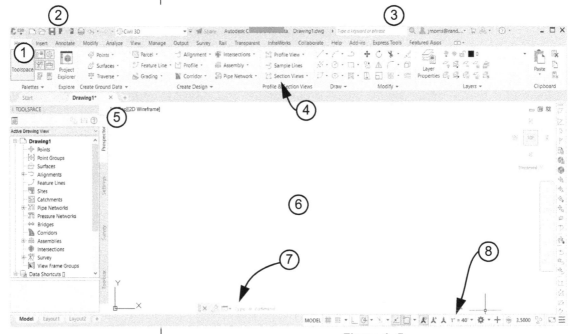

Figure 1–5

1. Application Menu	5. Tooltips
2. Quick Access Toolbar	6. Drawing Window
3. InfoCenter	7. Command Line
4. Ribbon	8. Status Bar

1. Application Menu

The *Application Menu* provides access to commands, settings, and documents, as shown in Figure 1–6. With the Application Menu, you can:

- Perform a search of menus, menu actions, tooltips, and command prompt text strings.

- Browse for recent documents, currently open documents, and commands you have recently executed.

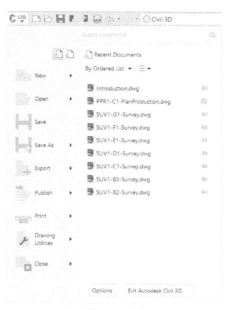

Figure 1–6

2. Quick Access Toolbar

The *Quick Access Toolbar* provides access to commonly used commands, such as **Open**, **Save**, **Print**, etc. You can add more tools to the Quick Access Toolbar by clicking the down arrow on the right, as shown in Figure 1–7.

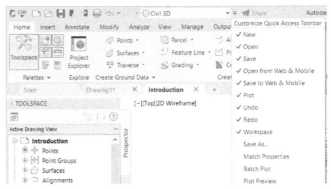

Figure 1–7

Share

Share your current drawing by using the  (Share) command in the Quick Access Toolbar. It opens a dialog box to create a copy of the current drawing for viewing only or for editing and saving it, as shown in Figure 1–8.

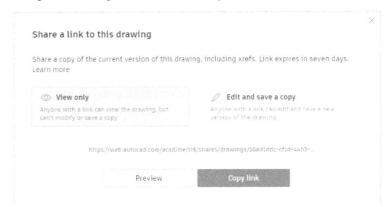

Figure 1–8

3. InfoCenter

The *InfoCenter* enables you to quickly search for help. You can specify which Help documents to search, and collapse or expand the search field (as shown in Figure 1–9) to save screen space. You can also sign in to the Autodesk 360 service, where you can use various tools in the Autodesk cloud.

(Autodesk App Store) provides the ability to connect to the Autodesk App Store to find additional efficiency-enhancing applications.

Figure 1–9

4. Ribbon

The *ribbon* provides a single, compact location for *commands* that are relevant to the current task. Most of the time, you work in the *Home* tab. When annotating the model, you switch to the *Annotate* tab. It contains tools in a series of *tabs* and *panels* to reduce clutter in the application and maximize drawing space. Selecting a tab displays a series of panels. The panels contain a variety of tools, which are grouped by function, as shown in Figure 1–10.

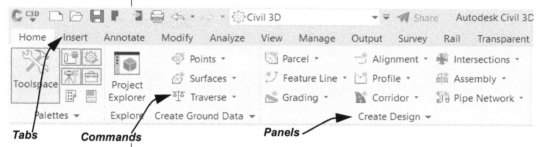

Figure 1–10

Clicking the drop-down arrow expands the panel to display additional tools, as shown in Figure 1–11. Clicking an arrow pointing to the bottom right opens the tool's dialog box, which contains additional options.

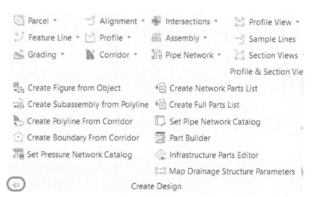

Figure 1–11

The expanded panel collapses again to its normal state when you either select a command or move your cursor off of the panel. To prevent this, you can pin the expanded panel by clicking on the pin icon ( ) in the lower left corner of the panel. When a panel is pinned, the icon changes to a pinned state ( ).

You can minimize the ribbon by clicking the arrow successively on the far right of the tabs, as shown in Figure 1–12.

Figure 1–12

There are two classifications of ribbons: static and contextual.

- **Static Ribbons:** Display the most commonly used tabs, panels, and commands.

- **Contextual Ribbons:** Display the tabs, panels, and commands that are only applicable to the selected object. An example of a contextual ribbon is shown in Figure 1–13. The contextual ribbon tabs are always the last tab on the far right of the tabs.

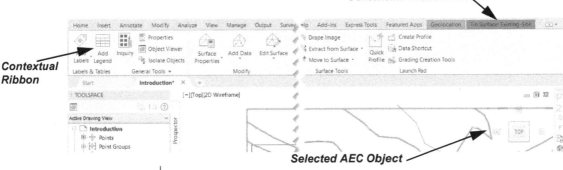

Figure 1–13

Depending on your screen size, screen resolution, and the menu or workspace you have, there may not be enough room for all tabs to display. In that case, a double arrow icon (▶▶) appears. When you select it, it lists the hidden tabs for you to select, as shown in Figure 1–14.

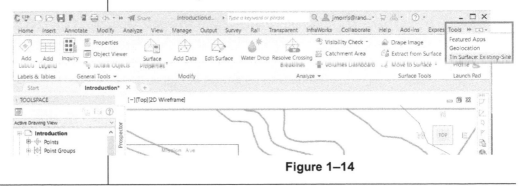

Figure 1–14

---

5. Tooltips

Tooltips display the item's name, a short description, and sometimes a graphic. They provide information about tools, commands, and drawing objects, as shown in Figure 1–15.

Tooltips can be turned off and a display delay can be set in the Options dialog box> Display tab.

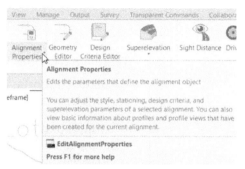

Figure 1–15

6. Drawing Window

The *Drawing Window* is the area of the screen where the drawing displays.

7. Command Line

The *Command Line* is a text window that is located at the bottom of the screen and displays command prompts and a history of commands, as shown in Figure 1–16.

To toggle the Command Line display on or off, press <Ctrl>+<9>.

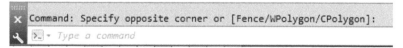

Figure 1–16

8. Status Bar

The *Status Bar* enables you to change many of AutoCAD's drafting settings, such as Snap, Grid, and Object Snap. Not all the available tools are shown by default (e.g., Coordinates).

Click ☰ (Customization) to toggle on more available tools in the Status Bar, as shown in Figure 1–17.

Customization

Figure 1–17

Practice 1a

Overview of Autodesk Civil 3D and the User Interface

Practice Objective

- Locate the basic features and commands of the Autodesk Civil 3D software interface which includes the Ribbon, Toolspace, Drawing Window, Command Line, etc.

In this practice, you will become familiar with Autodesk Civil 3D's capabilities and learn about its interface.

Task 1 - Set up the practice.

In this task, you will add a folder shortcut in the pane on the left side of the Select File dialog box. This enables you to quickly access the practice files folder in the Open dialog box.

1. If required, start the Autodesk Civil 3D 2022 Imperial application.

2. In the *Start* tab, click ⌒ (Open), or expand

   ⌒ C3D (Application Menu) and select **Open**. In the Select File dialog box, browse to the *C:\Civil 3D Projects\ Working* folder.

3. Expand the Tools drop-down list and select **Add Current Folder to Places**, as shown in Figure 1–18.

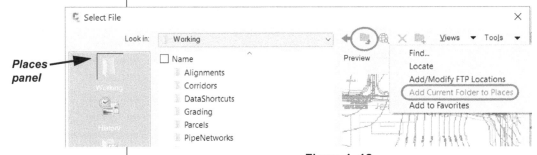

Figure 1–18

4. After you create the new entry into your *Places*, use the up arrow as shown in Figure 1–18 to go up one folder. Alternatively to adding an entry via the drop-down list as you did in the previous step, you could drag and drop the *Working* folder to the Places panel from this level.

5. Browse to the *References\DWG* folder.

6. Select **Introduction.dwg** and then select **Open.**

*If prompted to save the changes to your Places panel, click **Yes**.*

7. When the drawing opens, a notification bubble pops up in the lower right corner regarding *Unreconciled New Layers*, as shown in Figure 1–19. This means that some new layers have been discovered since the last time the drawing was opened.

Figure 1–19

Consult with your organization's CAD Management standards how to manage Layer Reconciliation.

8. Click on the blue **View unreconciled new layers...** link to open up the Layer Properties Manager. Click ⚙ (Layer Settings) in the top right corner, and in the Layer Settings dialog box, uncheck the **New Layer Notification** option, as shown in Figure 1–20. This will not reconcile the layers, but it will prevent the notification from appearing the next time you open this drawing.

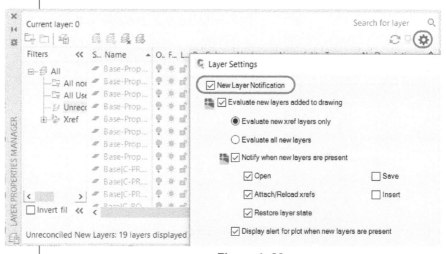

Figure 1–20

9. Click **OK** to close the Layer Settings dialog box, and then close the Layers Properties Manager dialog box.

10. In the Status Bar, confirm that **Civil 3D** is the active workspace. The Workspace icon is located in the Status Bar (bottom right of the interface) and in the Quick Access Toolbar (top left of the interface), as shown in Figure 1–21.

Figure 1–21

11. Click on the *Insert* tab and then click on the down arrow on the Import panel. The panel expands, as shown in Figure 1–22. Move your cursor back to the drawing area and the panel contracts. Click on the down arrow once again, then click on the pin icon ( ). This time when you move the cursor, the panel remains expanded. Click on the unpin icon

( ) to let the panel contract again.

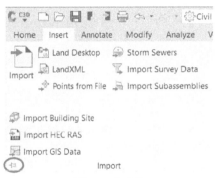

Figure 1–22

12. Click on the *Home* tab to return to the Home ribbon.

By default, the Toolspace is docked to the left side of your drawing window.

13. Locate the Autodesk Civil 3D Toolspace (as shown in Figure 1–23). If you cannot find it, click 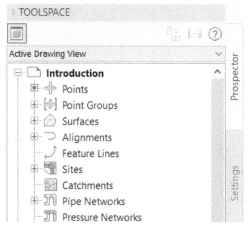 (Toolspace) in the *Home* tab>Palettes panel.

Figure 1–23

14. Save the drawing as **Intro-A1.dwg**. To do this, expand

     (Application Menu) and select **Save As**. Browse to the *C:\Civil 3D Projects\References\DWG* folder and in the *File Name* field, type **Intro-A1**. Click **Save**.

Task 2 - Review Autodesk Civil 3D's dynamic object model.

---

1. In the top left corner of the drawing window, select **-** (dash or minus symbol) for Viewport Control. Expand **Viewport Configuration List>Custom Viewport Configuration** and select **Plan-Profile**, as shown on the top in Figure 1–24.

   - Alternatively, in the *View* tab>Model Viewports panel, select **Named**, then select **Plan-Profile** from the *Named Viewports* tab of the Viewports dialog box, as shown on the bottom in Figure 1–24.

   This will divide the screen horizontally and zoom into the alignment in the bottom portion and the surface profile to the upper portion.

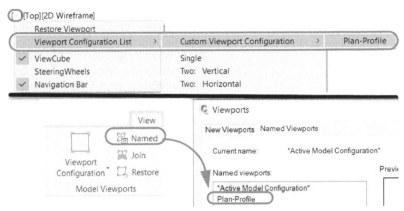

Figure 1–24

You may need to disable the Osnap (press <F3>) to be able to relocate the grip.

2. Select the **Jeffries Ranch Rd** alignment to activate its grips, as shown in Figure 1–25. (If there is a series of cyan square grips, it means you have selected the alignment labels, not the alignment. Press <Esc> and try again.) Select the eastern triangular grip and reposition it northward. The alignment and profile both update. The constraints built into the Civil 3D alignment will not allow you to drag it too far.

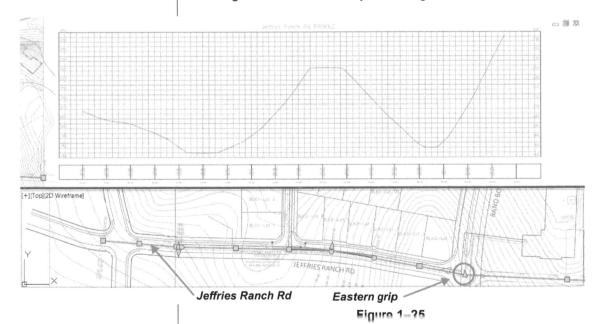

Jeffries Ranch Rd   Eastern grip

Figure 1–25

3. Hover the cursor near the alignment in its new position. Ensure that you are hovering over a blank section of the drawing, not over the alignment, surface contour, etc. The station, offset, and surface elevation information display through tooltips.

4. Select the eastern grip and reposition it back near its original position. The alignment and profile both update again.

5. In the top left corner of the drawing window, select **+** (plus symbol) for Viewport Control. Expand **Viewport Configuration List** and select **Single**.

6. Save and close the drawing.

1.4 Autodesk Civil 3D Toolspace

The Autodesk Civil 3D software uses a Toolspace to manage objects, settings, and styles. Each tab uses a hierarchical tree interface to manage objects, settings, and styles. Branches in these hierarchical trees are referred to in the Autodesk Civil 3D software as *collections*. The Toolspace is an interactive data management tool.

Toolspace operates similar to an AutoCAD tool palette in that it can be resized, set to dock or float, and when floating can be set to auto-hide. The Toolspace is shown floating on the left in Figure 1–26 and docked on the right in Figure 1–26. Note that the *TOOLSPACE* title is vertical in the floating position, whereas it is horizontal on top when docked.

Right-clicking on a collection or on an individual object provides many commonly used commands in the shortcut menus.

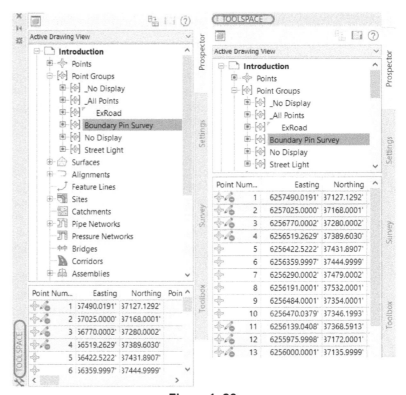

Figure 1–26

- The Toolspace can be closed by selecting the **X** in the upper left or right corner.

- Once closed, it can be opened by clicking ✳ (Toolspace) in the *Home* tab>Palettes panel.

- By right-clicking on the vertical title bar (when the palette is floating), you can anchor the palette either on the right or left side of the screen, as shown in Figure 1–27. It will be contracted when not in use, but when you hover over it, it will expand. When you hover over another space on your screen, it will contract again.

Figure 1–27

> **Hint: Anchoring the Toolspace**
>
> If you have multiple screens, it is best to keep the Toolspace floating and leave **Auto-hide** unchecked on the second screen. If you only have one screen, it is recommended to have the Toolspace anchored left or right. You need to activate the **Allow Docking** feature before the Anchor options become active.

Prospector Tab

The Toolspace, *Prospector* tab lists the Autodesk Civil 3D objects that are present in open drawings and other important information. Its hierarchical structure dynamically manages and displays objects and their data. As objects are created or deleted, they are removed from the *Prospector* tab. A drop-down list at the top contains the following options:

- **Active Drawing View:** Displays only the Autodesk Civil 3D objects that are present in the active drawing. If you switch to another drawing, the tree updates to reflect the currently active drawing.

- **Master View:** Displays a list of all open drawings and their objects, project information, and a list of drawing templates. The name of the active drawing is highlighted.

The Toolspace, *Prospector* tab is shown in Figure 1–28.

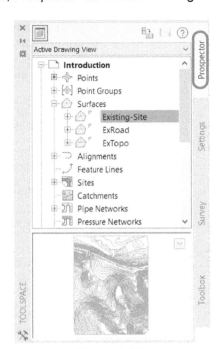

Figure 1–28

- To toggle the display of the Toolspace, *Prospector* tab on or off, click (Prospector) in the *Home* tab>Palettes panel.

- Each object type (Points, Point Groups, Alignments, Surfaces, etc.) is allotted a collection, and objects present in a drawing are listed below the respective collection.

- The bottom of the Toolspace, *Prospector* tab displays a list view of items in the highlighted collection or a preview of an object that has been selected in the Toolspace, *Prospector* tab. The preview options are toggled off by default. You will learn how to turn on the preview functions.

- The icon at the top of the Toolspace, *Prospector* tab controls how items in the Prospector tree display. Icons next to objects provide additional information about the object. A list of common icons is as follows:

	Toggles the Toolspace item preview on or off.
	Toggles floating Toolspace window orientation from Top / Bottom to Left/Right
	Opens (or closes) the Panorama window. This window only opens if vistas are available to be displayed in the Panorama.
	Opens the Autodesk Civil 3D Help system.
	Indicates that the object is currently locked for editing.
	Indicates that the object is referenced by another object. In the Toolspace, *Settings* tab, this also indicates that a style is in use in the current drawing.
	Indicates that the object is being referenced from another drawing file (such as through a shortcut or Vault reference).
	Indicates that the object is out of date and needs to be rebuilt, or is violating specified design constraints.
	Indicates that a vault project object (such as a point or surface) has been modified since it was included in the current drawing.
	Indicates that you have modified a vault project object in your current drawing and that those modifications have yet to be updated to the project.

Hint: Project Explorer

The new Project Explorer offers a lot of the same features as the *Prospector* tab, but with many improvements. For more information, see *Appendix B: Project Explorer*.

Settings Tab

To toggle the Toolspace, Settings tab display on or off, click

 *(Settings) in the Home tab>Palettes panel.*

The Toolspace, *Settings* tab is used to configure how the Autodesk Civil 3D software operates and the way Autodesk Civil 3D objects are displayed and printed, as shown in Figure 1–29.

Figure 1–29

Different settings are accessed by right-clicking on the name of a drawing file or on one of the collections located inside the tab.

The collections (such as the *Parcel* collection shown in Figure 1–29) can contain object styles, label styles, command settings, and related controls.

Changes to settings affect all lower items in the tree. For example, assigning an overall text height in the drawing's Edit Label Style Defaults dialog box applies that height to all other settings and styles in the drawing. Applying the same setting in the *Surface* collection's Edit Label Style Defaults only applies the text height to the surface label styles. (Lower items in the tree and styles can be set to override these changes individually as required.)

- All drawing settings originate from the reference template attached to the drawing or, if no reference template is used, the drawing template that is used to create an Autodesk Civil 3D drawing.

- To toggle the display of the Toolspace, *Settings* tab on or off, click (Settings) in the *Home* tab>Palettes panel.

Survey Tab

To toggle the Toolspace, Survey tab display on or off, click

 (Survey) in the Home tab>Palettes panel.

The Toolspace, *Survey* tab is used to manage survey observations data, as shown in Figure 1–30. Selecting this tab enables you to create a survey database, a survey network, points, and figures, and import and edit survey observation data.

Figure 1–30

Toolbox Tab

The Toolspace, Toolbox tab can be toggled on and off by clicking

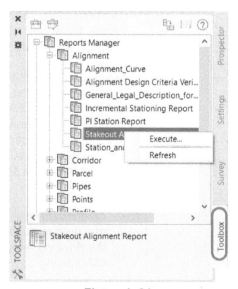 (Toolbox) in the Home tab>Palettes panel.

The Toolspace, *Toolbox* tab is used to access the Reports Manager and to add custom tools to the Autodesk Civil 3D interface, as shown in Figure 1–31.

Figure 1–31

The Reports Manager, the only set of tools that displays in the toolbox by default, enables you to generate a large variety of survey and design reports. For example, to launch a Stakeout Alignment Report, right-click on it in the *Alignments* collection and select **Execute**.

The icons in the upper left area of the Toolspace, *Toolbox* tab enable you to:

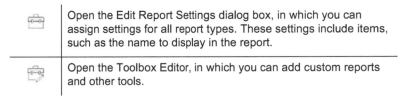	Open the Edit Report Settings dialog box, in which you can assign settings for all report types. These settings include items, such as the name to display in the report.
	Open the Toolbox Editor, in which you can add custom reports and other tools.

Open the Edit Report Settings dialog box by clicking on the (Edit Report Settings) in the top left corner to enter all the pertinent information for the reports, such as the client's and your company's name, addresses, etc., as well as the units to be used for the various Civil 3D objects the reports will be accessing, as shown in Figure 1–32.

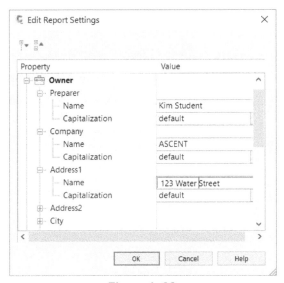

Figure 1–32

Once a report has been executed, it can be saved in multiple formats, including .HTML, .DOC, .XLS, .TXT, and .PDF. To save it in a format other than the default .HTML, expand Files of type and select the type of file required, as shown in Figure 1–33.

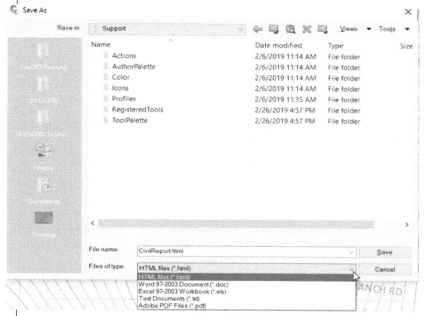

Figure 1–33

Hint: Project Explorer

The new Project Explorer offers alternatives to creating tables and reports, providing additional flexibility and improvements. For more information, see *Appendix B: Project Explorer*.

1.5 Autodesk Civil 3D Panorama

The Autodesk Civil 3D software includes a multi-purpose grid data viewer called the *Panorama window*. It is similar to an AutoCAD tool palette in that it can be docked or floating, and set to auto-hide. Each tab in the Panorama is called a *vista*. The Panorama can be opened from the Autodesk Civil 3D Toolspace by clicking ⬚ (Panorama), and can be closed by selecting the **X** in the upper left or right corner of the window. You can only display the Panorama after launching a command that uses it, such as **Edit Points** (right-click on a Point Group in the Toolspace, *Prospector* tab in the Toolspace to access this option). The Panorama can display many different kinds of data, such as point properties, alignment, and profile data, as shown in Figure 1–34.

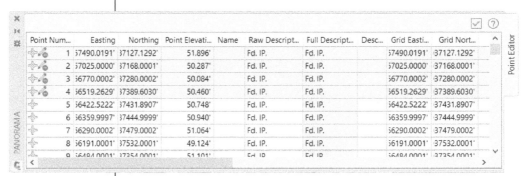

Figure 1–34

*If a Panorama contains multiple vistas, selecting a green checkmark only closes the current vista. To close (hide) the Panorama, click the **X** in the top right or left corner.*

The Panorama can also display a special vista called the *Event Viewer*, as shown in Figure 1–35. The *Event Viewer* opens prompting you about the status of the performed action. If every thing was successful, it displays a white circle containing a blue **i**, indicating that it is for informational purposes only. When there are items of interest or an item needs attention, a yellow triangle containing a black **!** (exclamation point) displays.

When the Autodesk Civil 3D software encounters a processing error, such as when surface breaklines cross or a road model passes over the edge of the existing ground surface, a red circle containing a white **x** displays. When working through a large number of events, you can use **Action>Clear All Events** to clear all of the old entries in the Panorama.

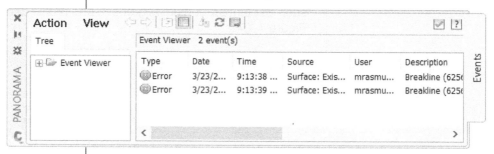

Figure 1–35

Hint: Project Explorer

The new Project Explorer offers a lot of the same features as the Panorama and its vista tabs, but with many improvements. For more information, see *Appendix B: Project Explorer*.

Practice 1b

Autodesk Civil 3D Toolspace

Practice Objective

- Access commands and change the drawing using the Autodesk Civil 3D Toolspace.

In this practice, you will explore the tabs in the Autodesk Civil 3D Toolspace.

Task 1 - Review the Toolspace, *Prospector* tab.

1. Open **Introduction.dwg** from the *C:\Civil 3D Projects\References\DWG* folder.

If the Toolspace is not displayed, click

(Toolspace) in the Home tab>Palettes panel.

2. Ensure that the Autodesk Civil 3D Toolspace displays.

3. Select the Toolspace, *Prospector* tab to make it active. (The tabs are listed vertically along the right side of the Toolspace.)

4. Select the **+** signs to open the collections and the **-** signs to close them. Items displayed in the Toolspace, *Prospector* tab are the design data (also known as AEC objects) currently in the drawing file (such as points, alignments, and surfaces).

5. Collections, such as *Points*, do not have a **+** or **-** sign because they are not intended to be expanded in the tree view of the Toolspace, *Prospector* tab. Select the **Points** collection and the list view displays in the Preview area, describing the Autodesk Civil 3D points that are currently in the drawing file.

6. Under the *Surface* collection, look for the surface called **ExTopo**. Expand its branch and the *Definition* area inside it. Highlight the items below (breaklines, boundaries, etc.) and note the components displayed in the list view.

7. With ExTopo's breaklines expanded and highlighted in the list view, right-click on *Ridge* and note the commands available in the shortcut menu, as shown on the left in Figure 1–36. Select **Zoom to**.

Similar shortcut menus are available for nearly all of the objects displayed in the Toolspace, Prospector tab.

8. Expand the Point Groups and select the **Boundary Pin Survey** point group. In the Preview area at the bottom, press <Shift> to select both point numbers **2** and **3**, as shown on the right in Figure 1–36. Right-click and select **Zoom To**. Although the points are not displayed, the software knows where they reside in the drawing. Use the **AutoCAD Zoom Previous** command to return to the previous zoom level.

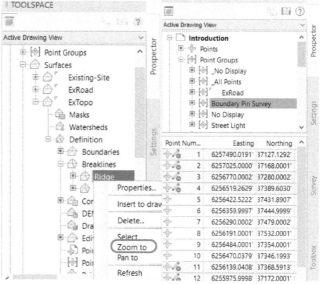

Figure 1–36

Task 2 - Review the Toolspace, *Settings* tab.

1. Select the Toolspace, *Settings* tab, as shown in Figure 1–37.

Figure 1–37

2. In the Toolspace, *Settings* tab, right-click on the drawing's name (**Introduction**, at the top), and select **Edit Drawing Settings**.

3. In the Drawing Settings dialog box, select the *Units and Zone* tab, as shown in Figure 1–38.

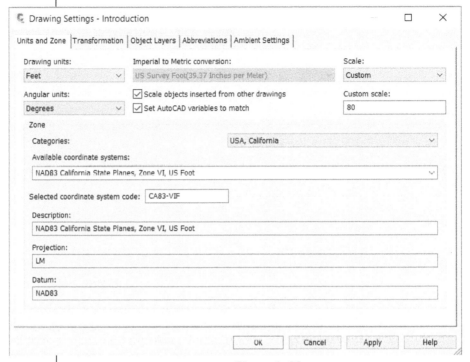

Figure 1–38

4. Expand the Scale drop-down list in the upper right corner and select **1"=40'**.

5. Note the coordinate systems that are available in the *Zone* area, such as CA83-VIF, NAD83 California State Planes, Zone VIF, US Foot.

6. Click **OK** to close the dialog box.

7. You can also change the Model Space display scale using the **Annotation** icon in the Status Bar. Change it to read **1"=80'**. Note that as you change the scale, all of the labels also change in size, as shown in Figure 1–39.

- Because Autodesk Civil 3D labels are annotative, the label annotation size has changed to match the new Drawing Scale. If the AutoCAD text within the XREFs is set to annotative to the proper drawing scales, it too will change.

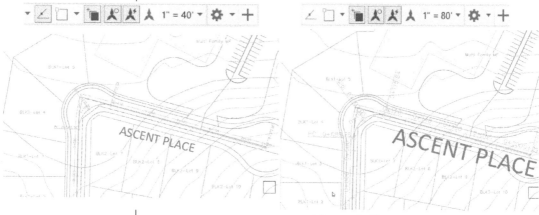

Figure 1–39

8. You can change the display of the contours by changing the style of the surface. In the drawing, select the surface object (for example, select a contour), so that the contextual tab displays in the ribbon, as shown in Figure 1–40.

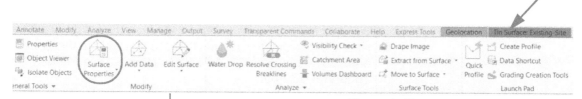

Figure 1–40

Alternatively, you can right-click and select Surface Properties.

9. In the Modify panel, click (Surface Properties).

10. In the *Information* tab, select the drop-down arrow for the surface style, as shown in Figure 1–41. Select any of the predefined styles and click **Apply** to apply the selected style to the surface to preview the results before they display in the dialog box.

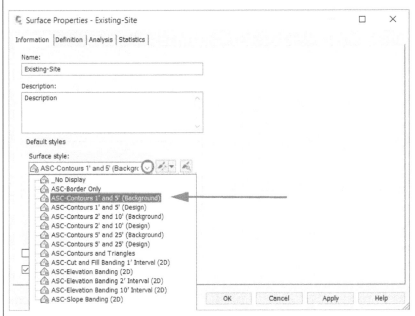

Figure 1–41

11. Click **OK** to exit the Surface Properties dialog box.

12. Save the drawing.

Task 3 - Review Autodesk Civil 3D's Reports Manager.

1. In the Toolspace, select the *Toolbox* tab.

2. Click (Edit Report Settings) in the top left corner.

3. Expand the **Owner** category and add your name as the **Preparer**, your **Company**, and other information, as shown in Figure 1–42.

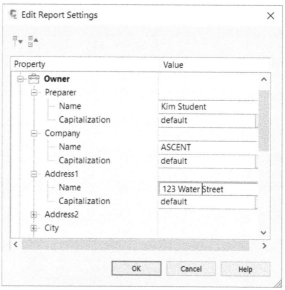

Figure 1–42

4. Time permitting, also fill out some of the information under Client, then click **OK** to accept the values.

5. Expand Reports Manager>Alignment, then right-click on **PI Station Report**, and select **Execute**, as shown in Figure 1–43.

*As a shortcut, you can double-click to launch the **Report** without having to select the **Execute** command.*

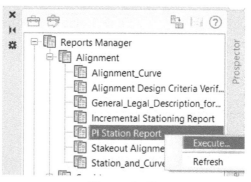

Figure 1–43

6. Accept all of the defaults and click **Create Report**. The report displays, as shown in Figure 1–44.

Alignment PI Station Report

Client:
Client
Client Company
Address 1
Date: 4/14/2020 5:52:03 PM

Prepared by:
Preparer
Your Company Name
123 Main Street

Alignment Name: Ascent PI
Description:
Station Range: Start: 0+00.00, End: 6+98.38

PI Station	Northing	Easting	Distance	Direction
0+00.00	2,036,643.0632'	6,256,521.2052'		
			353.170'	N1° 18' 05"E
3+53.17	2,036,996.1421'	6,256,529.2258'		
			381.930'	S75° 03' 44"E
6+98.38	2,036,897.6924'	6,256,898.2491'		

← # 7

Figure 1–44

7. Review the report and close the Internet Browser.

8. In the Create Reports dialog box, click **Done**.

9. In the Toolspace, *Toolbox* tab, expand the *Surface* collection. Select **Surface Report**, right-click, and select **Execute**, as shown in Figure 1–45.

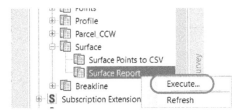

Figure 1–45

10. Accept all of the defaults and click **OK**. Type a filename for the saved report or accept the default. Expand the Files of type drop-down list, select **.XLS** and select **Save**. The report displays in Microsoft Excel, as shown in Figure 1–46. Review and close the report.

If an error occurs when trying to output the report to an .XLS format, try the HTML format instead.

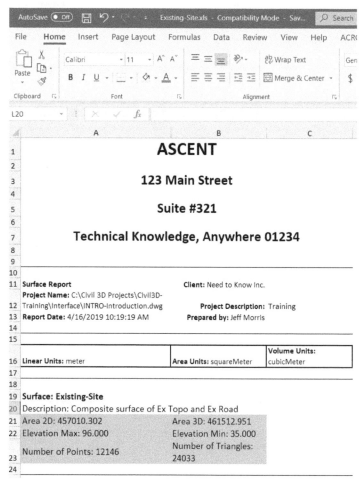

Figure 1–46

1.6 Autodesk Civil 3D Templates and Settings

A drawing template (.DWT extension) contains all blocks, Paper Space title sheets, settings, and layers for a new drawing. As with the AutoCAD software, a template (.DWT) file in the Autodesk Civil 3D software is the source file from which new drawings acquire their settings, units, layers, blocks, text styles, etc., and therefore, enforces standardization. With the Autodesk Civil 3D software, in addition to the AutoCAD components noted, the drawing template is also the source for specific Autodesk Civil 3D styles and settings.

As you will learn, Autodesk Civil 3D styles and settings (Feature and Command) have a profound impact on the appearance of objects, labels, and tables. These styles and settings also act as the primary mechanism that controls the behavior and default actions. Selecting the correct template for your intended design and standards needs is a significant component of fully using the benefits that the Autodesk Civil 3D software offers. Therefore, it is highly recommended that all styles and setting be set up in the template file before you use the Autodesk Civil 3D software in a project.

To use the Autodesk Civil 3D software efficiently and effectively, you need to understand the nature of the AEC Object styles and configure styles and settings to control the object display. All of these styles and settings affect the final delivered product and enable you to deliver a product with consistent quality.

Drawing Settings in Detail

The values in Drawing Settings influence every aspect of the drafting environment. Each tab has values affecting a specific drawing area. For example, layer naming properties, coordinate systems, default precisions, input and output conventions, abbreviations for alignment, volume units, etc. After implementing the Autodesk Civil 3D software, most of the time you will only need to access the first two tabs. The other tabs are used for tweaking your current drawing environment, when needed.

To access Drawing Settings, in the Toolspace, Settings tab, select and right-click on the drawing name (at the top), and select **Edit Drawing Settings**.

Units and Zone

In the Drawing Settings dialog box, the *Units and Zone* tab (as shown in Figure 1–47), sets the Model Space plotting scale and coordinate zone for the drawing. The scale can be a custom value or selected from a drop-down list. A zone is selected from a drop-down list of worldwide categories and coordinate systems.

A drawing which has been assigned a coordinate system enables points to report their grid coordinates and/or their longitude and latitude. Conversely, when assigning a coordinate system, grid coordinates and Longitude and Latitude data can create points in a drawing.

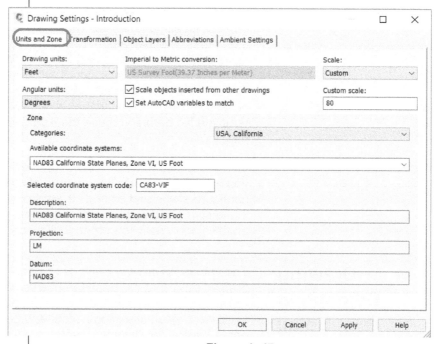

Figure 1–47

When plotting from the *Model* tab, the drawing scale in the upper right corner is the scale at which you would prefer the drawing to be printed. When in the *Model* tab, changing this scale automatically updates all Autodesk Civil 3D annotations that are scale-dependent. (Autodesk Civil 3D annotations are automatically resized for correct plotting in each viewport that displays them based on that viewport's scale.)

*Refer to the AutoCAD Help if you need more information on variables, such as **ltscale**, **msltscale**, and **psltscale**.*

Changing the drawing scale does not automatically change the **ltscale** variable. It is recommended that you set **ltscale** to **1** and ensure that **msltscale** and **psltscale** are also set to **1**. If this is not the case, you need to assign this variable manually.

You can also set the drawing scale by assigning a different annotation scale in the Status Bar, as shown in Figure 1–48. In layouts you can change either the VP Scale or Annotation Scale and have both update.

Figure 1–48

Transformation

During the life of a project, there can be reasons to change assumed point coordinates to a coordinate system. The values in the *Transformation* tab (as shown in Figure 1–49) transform local coordinates to a State Plane Coordinate system, UTM system, or other defined planar system.

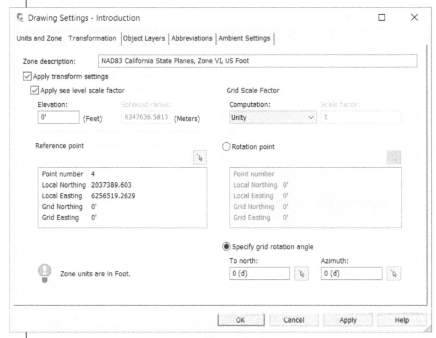

Figure 1–49

Object Layers

The *Object Layers* tab (shown in Figure 1–50) assigns layer names to Autodesk Civil 3D objects. A modifier, which can be a prefix or a suffix, is associated with each layer's name. The value of the modifier can be anything that is typed into its *Value* field. Traditionally, the value is an * (asterisk) with a separator (a dash or underscore). The Autodesk Civil 3D software replaces the asterisk with the name of the object of the same type. For example, the base surface layer name is **C-TOPO** with a suffix modifier of -* (a dash followed by an asterisk). When a surface named **Existing** is created, it is placed on the layer **C-TOPO-EXISTING**, and when a surface named **Base** is created it is placed on the layer **C-TOPO-BASE**.

The last column of the *Object Layers* tab enables you to lock the values. When a value is locked at this level, the Autodesk Civil 3D software does not permit it to be changed by any lower style or setting.

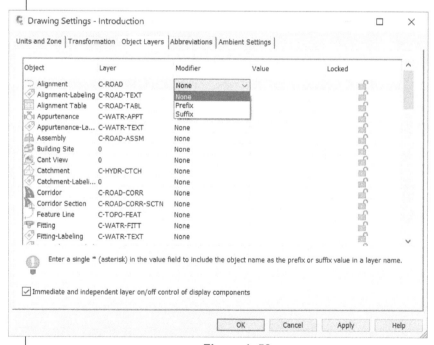

Figure 1–50

To change the listed object layers, double-click on a layer name. In the Layer Selection dialog box (shown in Figure 1–51), select the layer from the list. If the layer does not exist, click **New** in the Layer Selection dialog box. This opens a second dialog box, in which you can define a new layer for the object type.

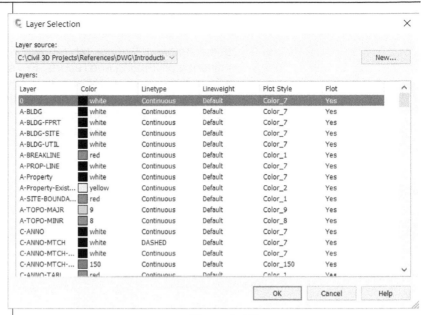

Figure 1–51

Abbreviations

The *Abbreviations* tab (shown in Figure 1–52) sets standard values for reports referencing alignment or profile data. Some entries in this panel have text format strings that define how the values associated with the abbreviation display in a label.

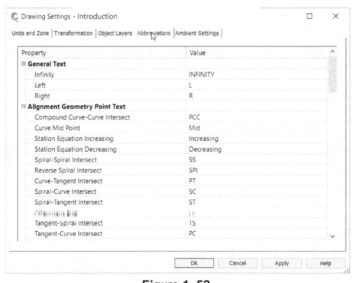

Figure 1–52

Ambient Settings

In the *Ambient Settings* tab (shown in Figure 1–53), the values influence prompting and reports. For example, the *Direction* area affects the prompting for direction input: **Decimal Degrees**, **Degrees Minutes and Seconds** (with or without spaces), or **Decimal Degrees Minutes and Seconds**. Any value set at this level affects everything (labels and commands) in the drawing.

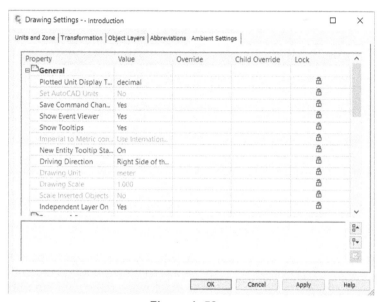

Figure 1–53

Edit Label Style Defaults

The values assigned in the Edit Label Style Defaults dialog box (shown in Figure 1–54) control text style, plan orientation, and the basic behavior of label styles. Similar to Feature Settings, this dialog box is available at the drawing level and at the individual objects level. Editing Label Style defaults at the drawing level affects all label styles in the drawing. Editing them at the object level (such as surfaces) only affects that object's labels.

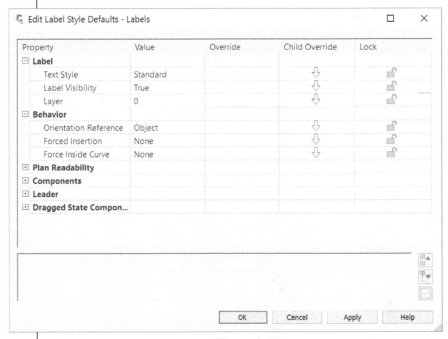

Figure 1–54

In the *Label, Behavior,* and *Plan Readability* areas, the values affect the overall visibility of labels, their default text style, label orientation, and the rotation angle that affects plan readability.

The values in the *Components, Leader,* and *Dragged State Components* areas affect the default text height for the label, colors for the text, leader, surrounding box, and type of leader. There are also several settings defining what happens to a label when you drag it from its original position.

Edit Autodesk LandXML Settings

The LandXML Settings dialog box (shown in Figure 1–55) provides settings that control how Autodesk LandXML data is imported and exported from the Autodesk Civil 3D software. Autodesk LandXML is a universal format for storing Surveying and Civil Engineering data that enables you to transfer points, terrain models, alignments, etc., between different software platforms. For more information, see *www.landxml.org* and the Autodesk Civil 3D Help system. The dialog box can be opened by right-clicking on Drawing Name in the Toolspace, *Settings* tab and selecting **Edit LandXMLSettings**.

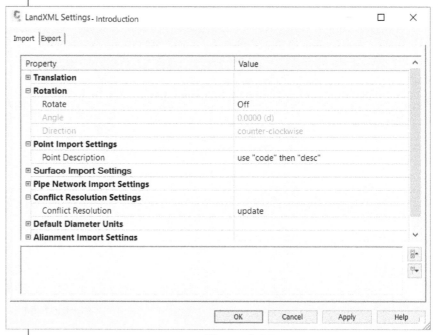

Figure 1–55

Feature Settings

In the Toolspace, *Settings* tab, each object type collection has an Edit Feature Settings dialog box, as shown for Surface in Figure 1–56. Its main function is to assign default naming values, initial Object and Label styles, and overriding the default values found in Edit Drawing Settings for that object type. You can access the feature settings by right-clicking on the object tree in the Toolspace, *Settings* tab and selecting **Edit Feature Settings**.

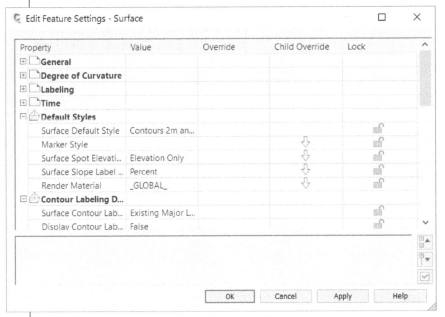

Figure 1–56

Command Settings

Similar to feature settings, in the Edit Command Settings dialog box (shown in Figure 1–57), you can set the default object and label styles used when creating objects with a specific command. Each object type contains a unique set of commands. Typical values in these dialog boxes include the name format (surface 1, parcel 1, etc.), design criteria (minimum area, frontage, length of vertical curve, and minimum horizontal curve), etc. To open the dialog box, expand a collection in the Toolspace, *Settings* tab until the commands display. Right-click on the command to which you want to assign default settings and select **Edit Command Settings**.

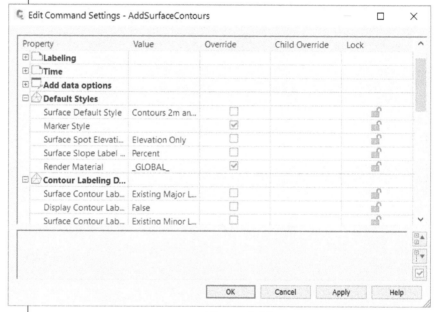

Figure 1–57

Hint: Style and Setting Overrides

In the Edit Label Style Defaults, Feature Settings and similar dialog boxes, a downward pointing arrow in the Child Override column indicates that a setting or style lower in the settings tree has a different value than the one displayed. Selecting the arrow (which creates a red **x** over the icon) and clicking **OK** removes the variant settings and makes all lower settings and styles match those assigned in the dialog box. This can be a quick way of standardizing multiple settings dialog boxes and styles at the same time.

For example, in the Surface Label Style defaults window (shown in Figure 1–58), some surface label styles are assigned a layer other than 0 and a visibility of false, because an arrow is present in the *Child Override* column. Since an arrow is not shown for the Text Style property, all surface label styles are using a text style of **Standard**.

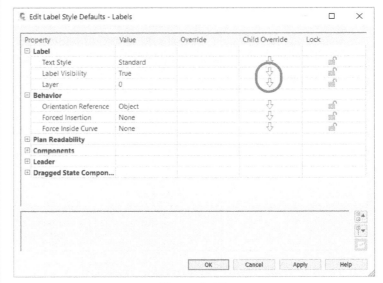

Figure 1–58

The *Override* column indicates whether a value in this window is overriding a higher settings dialog box. Clicking the **Lock** icon prevents you from changing that value in a lower setting's dialog box or style.

Hint: Styles and label styles are covered throughout the book in various chapters and exercises as required.

Practice 1c | Autodesk Civil 3D Settings

Practice Objective

- Modify Civil 3D settings.

In this practice, you will modify Autodesk Civil 3D settings and create styles.

1. Continue working in the drawing from the last practice. If you closed it, open **Introduction.dwg** from the *C:\Civil 3D Projects\References\DWG* folder.

2. Select the Toolspace, *Settings* tab to make it active.The tabs are listed vertically along the right side of the Toolspace.

3. In the Toolspace, *Settings* tab, right-click on the drawing's name (**Introduction**, at the top), and select **Edit Drawing Settings**.

4. In the Drawing Settings dialog box, select the *Object Layers* tab, as shown in Figure 1–59.

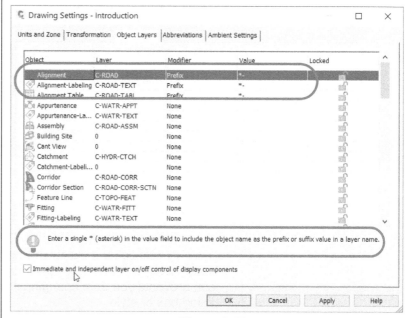

Figure 1–59

5. For the first three rows dealing with alignments, use the drop-down list in the *Modifier* column to select **Prefix**, in the *Value* column type ***-** (asterisk dash). Note in the lower part of the notice that an asterisk is a substitute for the object's name.

6. Select the *Abbreviations* tab.

7. Under *Alignment Geometry Point Text*, *Curve Mid Point*, change the existing **Mid** text to **MD**, as shown in Figure 1–60.

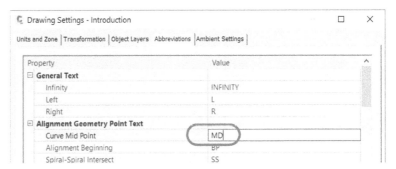

Figure 1–60

8. Select the *Ambient Settings* tab.

9. Under *Elevation>Unit*, use the drop-down list to select **meter**, as shown in Figure 1–61.

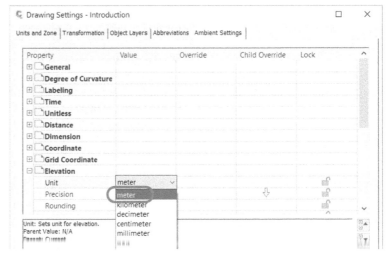

Figure 1–61

10. Click **OK** to dismiss the Drawing Settings dialog box.

11. Zoom into the knuckle bend of the Ascent Place alignment.

12. Hover the cursor over an empty space until the tooltip appears displaying the surface elevation information. Note that the surface elevation is shown in meters, whereas the distance of the Station Offsets (SO) of the alignments remain in feet, as shown in Figure 1–62.

13. Note that the curve midpoint text still shows as **Mid**. Type **RE** (for Regen) at the command line. The drawing regenerates and now the curve midpoint text displays as **MD**, as shown in Figure 1–62.

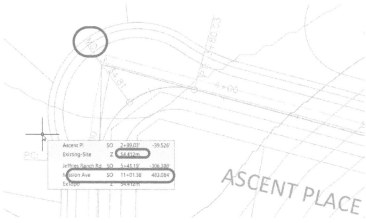

Figure 1–62

14. Pan southward to the intersection of Jeffries Ranch Rd and Ascent Place.

15. To the right of the existing Alignment Station Offset label, create another label. A convenient way of doing this is to select the Jeffries Ranch Rd alignment (the green line running east to west). In the contextual ribbon, from the *Add Labels* drop-down list, select **Station/Offset Fixed Point,** as shown in Figure 1–63.

Figure 1–63

16. Select a point to the west of the existing label.

17. Click on the existing label, right-click and pick Properties.
    Note the layer of the label - it is *C-ROAD-TEXT.*

18. Press <Esc> to deselect the first label and repeat the
    procedure for the label you just added. Its layer is *Jeffries
    Ranch Rd-C-ROAD-TEXT,* as shown in Figure 1–64. This is
    because you set the alignment labels (and other alignment
    objects) to have a prefix of the alignment name and a dash.

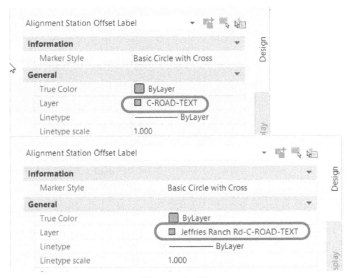

Figure 1–64

19. Save and close the drawing.

Chapter Review Questions

1. Which Workspace should you be in if you want to create an AEC object (surfaces, alignments, profiles, etc)?

   a. 2D Drafting and Annotation

   b. 3D Modeling

   c. Civil 3D

   d. Planning and Analysis

2. What does the Toolspace, *Prospector* tab do?

   a. Sets the layers for AEC objects.

   b. Lists the AEC objects and provides access to their information.

   c. Sets the workspace in which you want to work.

   d. Enables you to connect to GIS data from a number of sources.

3. What does the Toolspace, *Settings* tab do?

   a. Sets the layers and display styles for AEC objects.

   b. Creates templates from which new drawings are based.

   c. Creates new drawings with references to data.

   d. Generates Sheets for printing purposes.

4. How do you open the Edit Drawing Settings dialog box?

   a. Type **CUI** in the Command Line to open the Customize User Interface dialog box.

   b. **Application menu>Drawing Utilities**.

   c. In the Toolspace, *Prospector* tab, right-click on the drawing name.

   d. In the Toolspace, *Settings* tab, right-click on the drawing name.

5. What is the main function of the Panorama window?

   a. Setting up styles for AEC objects.

   b. Reviewing and editing tabular AEC object data.

   c. Pan inside the drawing.

   d. Look at the AEC objects in 3D views.

Command Summary

Button	Command	Location
☒	Close	• **Drawing Window** • **Application Menu** • **Command Prompt:** close
	Close Current Drawing	• **Application Menu**
	Open	• **Quick Access Toolbar** • **Application Menu** • **Command Prompt:** open, <Ctrl>+<O>
	Prospector	• **Ribbon:** *Home* tab>Palettes panel • **Command Prompt:** prospector
	Settings	• **Ribbon:** *Home* tab>Palettes panel • **Command Prompt:** settings
	Surface Properties	• **Contextual Ribbon:** *Surface* tab> Modify panel • **Command Prompt:** editsurfaceproperties
	Survey	• **Ribbon:** *Home* tab>Palettes panel • **Command Prompt:** survey
	Toolbox	• **Ribbon:** *Home* tab>Palettes panel • **Command Prompt:** toolbox
	Toolspace	• **Ribbon:** *Home* tab>Palettes panel • **Command Prompt:** toolspace

Survey, Points, and Linework

This chapter focuses on automated Field to Finish tools that aid in drafting an accurate and efficient Existing Conditions Plan. These tools create a correct existing topography, property lines, right-of-ways, and center line locations based on survey data collected in the field. You will learn how to create parcels from a legal description using the Autodesk® Civil 3D® Lines and Curves commands and the transparent commands. The chapter also covers the important topic of Civil 3D Styles and how they are managed. Styles will be modified and new styles will be created.

Learning Objectives in This Chapter

- List the steps used to create linework from coordinate files, in a typical survey workflow.
- Create a figure database for stylizing linework automatically.
- Create point marker and label styles to annotate points.
- Set the appropriate point creation settings and the next available point number.
- Create points manually using the Create Points toolbar.
- Assign point symbols, labels, layers, etc., automatically when importing points by setting up Description Key Sets.
- Import points from ASCII files created from the field survey.
- Group points together using common properties, such as name, elevation, description, etc.
- Review and edit points using the Panorama window to ensure accuracy.
- Share information about points used for error checking or stake out points using predefined reports.
- Draw parcels from a legal description.

2.1 Survey Workflow Overview

Workflow

To create linework from coordinate files, use the following survey workflow:

1. Data needs to be entered into the data collector. The correct language, methodology, and basic rules regarding data entry into the data collector begin with an understanding of Figure Commands and Field Codes (raw descriptions).

2. Data can be transferred from the data collector to the computer using an ASCII file or an electronic field book. An ASCII file can be opened in Notepad and data can be separated or delineated by spaces or commas. The most popular transfer format is Comma Delimited Point Number, Northing, Easting, Elevation, Description (PNEZD) format. This material focuses on the different types of Descriptions that can be entered into a data collector so that the user obtains the required automated symbology and linework.

3. If using an electronic field book file (a type of ASCII file), data needs to be converted from the raw coordinate file to a field book (*.FBK) using Survey Link or other methods of the Autodesk® Civil 3D® software. Autodesk has collaborated with major survey equipment vendors to develop API and drivers that interface their specific survey equipment (Trimble Link, TDS Survey Link, Leica X-Change, TOPCON Link, etc.) with the Autodesk Civil 3D software.

   If following the **Linework Code Set** command format, you do not need to convert the coordinate file to a field book. The Autodesk Civil 3D software needs to have all of the necessary Styles, Settings, and Figure Prefixes to create, sort, and place points and linework on the required layers.

2.2 Survey Figures

Survey figures consist of linework generated by coding and placed in a file that is imported into a Survey Database. A figure represents linear features (edge-of-pavement, toe-of-slopes, etc.).

A figure has many functions, which include:

- Acting as linework in a drawing.
- Acting as breaklines for a surface definition.
- Acting as parcel lines.
- Acting as a pipe run.
- Acting as targets for *Width* or *Offset Targets* in a Corridor.
- Acting as targets for *Slope* or *Elevation Targets* in a Corridor (e.g., limits of construction for a road rehab project might be to the face of walk, which exists in the drawing as a Survey Figure, hence a target).

The Figure Prefix database should be set up before importing any survey data to obtain the required entities in a drawing. As point and label styles and the Description Key Set need to exist before importing points, figure styles and entries in the Figure Prefix database need to exist before importing survey data.

Figure Styles

Figure styles (found in the Toolspace, *Settings* tab, under Survey>Figures>Figure Styles) affect how the survey linework displays in a drawing. They should be part of your template file. These styles are not critical. However, to make figures work more efficiently, you should define the layers they use in the drawing.

- Figure styles are tied to the Figure Prefix database. The Figure Prefix database assigns a figure style to a figure that is imported into a drawing.
- A figure style includes the layers for its linework and markers.
- A marker is a symbol placed on the figure's segment midpoints and end points. They call attention to the figure's geometry. Although a figure style includes marker definitions, they typically do not display.
- In the Figure Style dialog box, the *Information* tab assigns a name to a style. The *Profile*, and *Section* tabs define how the marker displays in various views.

- The *Display* tab defines which figure's components display and which layers they use for plan, model, profile, and section views, as shown in Figure 2–1.

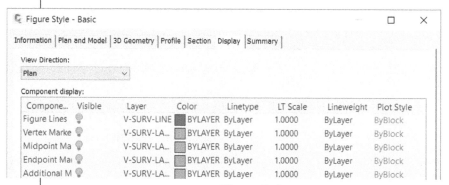

Figure 2–1

Figure Prefix Database

The Figure Prefix database (found in the Toolspace, *Survey* tab) assigns the figure a style, a layer, and defines whether the figure is a surface breakline and/or lot line (parcel segment). If you did not define any figure styles, you should at least assign a layer to correctly place the figure in the drawing. Toggling on the *Breakline* property, as shown in Figure 2–2, enables you select all of the tagged survey figures and assign them to a surface without having to insert or select from a drawing. Toggling on the *Lot Line* property creates a parcel segment from the figure in the drawing and, if there is a closed polygon or intersecting lines to form an enclosure, assigns a parcel label and creates a parcel in the designated site.

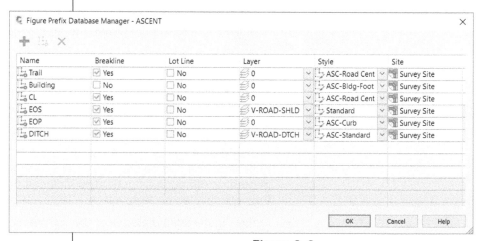

Figure 2–2

If the *Name* is **EOP** (as shown in Figure 2–2), any figure starting with EOP uses these settings. This is similar to using a Description Key Set, except that the entry in the Figure Prefix database does not need an asterisk (*). The entry Name matches EOP-R or EOP-West or EOP-Main-East. When inserting survey figures in the drawing, Survey checks the Figure Prefix database for style or layer values.

Practice 2a

Creating Figure Prefixes

Practice Objective

- Create a figure database for automatically stylizing linework when importing field book or ASCII files.

1. Open **SUV1-A.dwg** from the *C:\Civil 3D Projects\Working\ Survey* folder.

2. In the Toolspace, select the *Survey* tab. Right-click on *Figure Prefix Databases*, and select **New…**. Type **ASCENT** for the name.

3. Right-click on the newly created ASCENT Figure Prefix database, and select **Make Current**.

4. Right-click on the ASCENT Figure Prefix database again, and select **Manage Figure Prefix Database…**.

5. Click ✚ to create a new Figure definition. Set the following options, as shown in Figure 2–3:

   - Change the *Name* to **TRAIL**.
   - Select *Breakline*.
   - Set *Style* to **ASC-Road Centerline**.

   Any figure starting with **TRAIL** will now be selectable for a surface breakline and will use the style **ASC-Road Centerline**. As noted earlier, unlike the Description Key Set, an asterisk (*) is not necessary to match Trail1, Trail2, etc.

You might have to change the draw order of the image to be able to view other objects. In Model Space, select the image, right-click, and select Display Order>Send to Back.

Figure 2–3

6. Click ✚ to create a new Figure definition.
   - Change the name to **BLDG**.
   - Set the *Breakline* to **No**.
   - Set the *Style* to **ASC-Buildings**.

7. Click **OK** to exit the dialog box.

8. Save the drawing.

2.3 Styles

Styles are preconfigured groups of settings (specific to an individual object type or label) that make the objects display and print the way you want them to. For example, in the list of surface styles shown in Figure 2–4, each surface style is configured differently to display different features, such as contours at different intervals and on the correct layers. The display of a terrain model could be changed by swapping one surface style for another. Styles enable an organization to standardize the look of their graphics by providing preconfigured groupings of display settings.

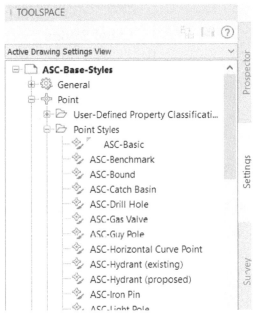

Figure 2–4

The two categories of styles you work with most often are Object Styles and Label Styles. Some objects have table styles as well. Object styles control how Autodesk Civil 3D objects (points, surfaces, alignments, etc.) display, what combination of components the object displays, which layers they display on, and many other settings. Label Styles are similar except that they control the text and other annotations associated with the objects.

For example, an alignment object style specifies many settings including the layers on which to draw tangents and curve segments (which might be different) and the symbols to add at certain points as required (such as a triangle at the PI point). Alignment label styles include major and minor station labels, the display of station equations, design speeds, and similar annotation. By separating object and label styles, you can mix and match the right combination for a specific object.

Styles are the lowest items in the Toolspace, *Settings* tree and are typically dependent on other settings above them. If a style is given a unique setting, different from feature settings or label style defaults (such as a different text height), then that style is considered to have an override.

Label Styles

Label styles produce annotation of values from existing conditions or a design solution. A label annotates a contour's elevations, a parcel's number and area, a horizontal geometry point's station on an alignment, etc.

A label style can have text, vectors, AutoCAD blocks, and reference text. The content of a label depends on the selected object's components or properties. For instance, a Line label can annotate bearing, distance, and coordinates, and use a direction arrow. A Parcel Area label can contain a parcel's area, perimeter, address, and other pertinent values. A surface label can include a spot elevation, reference for an alignment's station and offset, or other pertinent surface information.

- To access the values of a label style, in the Toolspace, *Settings* tab, select the style, right-click on its name, and select **Edit**.

- A style's initial values come from Edit Label Style Defaults and the style's definition.

- All labels use the same interface.

- The object properties available for each label vary by object type.

Each label style uses the same tabbed dialog box. The *Information* tab describes the style as well as who defined and last modified its contents. The values of the *General* tab affect all occurrences of the label in a drawing. For example, if Visibility is set to False, all labels of this style are hidden in the drawing. Other settings affect the label's text style, initial orientation, and reaction to a rotated view.

The *Layout* tab lists all of a label's components. A label component can be text, line, block, or tick. The Component name drop-down list (shown in Figure 2–5), contains all of the defined components for the style. When selecting a component name in the drop-down list, the panel displays information about the component's anchoring, justification, format, and border.

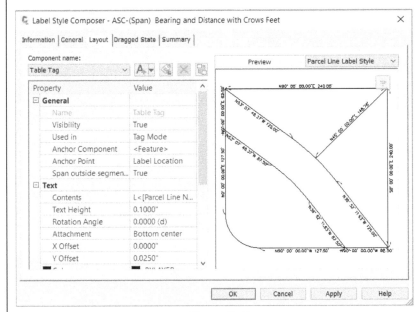

Figure 2–5

When defining a new text component, you assign it an object property by clicking ⋯ (Browse) for Contents. This opens the Text Component Editor dialog box, as shown in Figure 2–6. The Properties drop-down list displays the available object properties. The number and types of properties varies by object type. For example, a parcel area label has more and different properties than a line label does. Once a property has been selected, units, precision, and other settings can be set to display the property correctly in the label. Click ⇨ next to Properties to place the property in the label layout area to the right.

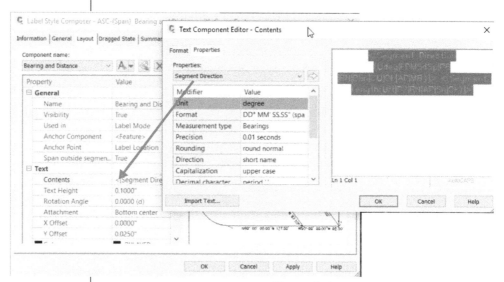

Figure 2–6

The values in the *Dragged State* tab define a label's behavior when it is dragged to a new location in the drawing.

The key to having the label display correctly when it is not in the dragged state, is to line up the Anchor Point of the component with the **Attachment** option for the text. Each has nine options from which to select. The options are shown in Figure 2–7.

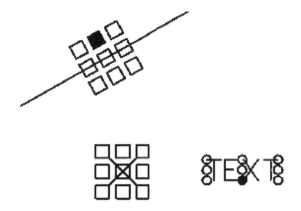

Figure 2–7

Lining up the square hatched Anchor Point with the circular hatched attachment option results in the text centered above the object similar to the bearing distance label shown in Figure 2–8.

Figure 2–8

2.4 Points Overview

Survey Points are often used at the beginning of a project and COGO Points (for stakeout) at the end of a project. Surveyors collect data about existing site conditions (elevations, utilities, ownership, etc.) for the project. Their world is coordinates, which are represented by points. Each point has a unique number (or name) and a label containing additional information (usually the elevation of the coordinate and a short coded description).

There are no national standards for point descriptions in the Surveying industry. Each company or survey crew needs to work out its own conventions. There are no standards for symbols either. Each firm can have its own set of symbols. The symbols used in a submission set can be specified by the firm contracting the services.

Autodesk Civil 3D cogo / survey points are a single object with two elements: a point style and a point label style. A cogo / survey point definition is shown in Figure 2–9.

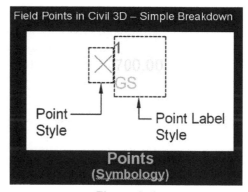

Figure 2–9

The following is important point information:

- A point style (no matter what it displays), an AutoCAD node, a custom marker, or a block is selectable with an AutoCAD **Node** object snap.

A point label is not limited to the point's number, elevation, and description. A point label can contain lines, blocks, and other point properties. One can set up User-Defined point properties as well. For example, point labels might only display an elevation or description. This text can be manually overridden (as shown in Figure 2–10) or it can consist of intelligent variables that represent point characteristics (such as its convergence angle).

In assigned coordinate systems, the convergence angle is the difference between a geodetic azimuth and the projection of that azimuth onto a grid (grid azimuth) of a given point.

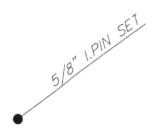

Figure 2–10

Point Marker Styles

A surveyor interacts with points daily. To easily use Autodesk Civil 3D points, you need to have a basic understanding of their related styles.

The Autodesk Civil 3D software provides metric and imperial template files that contain several point styles: *Autodesk Civil 3D Imperial (NCS)* and *Autodesk Civil 3D Metric (NCS)*. These two templates use the National CAD standards for their layers and provide examples of styles that you can use in a project. To customize these styles, you need to modify and expand the list of point styles.

Customizing styles needs to be managed carefully. Consult with your BIM Manager as to the standards and procedures for such customization. If you do modify an existing style or create a new one, be sure to put your name or initials in the *Created by:* field for easy identification, as shown Figure 2–11.

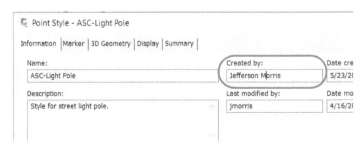

Figure 2–11

When installing the Autodesk Civil 3D software, the first thing you should do is set one of these two templates as your default template. Alternatively, your BIM Manager can develop styles to be used in your organization's drawing template file.

A point style defines a point's display, its 3D elevation, and its coordinate marker size. In the example shown in Figure 2–12, the point style is an X for a ground shot.

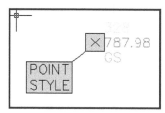

Figure 2–12

The Point Style dialog box has five tabs: *Information*, *Marker*, *3D Geometry*, *Display*, and *Summary*.

The *Information* tab sets the point style's name and description, as shown in Figure 2–13.

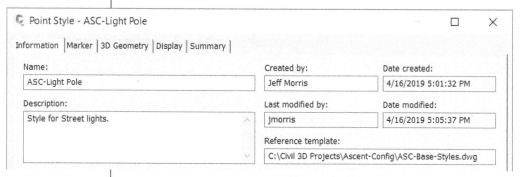

Figure 2–13

The *Marker* tab supports three marker definition methods, as shown in Figure 2–14.

Figure 2–14

- **Use AutoCAD POINT [node] for marker:** All points in the drawing follow AutoCAD's **PDMODE** and **PDSIZE** system variables. You do not have independent control over points using this option. (This option is seldom used.)

- **Use custom marker:** This option creates markers similar to an AutoCAD point (node). However, the marker is under the Autodesk Civil 3D software's control, and each point style can display a different combination of marker styles. When using this option, select the components of the style from the list of Custom marker style shapes. A custom marker can have shapes from the left and right sides. The first comes from one of the five icons on the style's left side, and you can optionally add none, one, or both shapes from the right.

- **Use AutoCAD BLOCK symbol for marker:** This option defines the marker using a block (symbol). The blocks listed represent definitions in the drawing. When the cursor is in this area and you right-click, you can browse to a location containing drawings that you want to include as point markers.

Options for scaling the marker display in the marker panel's top right corner. The most common option is **Use drawing scale** (as shown in Figure 2–15), which takes the marker size (0.1000") and multiplies it by the current drawing's annotation scale, resulting in the final marker size. When the annotation scale changes, the Autodesk Civil 3D software automatically resizes the markers and their labels to be the appropriate size for the scale.

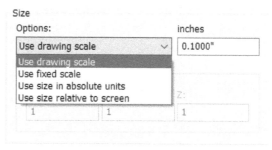

Figure 2–15

The other options are described as follows:

Use fixed scale	Specifies user-defined X, Y, and Z scale values.
Use size in absolute units	Specifies a user-defined size.
Use size relative to screen	Specifies a user-defined percentage of the screen.

The *3D Geometry* tab affects the point's elevation. The default option is **Use Point Elevation** (as shown in Figure 2–16), which displays the point at its actual elevation value.

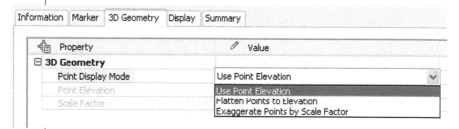

Figure 2–16

The other options are described as follows:

Flatten Points to Elevation	Specifies the elevation to which the point is projected (flattened). The Point Elevation cell highlights if this option is selected and is 0 elevation by default. When using an AutoCAD object snap to select a marker using this option, the resulting entity's elevation is the default elevation of 0. If selecting by point number or point object, the resulting entity is the point's actual elevation.
Exaggerate Points by Scale Factor	Exaggerates the point's elevation by a specified scale factor. When selecting this option, the Scale Factor cell highlights.

The *Display* tab assigns the marker and label layers, and sets their visibility and properties. Setting the property to **ByLayer** uses the layer's properties. Alternatively, you can override the original layer properties by setting a specific color, linetype, or lineweight.

A style's view direction value affects how the point and label components display in the plan, model, profile, and section views, as shown in Figure 2–17.

Figure 2–17

The *Summary* tab is a report of all of the style's settings. Controlling a leader arrow from a label in the dragged state, points to the boundary of the marker (yes) or the center of the marker (no). It is also changed under **Marker>Leader** and stops at marker. You can also edit style variables in this tab.

Point Label Style

The Autodesk Civil 3D point label style annotates point properties beyond the typical point number, elevation and description. A typical point label style is shown in Figure 2–18.

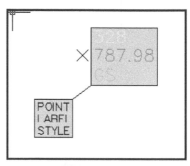

Figure 2–18

All Autodesk Civil 3D label style dialog boxes are the same. The basic behaviors for a label are in the settings in the Edit Label Style Defaults dialog box. The values in this dialog box define the label layer, text style, orientation, plan readability, size, dragged state behaviors, etc.

In the Toolspace, *Settings* tab, the drawing name and object collections control these values for the entire drawing (at the drawing name level) or for the selected collection (*Surface, Alignment, Point*, etc.) To open the Edit Label Style Defaults dialog box, select the drawing name or a heading, right-click, and select **Edit Label Style Defaults...**, as shown in Figure 2–19.

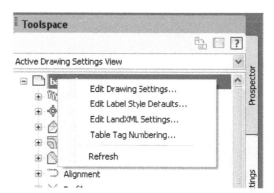

Figure 2–19

The Label Style Composer dialog box contains five tabs, each defining specific label behaviors: *Information*, *General*, *Layout*, *Dragged State*, and *Summary*.

The *Information* tab names the style, as shown in Figure 2–20.

Figure 2–20

The *General* tab contains three properties: *Label* (text style and layer), *Behavior* (orientation), and *Plan Readability* (amount of view rotation before flipping text to read from the bottom or the right side of the sheet), as shown in Figure 2–21.

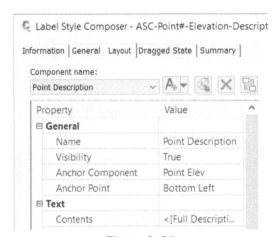

Figure 2–21

The *Label* property sets the *Text Style*, *Label Visibility*, *Layer*. Select the *Value* cell next to the *Text Style* and *Layer* to open browsers and change their values. Selecting the *Label Visibility* cell displays a drop-down list containing the options **true** and **false**.

The *Behavior* property sets two variables that control the label's location. The *Orientation Reference* variable contains the three label orientation options.

Object	Rotates labels relative to the object's zero direction. The object's zero direction is based on its start to end vector. If the vector changes at the label's anchor point, the orientation updates automatically. This is the default setting.
View	Forces labels to realign relative to a screen-view orientation in both model and layout views. This method assumes that the zero angle is horizontal, regardless of the UCS or Dview twist. If the view changes, the label orientation updates as well.
World Coordinate System	Labels read left to right using the WCS X-axis. Changing the view or current UCS does not affect label rotation. The label always references the world coordinate system.

Under the *Behavior* property, the **Forced Insertion** variable has three optional values that specify the label's position relative to an object. This setting only applies when the *Orientation Reference* is set to **Object** and the objects are lines, arcs, or spline segments.

None	Maintains label position as composed relative to the object.
Top	Adjusts label position to be above an object.
Bottom	Adjusts label position to be below an object.

- **Note:** If you select **Top** or **Bottom**, set the value of *Plan Readable* to **True**.

The *Plan Readability* property has three variables that affect how text flips when rotating a drawing view.

Under the *Plan Readability* property, the *Plan Readable* variable has two options.

True	Enables text to rotate to maintain left to right readability from the bottom or right side of the drawing.
False	Does not permit text to flip. The resulting text might be upside down or read from right to left.

The *Readability Bias* variable is the amount of rotation required to flip a label to become left to right readable. The angle is measured counter-clockwise from the WCS 0 (zero) direction.

The *Flip Anchors with Text* variable has two options:

True	If the text flips, the text anchor point also flips.
False	The label flips, but maintains the original anchor point. The behavior is similar to mirroring the original text.

The *Layout* tab defines the label contents, as shown in Figure 2–22. A label component is an object property that it labels. Point properties include northing, easting, raw description, etc. If User Defined properties are in use, they will also be available. A label might have one component with several properties or several components each containing an object property, as well as regular text (such as Northing:).

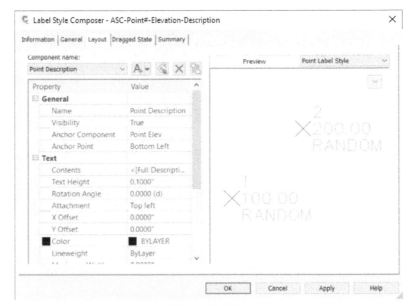

Figure 2–22

A point style label component can be text, lines, or blocks. Other object type label styles can include additional components, such as reference text, ticks, directional arrows, etc. To add a component, expand the drop-down list (as shown in Figure 2–23) and select the component type.

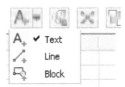

Figure 2–23

The remaining icons in the *Layout* tab are described as follows:

	Copies the current component and its properties.
	Deletes the current component.
	Changes the display order of a label's components. For example, use this icon to change the draw order of the label's component such as text above a mask.

Depending on the label component type, it might have any combination of three areas: *General*, *Text*, and *Border*. *General* defines how the label attaches to the object or other label components, its visibility, and its anchor point.

If the label component is text, the *Text* property values affect how it displays its object property. To set or modify a label's text value, select the cell next to *Contents* to display ⸱⸱⸱ (shown in Figure 2–24). Click ⸱⸱⸱ to open the Text Component Editor dialog box.

Figure 2–24

The Text Component Editor dialog box (shown in Figure 2–25), defines the properties that the label annotates. When creating a label component, double-click on the text in the right pane to highlight it. In the left pane, select the property that you want to add, set the property's format values, and then click ⇨ to add the new property to the label component.

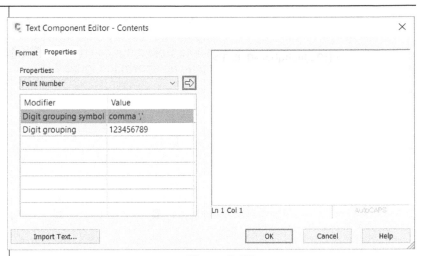

Figure 2–25

It is important to maintain the process order and to remember that the text on the right in brackets needs to be highlighted before you can revise its format values on the left.

The *Dragged State* tab has two properties: *Leader* and *Dragged State Components*. This tab defines how a label behaves when you are dragging a label from its original insertion point.

The *Leader* property defines whether a leader displays and what properties it displays. You can use the label's layer properties in the *General* tab (**ByLayer**) or override them by specifying a color, as shown in Figure 2–26.

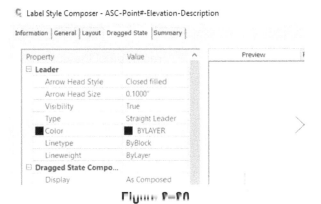

Figure 2–26

The *Dragged State Components* property defines the label component's display after it has been dragged from its original position. Select the cell next to *Display* to view the two display options, as shown in Figure 2–27.

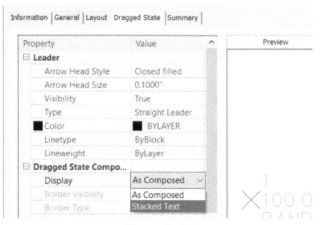

Figure 2–27

As Composed	The label maintains its original definition and orientation from the settings in the Layout panel. When you select **As Composed**, all of the other values become unavailable for editing.
Stacked Text	The label text becomes left justified and label components are stacked in the order listed in Layout's Component Name list. When you select **Stacked Text**, all of the blocks, lines, ticks, and direction arrows are removed.

The *Summary* tab lists the label component, general, and dragged state values for the label style. The label components are listed numerically in the order in which they were defined and report all of the current values.

Practice 2b

Point Marker Styles

Practice Objective

- Create a point marker and label style to ensure that the correct symbol is assigned to specific points.

In this practice, you will create a new point style and apply it to an existing group of points.

Task 1 - Add a block symbol.

1. Continue working on the drawing from the previous practice or open **SUV1-B1-Survey-.dwg** from the *C:\Civil 3D Projects\Working\Survey* folder.

The aerial image used in this chapter was attached using the AutoCAD® Map 3D FDO connection.

2. To toggle off the aerial image, in the *Home* tab>Palettes panel, click ⬜ (Map Task Pane). When prompted, select **ON**.

3. In the Task pane>*Display Manager* tab, clear the **Main Site Imperial** layer, as shown in Figure 2–28. Select *Map Base* again to clear the *Raster Layer* contextual tab. Close the map Task Pane.

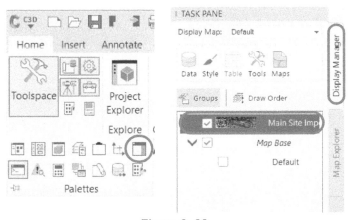

Figure 2–28

4. In the Toolspace, *Settings* tab, expand the *Point* collection until *Point Styles* displays. Expand the *Point Styles* collection.

Review the Point Styles list and note that there is no light pole style.

5. In the *Point Styles* list, select the **ASC-Guy pole** style, right-click, and select **Copy....**

6. In the *Information* tab, change the point style's name to **ASC-Light Pole** and enter your name or initials in the *Created by:* field.

7. Select the *Marker* tab. Select the **Use AutoCAD BLOCK symbol for marker** option. In the block list, scroll across as required and select the AutoCAD block **ST-Light**, as shown in Figure 2–29.

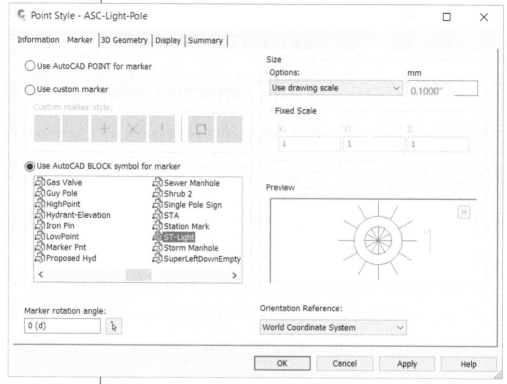

Figure 2–29

8. Select the *Display* tab and note that the layer settings are from the Guy Pole point style.

9. You can reassign the marker and/or label layer by selecting the layer name. Select the layer name to display the drawing layer list.

10. Click **New** in the top right corner of the Layer Selection dialog box. The Create Layer dialog box opens (as shown in Figure 2–30), enabling you to create new layers without having to use the Layer Manager.

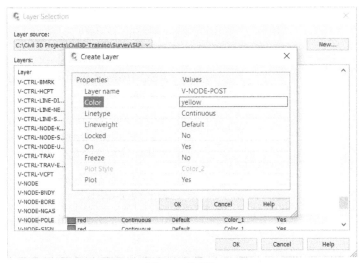

Figure 2–30

11. For the *Layer name*, type **V-NODE-POST**, and then set the *Color* to **yellow**, as shown in Figure 2–30. Click **OK** to exit the Create Layer dialog box. Click **OK** to exit the Layer Selection dialog box.

12. Click **OK** to create the point style.

13. Review the *Point Styles* list and note that **ASC-Light Pole** is now a point style, as shown in Figure 2–31.

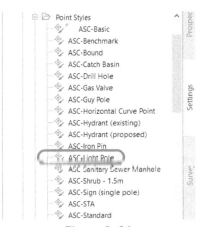

Figure 2–31

14. Save the drawing.

Task 2 - Create a point label style's components.

1. Continue working with the drawing from the previous task or open **SUV1-B2.dwg**.

2. In the Toolspace, *Settings* tab, expand the *Point* collection until the *Point Label Styles* list displays.

3. From the list of point label styles, select **ASC-Point#-Elevation-Description**, right-click, and select **Copy**.

4. In the *Information* tab, change the name to **ASC-Point#-Description-N-E** and enter your name or initials in the *Created by:* field.

5. Select the *Layout* tab and do the following (as shown in Figure 2–32):

    • Select **Point Number** in the *Component name* drop-down list.
    • Set the *Anchor Component* to **<Feature>**.
    • Set the *Anchor Point* to **Top Right**.
    • Set the *Attachment* to **Bottom left**.

These settings attach the bottom left of the label to the top right of the point object.

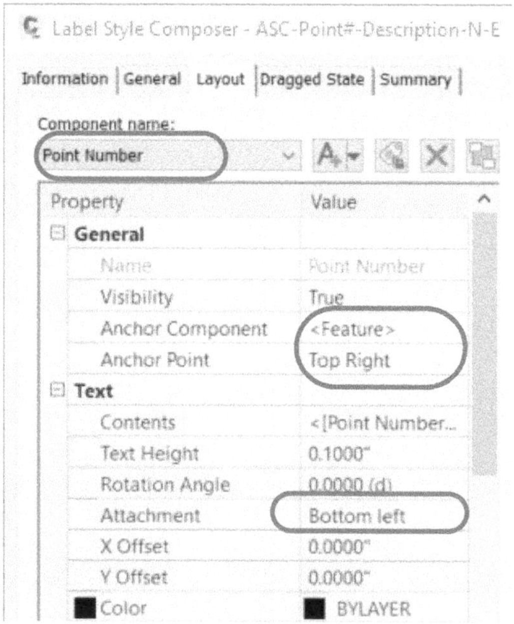

Figure 2–32

Since the elevation label is not required, you can delete it.

6. Select **Point Elev** in the Component name drop-down list and click , as shown in Figure 2–33. At the *Do you want to delete it?* prompt, click **Yes**.

Component name:

Point Description

Figure 2–33

7. Select **Point Description** in the Component name drop-down list and do the following (shown in Figure 2–34):

   • Set the *Anchor Component* to **Point Number**.
   • Set the *Anchor Point* to **Bottom Left**.
   • Set the *Attachment* to **Top Left**.

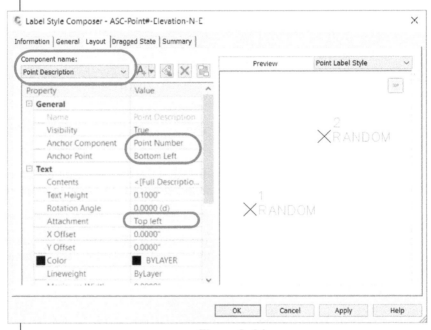

Figure 2–34

You will now add a new text component to display the Northing and Easting

8. Expand the **Create Text Component** flyout (shown in Figure 2–35) and select **Text** to create a text component.

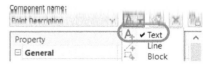

Figure 2–35

9. Change the default *Name* **text.1** to **Coordinates**, and then do the following:

- Set the *Anchor Component* to **Point Description**.
- Set the *Anchor Point* to **Bottom Left**.
- Set the *Attachment* to **Top Left**.

You will now change the contents from the default label set by the Autodesk Civil 3D software to display the coordinates.

10. Click  in the *Contents* cell, next to *Label Text*, as shown in Figure 2–36.

Figure 2–36

11. In the Text Component Editor dialog box, double-click on the text in the right side panel to highlight it and type **N:**.

12. Select **Northing** in the Properties drop-down list. Change the *Precision* to **0.001** and click 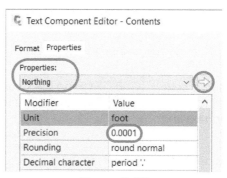, as shown in Figure 2–37, to add the code to display the northing.

Figure 2–37

13. Click at the end of the code. Press **<Enter>** to insert a new line followed by the letter **E** and a colon. Then select **Easting** in the Properties drop-down list and add it to post the code in the right side panel. The following should be displayed:

- N:<[Northing(Uft|P3|RN|AP|GC|UN|Sn|OF)]>
- E:<[Easting(Uft|P4|RN|AP|GC|UN|Sn|OF)]>

In the easting, the value will be displayed to the 4th decimal, P4. Change it so that it matches the northing.

14. Select all of the code for the easting. Change the *Precision* to **0.001** and click 🔄 to revise the easting code.

15. Select the *Format* tab and verify that *Justification* is set to **Left**. Click **OK** to accept the changes in the Text Component Editor dialog box, and click **OK** again to accept the changes in the Label Style Composer.

16. Save the drawing.

Task 3 - Apply style components.

1. Continue working with the drawing from the previous task or open **SUV1-B3.dwg**.

Point Groups will be covered in detail later in this chapter.

2. In the Toolspace, select the Toolspace, *Prospector* tab and expand the *Point Groups* collection until the *StreetLights* point group displays. Select the **StreetLights** group, right-click, and select **Properties**.

3. In the *Information* tab, expand the Point Style drop-down list and select **ASC-Light Pole**. Then expand the Point label style drop-down list and select **ASC-Point#-Description-N-E**, as shown in Figure 2–38.

Figure 2–38

4. Click **OK** to accept the changes and close the dialog box.

*If the symbol and label do not change, in the Toolspace, Prospector tab, right-click on the StreetLights point group and select **Update**.*

5. The symbols for the Light pole points have now been changed. Additionally, both the point symbols and point labels are annotative. In the Status Bar, expand the Annotation Scale drop-down list and change the scale of the drawing from *1"=80'* to **1"=40'**, as shown in Figure 2–39. The size of the labels and point symbols change.

Figure 2–39

6. Save the drawing.

2.5 Point Settings

When creating new points, you must determine the next point number, and which elevations and descriptions to assign and how to assign them. To set the current point number, default elevations, descriptions, and other similar settings, you can use

the expanded Create Points toolbar. Click ⬇ in the Create Points toolbar to display the *Points Creation* and *Point Identity* categories (shown in Figure 2–40), which contain the most commonly used values.

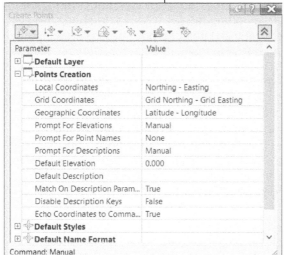
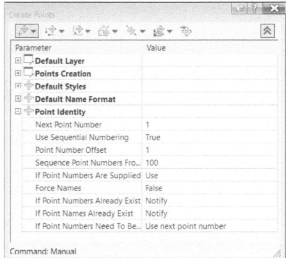

Figure 2–40

Points Creation Values

The *Points Creation* area affects prompting for elevations and/or descriptions. The two properties in this area are *Prompt For Elevations* and *Prompt For Descriptions*. These properties can be set as follows:

None	Does not prompt for an elevation or description.
Manual	Prompts for an elevation or description.
Automatic	Uses the **Default Elevation** or **Default Description** value when creating a point.
Automatic-Object	Creates points along an alignment whose description consists of the **Alignment name** and **Station**. This description is not dynamic and does not update if the alignment changes or the point is moved.

Point Identity Values

The *Point Identity* area sets the default method of handling duplicate point numbers. If there are duplicate point numbers, there are three ways to resolve the duplication:

1. Overwrite the existing point data.
2. Ignore the new point.
3. Assign it a new number.

This area's critical property is *Next Point Number*. It is set to the first available number in the point list. If a file of imported point data uses point numbers 1-131 and 152-264, the current point number is 132 after importing the file. This value should be set manually to the next required point number before creating new points with the Create Points toolbar.

You can also change these point settings by selecting the Toolspace, *Settings* tab and expanding the *Commands* collection under the *Point* collection. Right-click on **CreatePoints** and select **Edit Command Settings...**, as shown on the left in Figure 2–41. In the Edit Command Settings dialog box, you can set the defaults for Point Creation, as shown on the right. **Note:** Ideally, this will be preset for you by your BIM Manager, according to your organization's standards.

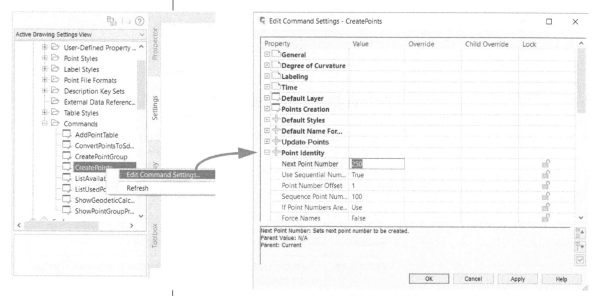

Figure 2–41

2.6 Creating Points

You can create points using the commands in the Create Points toolbar. These commands include:

- **Miscellaneous - Manual:** Creates a new point at specified coordinates.

- **Alignments - Station/Offset:** Creates a point at an alignment's specific station and offset. These points and their descriptions do not update if the alignment is modified or the point is moved. If you prefer a dynamic station and offset labels, consider using an Alignment label instead.

- **Alignments - Measure Alignment:** Creates point objects at a set interval, which is useful for construction staking. Again, these points do not update if the alignment changes.

- **Surface - Random Points:** Creates points whose elevation is from a specified surface. These points can update, but only if you manually force the update. If you prefer a dynamic spot label which will always be up to date, consider a Surface label instead.

Each icon in the Create Points toolbar has a drop-down list. If you expand it, you can select a command from the list to run, as shown in Figure 2–42.

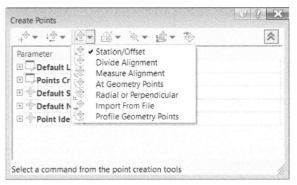

Figure 2–42

| Practice 2c | # Creating Autodesk Civil 3D Points |

Practice Objective

- Create a point manually then zoom to it using transparent commands.

In this practice, a fire hydrant was located by GPS. You will add a point object to locate it manually.

1. Continue working with the drawing from the previous practice or open **SUV1-C.dwg**.

2. In the *Home* tab>Create Ground Data panel, select **Points> Point Creation Tools** to display the Create Points toolbar. Expand the toolbar by clicking ⩔ .

3. In the *Point Identity* area in the dialog box, set the *Next Point Number* to **260** and collapse the toolbar, by clicking 🔼 .

4. Select the **Manual** option in the miscellaneous group in the toolbar as shown in Figure 2–43.

Figure 2–43

5. When prompted for a location, enter **6256069.30,2036634.25** and press <Enter>.

- When prompted for a description, type **HYD** and press <Enter>.

The period is a placeholder for the elevation field. Typing zero is not correct because 0 is a valid elevation.

- When prompted for an elevation, press <Enter> to accept the default value of **<.>** (period), because it is unknown.

- Press <Enter> again to finish the command and select **X** in the Create Points dialog box to close it.

- In the Transparent Command toolbar, click 🔍 (Zoom to Point), and type **260**.

6. Save the drawing.

2.7 Description Key Sets

Description Keys categorize points by their field descriptions (raw description). If a point matches a Description Key entry, the point is assigned a point and label style, and a full description (a translation of the raw description). Description Key Sets can also scale and rotate points.

The Description Key's first five columns are the commonly used entries, as shown in Figure 2–44.

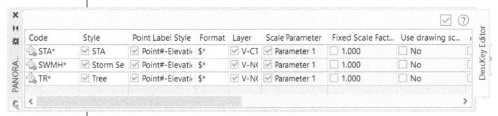

Code	Style	Point Label Style	Format	Layer	Scale Parameter	Fixed Scale Fact...	Use drawing sc...
☑ STA*	☑ STA	☑ Point#-Elevati	$*	☑ V-CT	☑ Parameter 1	☐ 1.000	☐ No
☑ SWMH*	☑ Storm Se	☑ Point#-Elevati	$*	☑ V-N(	☑ Parameter 1	☐ 1.000	☐ No
☑ TR*	☑ Tree	☑ Point#-Elevati	$*	☑ V-N(	☑ Parameter 1	☐ 1.000	☐ No

Figure 2–44

- To create a new Description Key row, select an existing code, right-click, and select **New**. To edit a code, double-click in the cell.

Code, Point, and Label Style

Description code is a significant part of data collection. Codes assigned to a raw description trigger action by the Description Key Set. Each entry in the set represents all of the possible descriptions that a field crew would use while surveying a job. When a raw description matches a code entry, the Key Set assigns all of the row's values to the matching point, including point style, label style, translates the raw description, and possibly assigns a layer. Codes are case-sensitive and must match the field collector's entered raw description.

A code might contain wild cards to match raw descriptions that contain numbering or additional material beyond the point's description. For example, MH? would match MH1, MH2, etc.,but not MH12, since the ? (question mark) symbol matches only single characters, whereas UP* would match UP 2245 14.4Kv Verizon, since the * (asterisk) matches any string characters. Common wild keys are described as follows:

# (pound)	Matches any single numeric digit. (T# matches T1 through T9.)
@ (at)	Matches any alphabetic character. (1@ matches 1A through 1Z.)
. (period)	Matches any non-alphanumeric character. (T. matches T- or T+.)
* (asterisk)	Matches any string of characters. (T* matches TREE, TR-Aspen, Topo, or Trench.)
? (question mark)	Matches any single character. (?BC matches TBC or 3BC.)

Matching a Key Set entry for the code assigns a Point Style at the point's coordinates. If the *Point Style* is set to **Default**, the *Settings* tab's Point feature *Point Style* is used (set in the Edit Feature Settings dialog box), as shown in Figure 2–45.

Matching a Key Set entry for the code assigns a point label style to annotate important point values. This is usually a number, elevation, and description. If the *Point Style* is set to **Default**, the *Settings* tab's Point feature *Point Label Style* is used (set in the Edit Feature Settings dialog box), as shown in Figure 2–45.

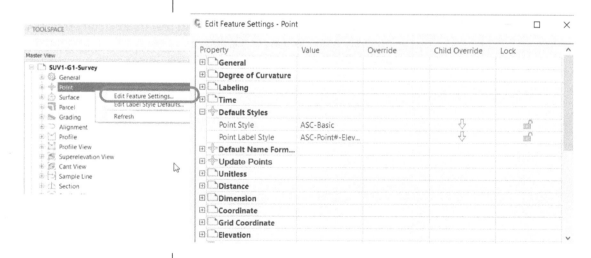

Figure 2–45

Format

The *Format* column translates the raw description (what the surveyor typed) into a full description (what you want it to read). When including spaces in a raw description, the Autodesk Civil 3D software assigns parameter numbers to each description element. Parameters are represented by a $ sign, followed by a number. For example, the description *PINE 6* has two elements: PINE and 6, with PINE as parameter 0 ($0) and 6 as parameter 1 ($1). When the *Format* column contains $*, it indicates that the software should use the raw description as the full description. The *Format* column can reorder the parameters and add characters to create a full description. For example, the raw description *PINE 6* can be translated to 6' PINE by entering **$1' $0**.

A complex raw description is as follows:

> TREE D MAPLE 9

For the raw description to match the Description Key Set entry, the entry **TREE** must have an asterisk (*) after TREE (as shown in Figure 2–46). The raw description elements and their parameters are TREE ($0), D ($1), MAPLE ($2), and 9 ($3). The *Format* column entry of **$3' $2 $0** creates a full description of **9' MAPLE TREE**.

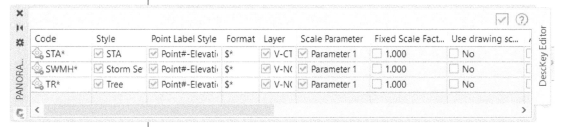

Figure 2–46

If a point does not match any Description Key Set entry, it receives the default styles assigned by the All Points group.

The *Layer* column assigns a layer to the matching point. If the Point Style already has a marker and label layer, this entry should be toggled off. The Description Key Set also contains the *Scale* and *Rotate Parameter* columns. In the example in Figure 2–46, the 3 for the trunk diameter can also be a tree symbol scaling factor when applied to the symbol's X, Y.

The most common parameter is the **Scale** parameter. With this parameter, a surveyor will enter the size of a tree as part of the description and the description key file will insert a symbol scaled to the value provided by the surveyor.

The **Rotate** parameter is used less frequently, but it can be useful. For example, you can edit the point file in the office (not in the field) once you have determined the bearing of a roadside curb. Then, you can append that rotation value as a parameter to the description of each hydrant, street sign, light standard, etc. along the road to have them inserted with the proper rotation so the symbols will be inserted with the proper angle to be perpendicular to the curb.

Practice 2d

Creating a Description Key Set

Practice Objective

- Assign point symbols, labels, layers, etc., on import by setting up Description Key Sets.

In this practice, you will learn to create a new Description Key Set entry and apply it to an existing point. In addition, you will update the Description Key Set to use parameters.

Task 1 - Create a new Description Key Set entry.

1. Continue working with the drawing from the previous practice, or open **SUV1-D.dwg**.

2. In the Toolspace, *Settings* tab, expand the *Point* collection until the *Description Key Set* collection and its list display.

3. Select **Civil 3D**, right-click, and select **Edit Keys...**

4. Right-click in any *Code* cell and select **New...**, as shown in Figure 2–47.

Figure 2–47

5. Double-click in the *Code* cell in the newly created row and type **HYD**, as shown in Figure 2–48.

Figure 2–48

6. In the *Style* cell, toggle on the Point Style and select the **Style** cell to open the Point Style dialog box, as shown in Figure 2–49. Select **ASC-Hydrant (existing)** in the drop-down list and click **OK** to assign the style to the code.

Figure 2–49

7. Leave **<default>** selected as the *Point Label Style* and **$*** as the *Format*. This means the label will be the same as the one entered by the surveyor.

8. Leave the check box toggled off in the *Layer* column.

You do not have a scale parameter and will not be using a fixed scale.

9. Select the **Yes** option in the *Use drawing scale* column, and clear the check box for the **Scale Parameter**, as shown in Figure 2–50.

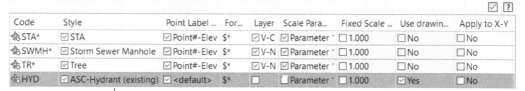

Code	Style	Point Label ...	For...	Layer	Scale Para...	Fixed Scale ...	Use drawin...	Apply to X-Y
☒ STA*	☑ STA	☑ Point#-Elev	$*	☑ V-C	☑ Parameter '	☐ 1.000	☐ No	☐ No
☒ SWMH*	☑ Storm Sewer Manhole	☑ Point#-Elev	$*	☑ V-N	☑ Parameter '	☐ 1.000	☐ No	☐ No
☒ TR*	☑ Tree	☑ Point#-Elev	$*	☑ V-N	☑ Parameter '	☐ 1.000	☐ No	☐ No
☒ HYD	☑ ASC-Hydrant (existing)	☑ <default>	$*	☐	☐ Parameter '	☐ 1.000	☑ Yes	☐ No

Figure 2–50

10. Close the DescKey Editor vista by clicking ☑ in the top right corner of the palette.

Task 2 - Apply the new Description Key Set to an existing point.

---

1. If not already zoomed into the new point, in the *Transparent* tab, click ⌖ (Zoom to Point), and then type **260**.

2. In the Toolspace, *Prospector* tab, select the **_All Points** group, right-click, and select **Apply Description Keys**, as shown in Figure 2–51.

The point updates to display the Hydrant symbol and its new description.

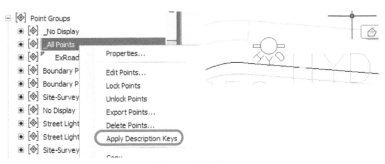

Figure 2–51

3. Save the drawing.

Task 3 - Update the Description Key Set to use parameters.

In this task, you will use the Parameters feature to control the display properties of symbols in your drawings.

In this case, you will use the **Rotate** parameter, so that the pumpers on the hydrant display correctly (i.e., running parallel to the road).

1. In the Toolspace, *Settings* tab, expand *Point>Description Key Sets*. Select **Civil 3D**, right-click, and select **Edit Keys...**, as shown in Figure 2–52.

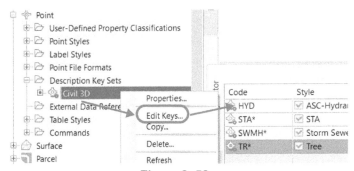

Figure 2–52

2. In the HYD row, *Code* column, type **HYD***. The asterisk symbolizes a wildcard, (i.e., any character after the letters HYD).

3. In the HYD row, select the check box in the *Marker Rotate* column (as shown in Figure 2–53), select the cell, and then select **Parameter1** in the drop-down list.

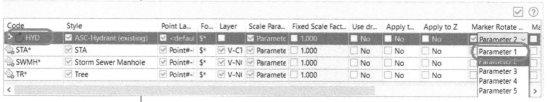

Figure 2–53

4. Click ☑ in the top right corner of the dialog box to close the Panorama view.

5. Using the AutoCAD **Distance** inquiry, you will note that the bearing of the curb is 5 degrees clockwise, as shown in Figure 2–54.

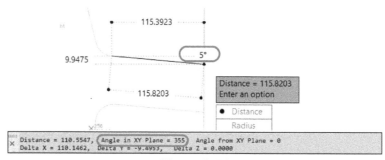

Figure 2–54

6. In Model Space, select the Hydrant point object, right-click, and select **Edit Points**.

The -5 indicates the required rotation.

7. Set the *Raw Description* from HYD to **HYD -5**. Ensure that you put a space after **HYD**.

8. Select the row, right-click, and select **Apply Description Keys**, as shown in Figure 2–55.

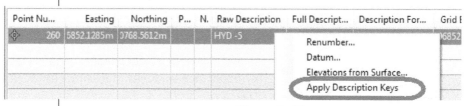

Figure 2–55

9. Click  in the top right corner of the dialog box to close the Panorama view.

The hydrant has now been rotated to display the hydrant pumpers following the bearing of the curb, as shown in Figure 2–56.

The curb line is accentuated in the figure for clarity. The rotation is slight and may be difficult to discern.

Figure 2–56

10. The label also displays the rotation angle text -5, which you do not want. In the Toolspace, *Settings* tab, expand the *Point* and *Description Key Sets* collections. Select **Civil 3D**, right-click, and select **Edit Keys...**

11. In the HYD row, change the *Format* from $* to **Hydrant**, as shown in Figure 2–57.

Code	Style	Point Label Style	Format	Layer	Scale Parameter	Fi	Marker Rotate ...	Ma
HYD*	☑ ASC-Hydrant (existing)	☑ <default>	Hydrant	☐	☑ Parameter 1		☑ Parameter 1	☐
STA*	☑ STA	☑ Point#-Elevati	$*	☑ V-C1	☑ Parameter 1		☐ Parameter 2	☐
SWMH*	☑ Storm Sewer Manhole	☑ Point#-Elevati	$*	☑ V-N(	☑ Parameter 1		☐ Parameter 2	☐
TR*	☑ Tree	☐ Point#-Elevati	$*	☑ V-N(	☑ Parameter 1		☐ Parameter 2	☐

Figure 2–57

12. Click  in the top right corner of the dialog box to close the Panorama view.

13. In Model Space, select the Hydrant point object, right-click, and select **Apply Description Keys**. The changes are now applied, as shown in Figure 2–58.

Figure 2–58

14. Save the drawing.

2.8 Importing Survey Data

The Autodesk Civil 3D software has methods to import point data from ASCII text files to Autodesk LandXML files, as well as methods to convert AutoCAD points to Autodesk Civil 3D points. The Toolspace, *Survey* tab also inserts points from a survey to a drawing.

Import Points Only

There are two methods of launching the import point feature, one is by using the *Insert* tab and the other is using the **Points** creation tool in the *Home* tab, Create Ground Data panel or the Toolspace, *Prospector* tab.

How To: Use the *Insert* Tab Method

1. In the *Insert* tab, click ⚛ (Points from File).This opens the Import Points dialog box.
2. In the Import Points dialog box, set the file format, select the files to import, set any advanced options, and click **OK** to import the points.

Alternatively, you can click ⚛ (Import Points) in the Create Points toolbar.

How To: Use the Point Creation Tools Method

1. Open the Create Points dialog box by expanding Points in the *Home* tab, expanding the drop-down list and selecting a **Create Points** option, as shown on the left in Figure 2–59. Alternatively, in the Toolspace, *Prospector* tab, select **Points**, right-click and select **Create…**, as shown on the right.

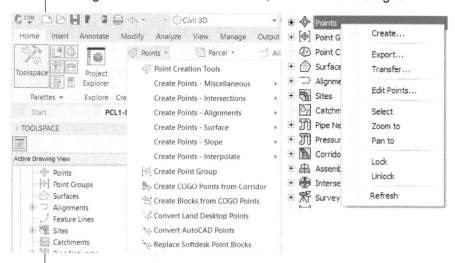

Figure 2–59

All commands in the Points drop-down list can also be accessed in the Create Points toolbar, as shown in Figure 2–60.

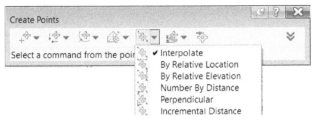

Figure 2–60

2. Click 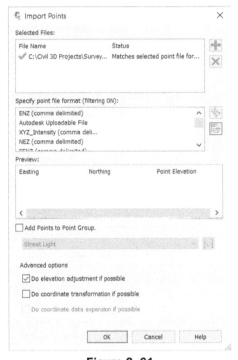 (Import Points) to open the Import Points dialog box (shown in Figure 2–61).

Figure 2–61

3. In the Import Points dialog box, under the *Specify point file format* area, select the required format.

4. After setting the format, click ✚ on the right to open the Select Source File dialog box.

You can select multiple files if they have the same file format.

5. In the Select Source File dialog box, browse to the import point file, select it, and select **Open**. Assign the imported points to a new or existing point group by selecting the **Add Points to Point Group** option and selecting the point group in the drop-down list. Select **Advanced options** as required.

Duplicate Point Numbers

If an imported file creates duplicate point numbers, the Autodesk Civil 3D software overwrites, merges, or reassigns them during the import process. When encountering duplicate point numbers, the Autodesk Civil 3D software can assign the next available number, add an offset value (add 5000 to each point number that conflicts), overwrite points (replaces the current point values with the file's values), or merge points (add the file's values to an existing point's values). If using the offset method, the new point numbers are kept unique in the drawing. If using the next available number method, the new points blend into the original points and are difficult to identify.

The offset method is preferred when resolving duplicate point numbers. When importing points that will potentially duplicate point numbers, the Create Points toolbar's *Point Identity* settings, as shown in Figure 2–62, is the default when handling duplicate point numbers.

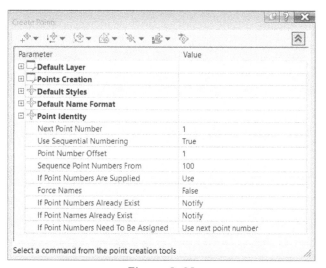

Figure 2–62

In the *Point Identity* settings, set the duplicate point resolution method for the *If Point Numbers Already Exist* variable. The four methods are **Renumber**, **Merge**, **Overwrite**, and **Notify**, as shown in Figure 2–63. The import process never overwrites point data unless you specify that it should do so.

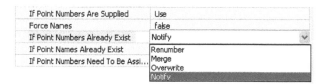

Figure 2–63

When encountering a duplicate point, the Duplicate Point Number dialog box opens. After you define a resolution, it can be assigned to the current duplicate point or to all encountered duplicate points.

Survey Toolspace

The Toolspace, *Survey* tab displays a panel through which all surveys are processed. Survey uses graphics to display field book imports, figure and network previews, and points. If you toggle off these graphics, you can process a survey without a drawing being open. If you want to display these graphics, you need to have a drawing open. Survey prompts you to open a drawing if you do not have one open.

The Toolspace, *Survey* tab contains Survey settings, Equipment defaults, Figure Prefixes, and Linework Code Sets. Survey's settings can be on a local or network folder. It is preferred to use a network folder in larger offices because all users can then standardize the file values.

How To: Display the Toolspace, *Survey* Tab

If your Toolspace does not display the *Survey* tab, click

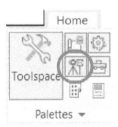 (Survey) in the *Home* tab>Palettes panel, as shown in Figure 2–64.

Figure 2–64

Import Points and Figures Using the Survey Database

After collecting and coding the data, and then downloading and converting it, the next step in Survey is to import the survey data, review it, and place the survey points and figures into a drawing. A working folder defines where the local Survey Database is located. The preferred location is a network folder, in which you place the local Survey Databases. The Survey User Settings dialog box sets the defaults for all new Survey Databases. You should set these before starting Survey. The Survey Working Folder is the location for all of the Survey Databases and can be local or on the network. The default working folder is *C:\Users\Public\Documents\Autodesk\Civil 3D Projects*.

How To: Set the Working Folder for the Survey Database

1. In the Toolspace, *Survey* tab, select **Survey Databases**.
2. Right-click and select **Set working folder...**, as shown in Figure 2–65.

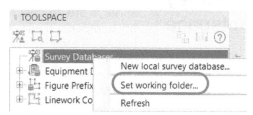

Figure 2–65

Survey Database

Survey Database Folders cannot be deleted in Autodesk Civil 3D Survey. If you want to delete the working folder, this process must be done through the Windows File Explorer, external to the Autodesk Civil 3D software.

A Survey Database is a subfolder in the working folder. The Survey Working Folder contains the Survey's settings and observation database. This database contains the Survey's Networks, Figures, and Survey Points.

To import a field book, you use the Survey's *Import Events* collection. *Import Events* provides access to an Import wizard, which guides you through the steps of importing a file.

1. To open the Import wizard, select **Import Events** in the Survey, right-click, and select **Import survey data...**.
2. The Specify Database page is shown in Figure 2–66. It sets the survey, creates a new survey, and edits the Survey's settings.

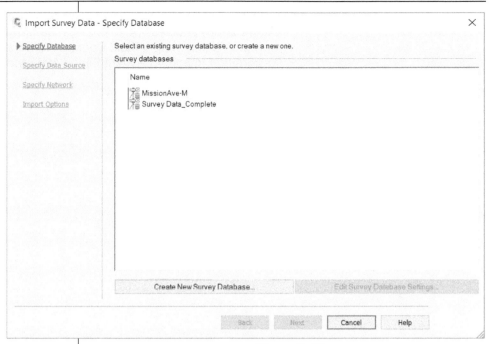

Figure 2–66

3. Click **Next**. The *Specify Data Source* page (shown in Figure 2–67), defines the file import type, the file's path, and its format (if it is a coordinate file).

Figure 2–67

4. Click **Next**. The *Specify Network* page (shown in Figure 2–68) enables you to change the network or create a new one. If importing a Field Book, a *Network* must be assigned. If Importing a Point File, a *Network* is optional.

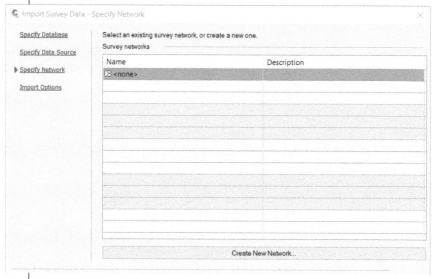

Figure 2–68

5. Click **Next**.

6. The *Import Options* page (shown in Figure 2–69) sets the values for the import. These settings affect what the import does and which support files it uses.

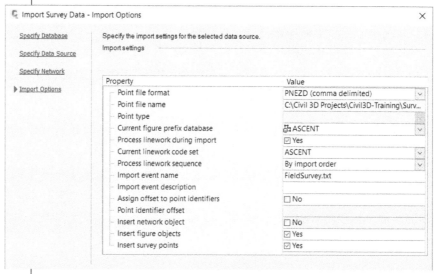

Figure 2–69

If the field book has figure coding from a conversion, you do not need to toggle on the *Process linework during import* property. This is for Point files other than field books that have **Linework Code Set** commands included in the point's description.

Inserting figures requires entries to be in the Figure Prefix database and figure styles to be in the drawing. This is required to point the figure and linework to the correct drawing layers and to specify whether the figure is also a breakline in a surface.

When inserting points, it is necessary to have a Description Key Set defined to assign points, point label styles, and layers, and to translate raw descriptions to full descriptions.

Open a Survey Database for Editing

Only one Survey Database can be edited at a time. When opened for editing, this prepares the survey for reading and writing. There are options to set the path or location for the Survey Database project files, and for all of the settings. When you create a new Survey Database, a Windows folder is created with the same name. If you close a drawing with a survey open, the Survey Database closes automatically. You must start a new drawing or open an existing drawing and then open the required Survey Database. You can only have one Survey Database open at a time.

How To: Open a Survey Database

1. In the Toolspace, *Survey* tab, expand the *Survey Database* collection.
2. Select the survey database that you want to open, right-click, and select **Open for edit** or **Open for read-only**, depending on your requirements, as shown in Figure 2–70. Contrary to most Civil 3D functions, where double-clicking invokes an edit function, double-clicking on a Survey Database will open it as read-only.

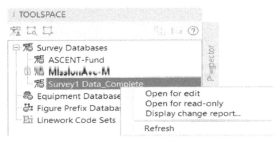

Figure 2–70

Hint: Survey Database Migration to 2020 and Above

The Survey Database format has changed in the 2020 Release. If you have existing Survey Databases created in an earlier format, they will be marked and must be migrated, Right-click on the Survey Database and pick *Migrate....*You will need to select a new location for the updated Survey Database, as shown in Figure 2–71.

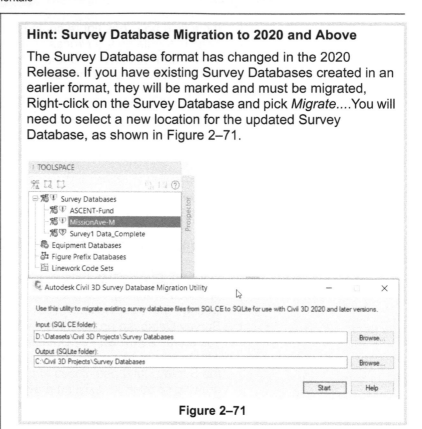

Figure 2–71

Practice 2e | Importing Survey Data

Practice Objective

- Import points from an ASCII file created from the field survey.

In this practice, you will import an ASCII file created in the field.

1. Continue working with the drawing from the previous practice or open **SUV1-E.dwg** from the *C:\Civil 3D Projects\ Working\Survey* folder.

2. On the *Survey* tab, right-click on **Survey Databases** and select **Set working folder**, as shown in Figure 2–72.

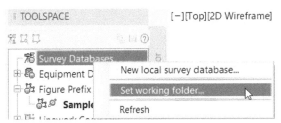

Figure 2–72

3. Browse to C:*Civil 3D Projects\Survey Databases* and click the **Select Folder** button in the lower right corner.

4. In the *Home* tab>expanded Create Ground Data panel, click (Import Survey Data).

5. On the Specify Database page, click **Create New Survey Database...**, as shown in Figure 2–73.

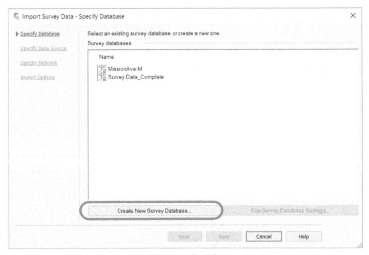

Figure 2–73

6. Type **ASCENT-Fund** for the name and click **OK**.

7. Click **Edit Survey Database Settings...** as shown in Figure 2–74.

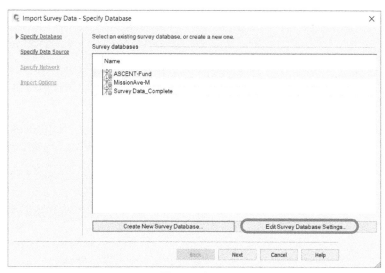

Figure 2–74

8. Under *Units* in the Survey Database Settings dialog box, for the *Coordinate Zone*, click the **Browse** icon. In the Select Coordinate Zone dialog box, select **NSRS 2007 California State Planes, Zone VI, US Foot** (as shown in Figure 2–75). Click **OK** twice and then click **Next**.

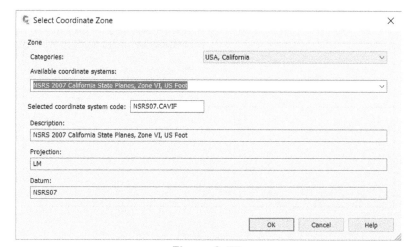

Figure 2–75

9. On the Specify Data Sources page, do the following, as shown in Figure 2–76:

- Expand the Data source type drop-down list and select **Point File**.

- Click ✚ (Add file) and browse to *C:\Civil 3D Projects\Survey Databases\Data*. Select **Field Survey.txt** and open it.

- For the file format, select **PNEZD (comma delimited)**.

- Click **Next**.

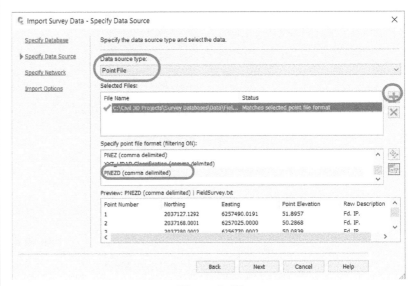

Figure 2–76

10. On the Survey Network page, click **Next**.

11. On the Import Options page, select **Process linework during import**, **Insert figure objects**, and **Insert survey points**, as shown in Figure 2–77. Click **Finish**.

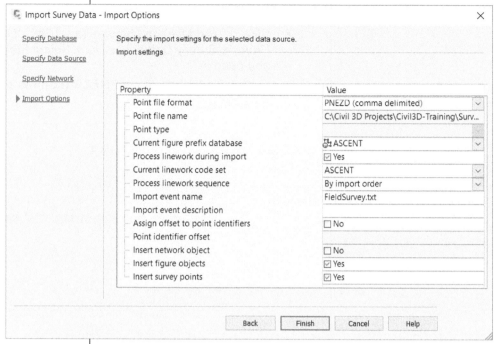

Figure 2–77

12. Save the drawing.

2.9 Reviewing and Editing Points

Reviewing and editing point data occurs throughout the Autodesk Civil 3D environment. It is as simple as selecting a point in the drawing, right-clicking, and selecting **Edit Points…**. You can also edit points using the shortcut menu in the *Points* heading in the Toolspace, *Prospector* tab. Alternatively, you can select a point entry in the Toolspace, *Prospector's* preview area.

Repositioning Point Labels

When selecting a point, it displays multiple grips. Click the move grip when you want to relocate the label.

Each point label style has **Dragged State** parameters. These parameters affect the label's behavior when moving the label from its original label position. Depending on the **Dragged State** parameters, a label can change completely (Stacked text) or display as it was originally defined (As composed). An example of a label is shown in Figure 2–78.

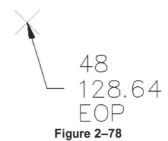

48
128.64
EOP

Figure 2–78

A point displays three grips when selected. Use the **Rectangle** label grip to Move, Rotate, and Toggle sub item grips and Reset the label. Use the Diamond point object grip to Move and Rotate both the label and marker, Rotate just the marker, reset marker rotation, and Reset all. The third grip is a plus symbol that enables you to add vertices to the leader, as shown in Figure 2–79.

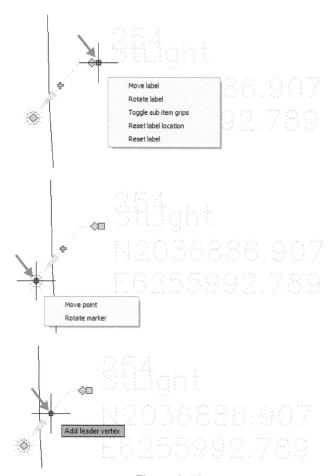

Figure 2–79

- Each label component can be modified and the change is only for that point.

- Point objects can be set to automatically rotate to match the current view using style settings. If this is not preferred, they can have a rotation assigned directly through the AutoCAD Properties dialog box.

- You can reset a label to its original position by selecting the point, right-clicking, and selecting **Reset Label**.

2.10 Point Reports

The surveyor needs to produce point reports. These can include a record list for the project, a checklist to find errors, reference for field crews, stakeout, etc. Incorporating survey data with an Autodesk Civil 3D engineering project is unique in that it relies on connection and communication with third party survey equipment and software. Autodesk has collaborated with the major survey equipment vendors (TDS Survey Link, TOPCON Link, Trimble Link, Carlson Connect, and Leica X-Change) and they have developed applications that interface their equipment with the Autodesk Civil 3D software.

Autodesk Civil 3D points can be exported and then uploaded to the survey equipment without relying on manually created lists. However, a documented point list might be required. There are several ways to create reports about points.

Point Reports - Reports Manager

The Autodesk Civil 3D Reports Manager produces several point reports. To create reports from the Reports Manager, the Toolspace, *Toolbox* tab must be available. To display the Toolspace, *Toolbox* tab, go to the *Home* tab>Palettes panel, and select **Toolbox**. Then select the Toolspace, *Toolbox* tab and expand the *Reports Manager* collection to display a list of object type reports, as shown in Figure 2–80.

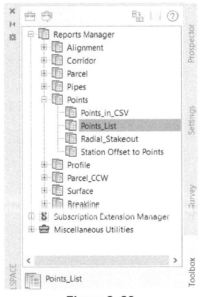

Figure 2–80

Points are easily organized into a convenient, legible list that displays the point number, northing, easting, elevation, and description (as shown in Figure 2–81). Another point report lists the points' station and offset values relative to an alignment. Another report calculates distances and angles from an occupied and a backsight. You can transfer points to Microsoft Excel spreadsheets using a CSV report. To create these reports, select the report's name, right-click, and select **Execute...**.

Number	Northing	Easting	Elevation	Description
1	632055.919	2208068.041	900.655	MON
2	631396.467	2207989.483	900.171	MON
3	630834.659	2207979.534	898.369	MON
4	631382.131	2207989.229	900.174	MON

Figure 2–81

Point Editor Reports

Another report method is to use the Point Editor vista. In the Toolspace, *Prospector* tab, select **Points**, right-click, and select **Edit...** to display the Point Editor vista, as shown in Figure 2–82.

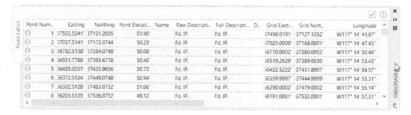

Figure 2–82

In the vista, you can select individual points using <Ctrl> or select blocks of points using <Shift>. When done selecting points, right-click and select **Copy to clipboard**. You can then paste the copied points into Microsoft Excel, Notepad, or any application that accepts the points, as shown in Figure 2–83.

Figure 2–83

Practice 2f

Manipulating Points and Point Reports

Practice Objectives

- Modify the label position for points to ensure that the plan is readable.
- Share information about points used for error checking or staking out points using predefined reports.

Task 1 - Modify the position of the labels.

1. Continue working with the drawing from the previous practice or open **SUV1-F**.dwg.

This positions the point at the center of the screen.

2. In the preview point list, scroll down until the point number **260** displays. Select it, right-click, and select **Zoom to**, as shown in Figure 2–84.

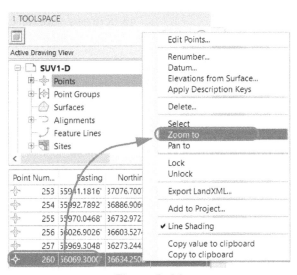

Figure 2–84

3. In a typical drafting workflow, points can overlap, making them illegible. Since the Point Style's text height is a function of the drawing scale, changing the *Annotation Scale* changes the text size. If need be, on the Status Bar, set the *Annotation Scale* to 1"=40', as shown in Figure 2–85, to change the point size in the drawing.

Figure 2–85

---

4. Select point 260 to display its grips. Select the Drag Label grip, as shown in Figure 2–86, to relocate the label.

Figure 2–86

5. With the label still displaying grips, hover on the Rectangle grip and select **Reset Label**.

6. With the label still displaying grips, hover over the Square label grip to display the options for moving, rotating, and additional sub item grips, as shown in Figure 2–87. Select **Rotate label** and rotate the label. Type **45** to rotate the label 45 degrees counter-clockwise.

Figure 2–87

7. With the label still displaying grips, hover over the diamond point grip to display the options to move, rotate label and marker, and Rotate marker, as shown in Figure 2–88. Select **Rotate marker** and rotate the marker. Type **45** to rotate the marker 45 degrees counter-clockwise.

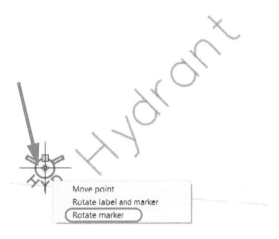

Figure 2–88

8. With the label still displaying grips, hover over the diamond point grip again and select **Reset all**, as shown in Figure 2–89.

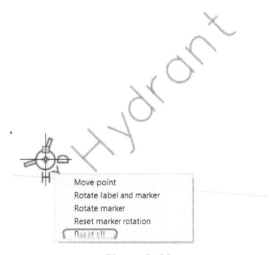

Figure 2–89

9. Save the drawing.

Task 2 - Create point reports.

1. If the Toolspace, *Toolbox* tab is not displayed in the
   Toolspace, select the *Home* tab and click 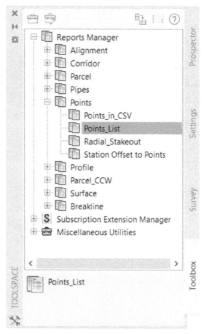 (Toolbox), to
   display the Toolspace, *Toolbox* tab.

2. Select the Toolspace, *Toolbox* tab and expand the *Reports Manager* collection to display the list of object type reports. Expand the *Points* collection, as shown in Figure 2–90.

Figure 2–90

3. Select **Point List**, right-click, and select **Execute**.

4. In the Export to LandXML dialog box, click **OK** to generate the report. In the Save As dialog box, browse to the *C:\Civil 3D Projects\Documents\Reports* folder and type **<Your Initials>-Points.html**, and save the file.

5. The point list displays in Internet Explorer. Review the report and when done, close it.

6. Save the drawing

2.11 Point Groups

Point groups organize points that share common descriptions and characteristics (such as existing storm, gas lines, building corners, etc.). If you consider the points in the project to be a database, then Point Groups can be considered a means of querying the point database.

Point groups also enable points to display different point or label styles. For example, a Landscape Architect needs to display different symbols for each tree species, while an Engineer only needs to display a generic tree symbol. The Description Key Set enables you to assign the tree species symbols for the Landscape Architect, and a point group enables generic tree symbols to override the symbols for the Engineer. Another function of a point group is to hide all of the points.

In the Autodesk Civil 3D software, point groups can be defined in the template along with a Description Key Set. When you create a new drawing from this template and import points, they are assigned their symbols and can be sorted into point groups.

All points in a drawing belong to the **_All Points** point group. Consider this point group as the point database. It cannot be deleted and initially is not in a drawing until you add points. All new point groups include all drawing points or a subset of drawing points (referenced points from the **_All Points** point group).

Defining Point Groups

To create a new point group, select the Toolspace, *Prospector* tab, right-click on the *Point Groups* collection and select **New…**. Alternatively, in the *Home* tab, expand *Points* and select **Create Point Group**.

When you select **New…** or **Create Point Group**, the Point Group Properties dialog box opens. It has nine tabs, each affecting the point group's definition.

The *Point Groups*, *Raw Desc Matching*, *Include*, and *Query Builder* tabs add points to the point group. The *Exclude* tab removes points from a point group.

The *Information* tab defines the point group's name. The *Point style* and *Point label style* should remain at their defaults, unless you want to use either style to override the assigned styles of the points in the point group. The points in the point group display their originally assigned styles until you toggle on the override. A point group can be locked by toggling on the **Object locked** option to prevent any changes to the group. The Point Group Properties dialog box is shown in Figure 2–91.

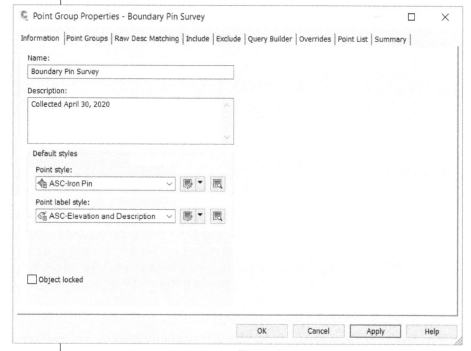

Figure 2–91

The *Point Groups* tab lists the drawing's groups. A point group can be created from other point groups, thereby creating a hierarchy of Point Groups. When you select a point group name, the group and its points become members of the new point group. For example, the point group **Trees** is created from the point groups *Maple*, *Walnut*, *Oak*, etc.

The *Raw Desc Matching* tab lists codes from the Description Key Code set. When you toggle on the code, any point matching the code becomes part of the point group.

If you cannot select a point with the previous two methods, the *Include* tab enables you to include points by specifically entering in the selection criteria. The criteria include the point number (point number list or by selection), elevation, name, raw description, full description, and all points.

- **With numbers matching:** Selects points by a point number range or list. When creating a list, sequential point numbers are hyphenated (1-20) and individual numbers are in a comma delimited list. A point list can include sequential and individual points (1-20, 14, 44, 50-60). Select **Selection Set in Drawing** to select the points in the drawing and list their point numbers at the top of the *Include* tab. If using the **Selection Set in Drawing** method, keep in mind that a Point Group defined by exact numbers will not be dynamic since it is fixed on individual point numbers.

- **With elevations matching:** Enables you to select points by entering a specific elevation or by specifying a minimum and/or maximum elevation. For example, valid entries include >100,<400, and >100. The first entry only includes points whose elevation is above 100, but less than 400. The second entry only includes points whose elevation is greater than 100. A point without an elevation cannot be selected using this method. An elevation range, defined by separating the start and end numbers with a hyphen, includes points whose elevation falls in the range (1-100). This can be combined with greater or less than symbols.

- **With names matching:** Selects points based on matching their point names. Enter one or more point names separated by commas.

- **With raw/full descriptions matching:** Selects points based on matching an entered raw or full description. Enter one or more descriptions separated by commas. You can use the same wildcards as the Description Key Set. Generally, this method uses the asterisk (*) as the wildcard after the description (e.g., PINE*, CTV*, CL*, etc.). By default, this is not case-sensitive.

- **Include all points:** Assigns all points in the drawing to the point group. When this option is toggled on, all other **Include** options are disabled.

The *Exclude* tab has the same options as the *Include* tab, except for the **Include All Points** option.

The *Query Builder* tab creates one or more expressions to select points. Each query is a row selecting points. As with all SQL queries, you combine expressions using the operators AND, OR, and NOT. You can also use parentheses to group expressions. It is here where you can make the criteria case-sensitive.

The *Overrides* tab overrides the points in the point group's raw description, elevation, point style, and/or point label style. For example, you can override specific tree species symbols with a generic tree symbol, override a label style when displaying this group, or override the point and label style with none (to hide all points).

The point group display order affects points and their overrides. To change how the point groups display, modify the Point Group display order.

The *Point List* tab displays the point group's points. This tab enables you to review points that are currently in the point group.

The *Summary* tab displays the point group's settings. You can print this tab as a report by cutting and pasting it into a document.

Updating Out-of-Date Point Groups

After defining point groups and adding points to a drawing, the group becomes out of date before assigning the points to the group. The point group will have an Alert symbol (!) next to it for easy recognition in the Prospector, as shown in Figure 2–92.

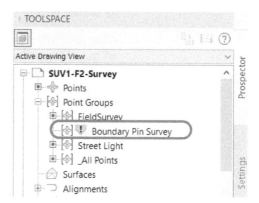

Figure 2–92

This enables you to verify that the point(s) should become part of the group. To review why a group is out of date, select the group, right-click, and select **Show Changes…** If the changes are correct, select **Update** to add the points to the group. If you know that all of the groups displaying as out of date should be updated, right-click on the *Point Groups* collection and select **Update**. At this level, the command updates all of the point groups.

Unlike other Civil 3D objects (such as Surfaces and Corridors), you cannot set Point Groups to be *Rebuilt Automatically*.

Overriding Point Group Properties

When working with points, you might want them to display different labels, not be displayed, or display different symbols. Each required change is a function of a point group override. A point group that contains all of the points and overrides their symbols and labels with none does not display any points. This is similar to freezing all of the layers involved with points. A point group that changes the symbols that a group displays overrides the label styles assigned to the point in the point group. To display a different symbol, the point group overrides the assigned point styles. To set the style and override the assigned styles, toggle on the point group in the *Overrides* tab and set the styles in the *Override* column of the point group, as shown in Figure 2–93.

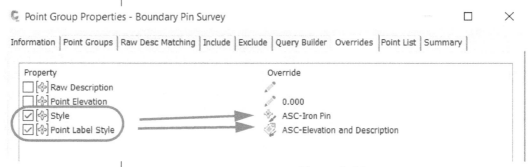

Figure 2–93

Point Groups Display Properties

When creating a point group, it is placed at the top of the point group list. The point group list is more than a list of point groups; it is also the Autodesk Civil 3D's point draw order. The Autodesk Civil 3D software draws the point groups starting from the bottom of the list to the top. If **_All Points** is the first drawn point group and the remaining point groups are subsets of all points, the individual point group does not display, but all of the points display.

To display point groups that are a subset of all points, you must create a point group whose purpose is to hide all points. This popular point group is commonly called *No Display*. With this group, any point group drawn after it displays its members without *seeing* the other points.

The Autodesk Civil 3D software draws point groups from the bottom to the top of the list. To manipulate the display order, right-click on the *Point Groups* collection in the Toolspace, *Prospector* tab and select **Properties**. The Point Groups dialog box opens, enabling you to modify the point group display order using the arrows on the right, as shown in Figure 2–94.

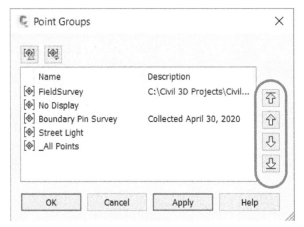

Figure 2–94

These arrows enable you to select the required point group and move it up or down in the list (or all of the way to the top or bottom of the list with one click, ⬆/⬇) in the hierarchy for display purposes. The Point Groups dialog box has two additional icons at the top. The first icon displays the changes that need to occur in the point groups and the second icon updates them.

If you use Description Key Sets, a point displays the assigned point and label style when it is part of any point group. The only time the point displays another style is when you override the style (in the Point Group Properties dialog box, in the *Overrides* tab).

With the Description Key Set and display order shown in Figure 2–95, the points display their originally assigned point label styles.

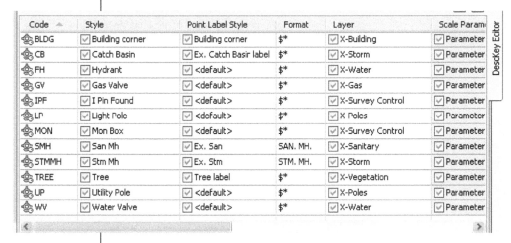

Code	Style	Point Label Style	Format	Layer	Scale Param
BLDG	Building corner	Building corner	$*	X-Building	Parameter
CB	Catch Basin	Ex. Catch Basin label	$*	X-Storm	Parameter
FH	Hydrant	<default>	$*	X-Water	Parameter
GV	Gas Valve	<default>	$*	X-Gas	Parameter
IPF	I Pin Found	<default>	$*	X-Survey Control	Parameter
LP	Light Pole	<default>	$*	X-Poles	Parameter
MON	Mon Box	<default>	$*	X-Survey Control	Parameter
SMH	San Mh	Ex. San	SAN. MH.	X-Sanitary	Parameter
STMMH	Stm Mh	Ex. Stm	STM. MH.	X-Storm	Parameter
TREE	Tree	Tree label	$*	X-Vegetation	Parameter
UP	Utility Pole	<default>	$*	X-Poles	Parameter
WV	Water Valve	<default>	$*	X-Water	Parameter

Figure 2–95

The *No Display* point group includes all of the points, but overrides the originally assigned point style and point label styles with **<none>**. When *No Display* is moved to the list's top, no points display. The Point Groups dialog box is shown in Figure 2–96.

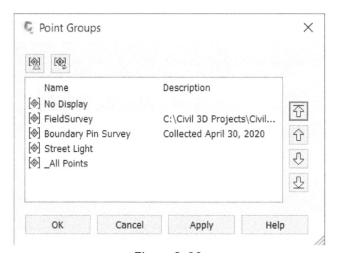

Figure 2–96

Practice 2g | Creating Point Groups

Practice Objective

- Create point groups and control the visibility of the points within the groups.

In this practice, you will create point groups.

Task 1 - Create point groups (Boundary Pin Survey).

1. Continue working with the drawing from the previous practice or open **SUV1-FG.dwg**.

2. In the Toolspace, *Prospector* tab, select **Point Groups**, right-click, and select **New...**, as shown in Figure 2–97.

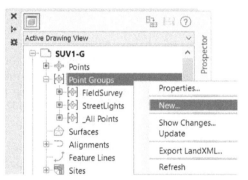

Figure 2–97

3. In the Point Group Properties dialog box, in the *Information* tab, type **Boundary Pin Survey** in the *Name* field, set the *Point style* to **ASC-Iron Pin**, and set the *Point label style* to **ASC-Elevation and Description**, as shown in Figure 2–98.

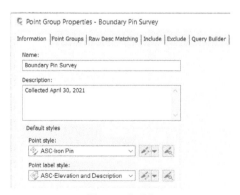

Figure 2–98

This will also select other Iron Pin descriptions beyond the "Found" ones, which the surveyor may use to determine Iron Pins.

4. Select the *Include* tab. Select the **With raw description matching** option. Type ***IP.** in the field to select all of the points that have the last three characters *IP.* (iron pin). (Verify that a period follows IP. By default, this is NOT case sensitive.) You can confirm this in the *Point List* tab, as shown in Figure 2–99.

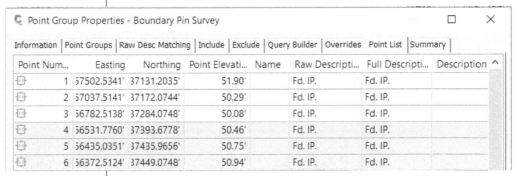

Point Num...	Easting	Northing	Point Elevati...	Name	Raw Descripti...	Full Descripti...	Description
1	57502.5341'	37131.2035'	51.90'		Fd. IP.	Fd. IP.	
2	57037.5141'	37172.0744'	50.29'		Fd. IP.	Fd. IP.	
3	56782.5138'	37284.0748'	50.08'		Fd. IP.	Fd. IP.	
4	56531.7760'	37393.6778'	50.46'		Fd. IP.	Fd. IP.	
5	56435.0351'	37435.9656'	50.75'		Fd. IP.	Fd. IP.	
6	56372.5124'	37449.0748'	50.94'		Fd. IP.	Fd. IP.	

Figure 2–99

5. Click **OK** to close the dialog box and apply the changes.

Task 2 - Create point groups (No display).

Continue working with the drawing from the previous task. In this task, you will use the point group to control the points display. Not only will you be able to display the same point differently, but you will also be able to control the visibility of the points. This eliminates needing to use the Layer command to thaw and freeze layers.

1. In the *View* tab>Named Views panel, select the preset view **Suv Main**.

2. As in Task 1, select **Point Groups**, right-click, and select **New...** to create a new point group. In the *Information* tab, type **No display** for the *Name*.

3. Select **<none>** for both the *Point style* and the *Point label style*, as shown in Figure 2–100.

Figure 2–100

4. Select the *Include* tab, select **Include all points** to set it to **True**. Select the *Point List* tab to confirm that all of the points have been included.

5. Select the *Overrides* tab and select **Style** and **Point Label Style**, as shown in Figure 2–101.

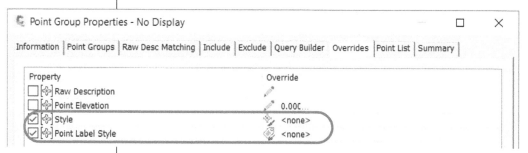

Figure 2–101

6. Click **OK** to create the point group. Note that the points have disappeared.

7. To control the hierarchy and the display of the point group style, select the Toolspace, *Prospector* tab, select **Point Groups**, right-click, and select **Properties**.

8. In the Point Groups dialog box, select the **Boundary Pin Survey** point group and move it to the top of the list by clicking ⬆, as shown in Figure 2–102.

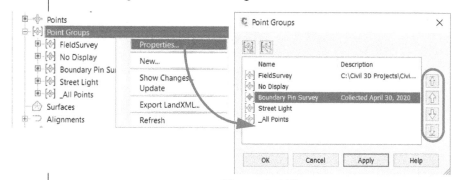

Figure 2–102

9. Click **OK** to apply the changes. Only the points in the Boundary Pin point group display. If the property pins are not displayed you might need to **regen** the drawing (type **RE**, and press <Enter).

10. Experiment with moving point groups up and down the list to control the display of points.

11. Save the drawing.

2.12 Lines and Curves

A typical land development project commences with plotting out the property being subdivided, based on the legal description. Planners need to enter lines and curves representing the property boundaries into the computer from legal text description. The Autodesk Civil 3D software makes this task easy with the many options under the **Lines** and **Curves** commands in the *Home* tab>Draw panel. Expanding the Lines or Curves commands displays several options that are not found in the ordinary AutoCAD® software, as shown in Figure 2–103.

Figure 2–103

A second option is to use transparent commands. These are similar to Object Snaps in that they are only accessible while in another command that is searching for a point.

Once the required command has been started, you can select the transparent commands as follows:

- From the Transparent Command toolbar
- From the *Transparent Command* ribbon tab
- By typing an apostrophe letter combination in the Command Line
- From the right-click menu>**Transparent Commands**

Icon	Command Line	Description
	'AD	**Angle Distance:** Specifies a point location at an angle and distance from a known point and direction.
	'BD	**Bearing Distance:** Specifies a point location at a bearing and distance from a known point (or the last point occupied).
	'ZD	**Azimuth Distance:** Specifies a point location at an azimuth and distance from a known point (or the last point occupied).
	'DD	**Deflection Distance:** Specifies a point location at an angle and distance from a known point and previous direction.
	'NE	**Northing Easting:** Specifies a point location using northing and easting coordinates.
	'GN	**Grid Northing Grid Easting:** Specifies a point location using a grid northing and grid easting. (Note: You must have the drawing zone, coordinate system and transformations set for grids.)
	'LL	**Latitude Longitude:** Specifies a point location using latitude and longitude. (Note: You must have the drawing zone, coordinate system, and transformations set.)
	'PN	**Point Number:** Specifies a point location using a point number found in the drawing or active project.
	'PA	**Point Name:** Specifies a point location using a point name found in the drawing or active project.
	'PO	**Point Object:** Specifies a point location by picking any part of an existing COGO point in the drawing.

	'ZTP	**Zoom to Point:** Zooms to a point in the drawing or active project by specifying the point number or name.
	'SS	**Side Shot:** Specifies a point location at an angle and distance from a known point and direction (uses the last two entered points to set the reference line).
	'SO	**Station Offset:** Specifies a point location at a station and an offset from an alignment in the current drawing.
	.g	**Point Object Filter:** Specifies a point location by picking any part of an existing COGO point in the drawing.
	'STAE	**Profile Station from Plan:** Specifies a profile view point location by specifying an alignment station in plan and an elevation.
	'SSE	**Profile Station and Elevation from Plan:** Specifies a profile view point location by specifying a surface, an alignment station, and a point in plan view.
	'SPE	**Profile Station and Elevation from COGO Point:** Specifies a profile view point location by specifying a COGO point and an alignment station in plan view.
	'PSE	**Profile Station Elevation:** Specifies a profile view point location by specifying a station and an elevation.
	'PGS	**Profile Grade Station:** Specifies a profile view point location using grade and station values from a known point.
	'PGE	**Profile Grade Elevation:** Specifies a profile view point location using grade and elevation values from a known point.
	'PGL	**Profile Grade Length:** Specifies a profile view point location using grade and length values from a known point (or the last point occupied).
	'MR	**Match Radius:** Specifies a radius equal to that of an existing object.
	ML	**Match Length:** Specifies a length equal to that of an existing object.
	'CCALC	**Curve Calculator:** Calculates curve parameters based on input.

The benefit to using these transparent commands to draw parcels over the **Lines** and **Curves** options (shown previously in Figure 2–103) is that a **Polyline** command can be used to create one entity rather than many individual lines that would need to be joined later.

Practice 2h

Beginning a Subdivision Project

Practice Objective

- Draw a parcel from a legal description.

In this practice, you will use the following legal description below to draw a parcel. Later, you will create a parcel from the linework.

*From the **POINT OF BEGINNING**; thence, S 00° 26' 42.2" W for a distance of 922.4138 feet to a point on a line. Thence, S 00° 24' 20.8" W for a distance of 508.3493 feet to a point on a line. Thence, S 66° 03' 35.8" W for a distance of 92.1845 feet to the beginning of a curve.*

Said curve turning to the right through 42° 35' 49.2", having a radius of 627.1788 feet, and whose long chord bears S 87° 21' 30.4" W for a distance of 455.6165 feet to the beginning of another curve.

Said curve turning to the left through an angle of 19° 13' 40.4", having a radius of 154.4828 feet, and whose long chord bears N 80° 57' 25.2" W for a distance of 51.6000 feet.

*Thence, S 89° 25' 44.6" W for a distance of 724.9442 feet to a point on a line. Thence, N 00° 11' 09.9" E for a distance of 1904.2647 feet to a point on a line. Thence, S 61° 50' 15.3" E for a distance of 135.9034 feet to a point on a line. Thence, S 64° 05' 35.8" E for a distance of 77.8201 feet to a point on a line. Thence, S 78° 09' 29.2" E for a distance of 63.8821 feet to a point on a line. Thence, S 66° 23' 19.5" E for a distance of 379.2248 feet to a point on a line. Thence, S 66° 17' 17.4" E for a distance of 278.5122 feet to a point on a line. Thence S 84° 58' 37.7" E a distance of 466.8116 feet to the **POINT OF BEGINNING**.*

1. Continue working on the drawing from the previous practice or open **SUV1 H Survey .dwg** from the *C:\Civil 3D Projects\Working\Survey* folder.

---

2. In effect, you will be tracing over the green perimeter in the drawing, using the legal information provided, as shown in Figure 2–104.

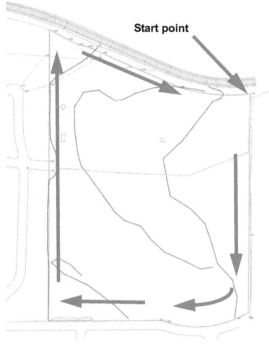

Start point

Figure 2–104

3. Start the **Line** command. For the starting point, type **6257490.0191,2037127.1292** and press <Enter>.

4. In the ribbon, in the *Transparent Commands* tab, click
   (Bearing Distance).

5. For the first line, type the following:
   - *Quadrant:* **3** (for the southwest quadrant)
   - *Bearing:* **0.26422**
   - *Distance:* **922.4138**

   Stay in the **Line** command with the **Bearing Distance** transparent command running for the next few lines.

6. For the next two line segments, use the following values:

Quadrant	Bearing	Distance
3	0.24208	508.3493
3	66.03358	92.1845

7. Press <Esc> twice to end the command.

8. In the *Home* tab>Draw panel, click (Create Curve from End of Object). Select the last line that was drawn using the Bearing Distance command.

Remember to press <Enter> after you input a value.

9. From the command options, select **Radius**. Set the radius to **627.1788**.

10. From the command options, select **Chord**. Set the chord length to **455.6165**.

11. In the *Home* tab>Draw panel, click (Create Reverse or Compound Curve). Select the last curve drawn.

12. From the command options, select **Reverse**. Set the radius to **154.4828**.

13. From the command options, select **Chord**. Set the chord length to **51.6**.

14. Start the **Line** command. For the starting point, pick the endpoint of the last arc drawn.

15. In the Transparent Command toolbar, click (Bearing Distance).

16. For the remaining line segments, use the following values:

Quadrant	Bearing	Distance
3	89.25446	724.9442
1	0.11099	1904.2647
2	61.50153	135.9034
2	64.05358	77.8201
2	78.09292	63.8821
2	66.23195	379.2248
2	66.17174	278.5122

The legal description at the beginning of this practice was used to find the bearings and distances to type.

17. Press <Esc> once to exit the **Bearing Distance** transparent command. Hold <Ctrl> as you right-click and select **Endpoint**, then select the starting point of the parcel to close on the point of beginning.

This prevents closure errors from occurring later.

18. Start the **Polyline Edit** command by typing **PE**. In the model, select one of the lines or curves you just created and press <Enter> to turn it into a polyline.

19. Select the **Join** option and then select all of the lines and curves you just created. Press <Enter> to create one closed polyline. Press <Esc> to end the command.

20. Save the drawing.

21. (Optional) Save the drawing as **<Your Initials>-Survey-Complete.dwg** in the *C:\Civil 3D Projects\References\DWG\ Survey* folder.

22. Update the relative paths of the referenced drawings in the alert box.

Chapter Review Questions

1. If you need linework, which method should you use to import survey data?

    a. Import survey data using the Survey Database.

    b. Import survey data using the **Import Points** command.

    c. Import survey data using the Map Explorer.

    d. Create points using the Toolspace, *Prospector* tab.

2. If you need to analyze the field data using the analysis tools available in the Survey Database, you must use a field book file rather than a text file.

    a. True

    b. False

3. Which of these is not a type of point object within the Autodesk Civil 3D software?

    a. COGO Point

    b. North Point

    c. Survey Point

    d. AutoCAD Point

4. Which of these is NOT an option within the Description Key manager?

    a. Rotating the Point

    b. Changing the Point Full Description

    c. Deleting the Point

    d. Assigning a Point Label

5. Which tab in the Point Label Style Composer dialog box controls the appearance of a point label when the point label grip is selected in the drawing and moved away from the point itself?

    a. *General* tab

    b. *Layout* tab

    c. *Dragged State* tab

    d. *Summary* tab

6. How do you control the next point number to be used in a drawing?

   a. The **Point Identity** parameters located in the expanded area in the Create Points toolbar.

   b. Under Label Styles in the Toolspace, *Settings* tab.

   c. In the Toolspace, *Survey* tab, right-click on Survey Points.

   d. In the Toolspace, *Prospector* tab, right-click on Survey Points.

7. Can the **_All Points** point group be deleted?

   a. Yes

   b. No

8. Can a point group be made out of point groups?

   a. Yes

   b. No

9. How do you draw a parcel boundary from a legal description in the most efficient way possible?

   a. Calculate the Cartesian coordinate angle for each bearing or azimuth within the legal description and type (distance)<(angle) for each line or curve.

   b. Calculate the Cartesian coordinate angle for each bearing or azimuth within the legal description, place the cursor in that direction, and type the distance.

   c. Use the extended **Lines** and **Curves** options in the *Home* tab>Draw panel or **Transparent** commands in the **Line** or **Polyline** command.

   d. There is no fast way to do this.

Command Summary

Button	Command	Location
	Create Points	• **Ribbon:** *Home* tab>Create Ground Data panel
	Import Points from File	• **Ribbon:** *Insert* tab>Import panel • **Toolbar:** Create Points • **Command Prompt:** ImportPoints
	Bearing Distance	• **Toolbar:** Transparent Commands • **Command Prompt:** 'bd
	Create Curve from End of Object	• **Ribbon:** *Home* tab>Draw panel • **Command Prompt:** CurveFromEndOfObject
	Import Survey Data	• **Ribbon:** *Home* tab>Create Ground Data panel • **Command Prompt:** ImportSurveyData
	Survey	• **Ribbon:** *Home* tab>Palettes panel
	Survey User Settings	• **Toolspace:** *Survey* tab
	Zoom To Points	• **Toolbar:** Transparent Commands • **Command Prompt:** 'ZTP

Surfaces

In this chapter, you will learn how to create a surface from contours and survey data. Then, you will refine the surface using breaklines, boundaries, and edits. Finally, you will analyze the surface and annotate it to communicate the existing conditions.

Learning Objectives in This Chapter

- List the steps required to build a surface in the Autodesk® Civil 3D® software.
- Adjust and edit a surface using surface properties and various commands.
- Add existing contour data to a surface to take advantage of data created by someone else.
- Add drawing objects to a surface to improve the accuracy of a TIN model.
- Add breaklines and boundaries to a surface to improve its accuracy.
- Analyze a surface using a quick profile or the object viewer.
- Label contour elevations, slope values, spot elevations, and watershed delineations to communicate surface information.
- Calculate the volume of cut and fill or adjusted cut and fill between two surfaces.
- Analyze a surface to determine the buildable area for the project conditions.

3.1 Surface Process

The surface building process can be divided into the following steps:

1. Assemble data.
2. Assign the data to a surface.
3. Evaluate the resulting surface.
4. Add breaklines, assign more data, modify the data, or edit the surface as required.

1. Assemble data

The first step in surface building is to acquire the initial surface data. This can be points, contours, 3D polylines, feature lines, AutoCAD® objects, ASCII coordinate files, and boundaries. Each data type provides specific information about a surface.

2. Assign data to a surface

Acquired data is assigned to a surface. Once assigned, the Autodesk Civil 3D software immediately processes this data and a surface object is created.

Surfaces are listed individually in the *Surfaces* collection in the Toolspace, *Prospector* tab. Each surface contains content information, as shown in Figure 3–1. The surface content includes *Masks, Watersheds,* and *Definition* elements. The *Definition* contains a list of all of the surface data that has been applied, including boundaries, breaklines, and points. The Toolspace, *Prospector* tab displays data for each type of surface data in the list view when one of these types is selected.

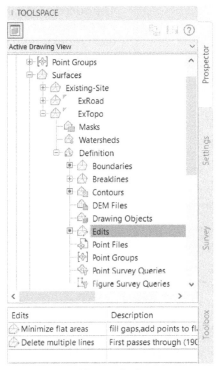

Figure 3–1

The Autodesk Civil 3D software processes the initial data into one of two types of surfaces. The first type, the **Triangulated Irregular Network** (TIN) surface, is the most common. With triangulated surfaces, surface points are connected to adjacent points by straight lines, resulting in a triangular mesh. Surfaces generated from contour lines have surface points created at their vertices, modified by weeding and supplementing factors. An example of this type of surface is shown in Figure 3–2.

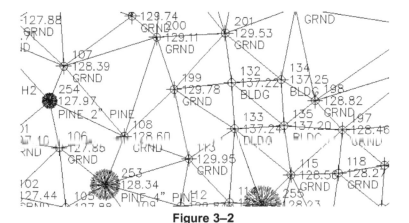

Figure 3–2

The second type of surface is a *Grid* surface. This surface interpolates and assigns an elevation from the surface data to each regular grid intersection. Most of the elevations at grid intersections are interpolated. **Digital Elevation Models** (DEMs) are a type of grid surface used in GIS applications. An example of this type of surface is shown in Figure 3–3.

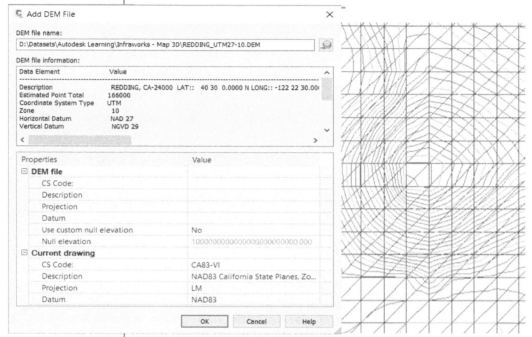

Figure 3–3

3. Evaluate the resulting surface

Surfaces, especially ones created from points, typically need some attention to represent them as accurately as possible. For any four adjacent surface points, there are two possible triangulations, as shown in Figure 3–4.

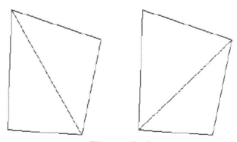

Figure 3–4

The differences can be difficult to envision when viewing the triangles from the TOP view, but these two configurations provide entirely different geometries. For example, note the surface shown in Figure 3–5.

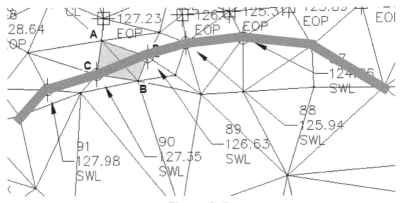

Figure 3–5

The triangulated points A, B, C, and D have a TIN line running from A to B. This configuration ignores the fact that C and D are both part of a continuous swale (SWL), indicated by the dashed line. In a 3D view, this configuration would resemble the example shown on the left in Figure 3–6. The correct triangulation has the triangle line *following* the linear feature rather than *crossing* it, as shown on the right.

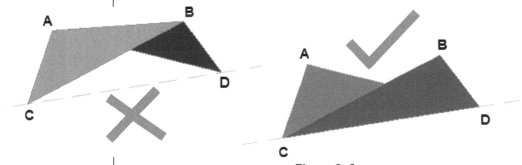

Figure 3–6

When creating surfaces, representing linear features correctly is very important. Examples of linear features include road center lines, edges-of-pavement, road shoulders, swales, berms, tops and bottoms of banks, and headwalls. Adding breaklines that follow linear features ensures that a terrain model is triangulated correctly along the features, rather than across them.

Other types of issues to watch out for include bad elevations (blown shots), elevations at 0 where there should be no chance of such elevation values, and points that were surveyed above or below the ground (e.g., the tops of fire hydrants). Unwanted triangles along the edges of the surface might connect points that should not be connected, which could also present problems.

In addition to the casual inspection of the triangles, surfaces can be evaluated by creating contour lines, reviewing the surface in 3D, and using the **Quick Profile** command.

4. Add breaklines, assign more data, modify the data, or edit the surface as required

After you have evaluated the surface, you can add the necessary breaklines or edit the surface directly to make adjustments. If the triangulation errors are isolated, editing the surface directly might be faster than creating and applying breaklines. For example, the triangulation issue in the previous *swale* example could be addressed by *swapping* the edge that crossed the swale center line. To do so, right-click on Edits under a Surface's definition in the Toolspace, *Prospector* tab and select **Swap Edge**, as shown in Figure 3–7.

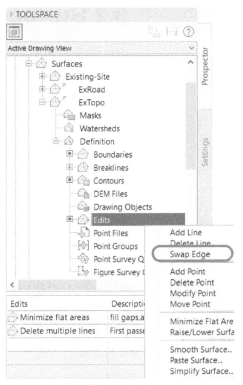

Figure 3–7

Other options enable you to add, move, modify, or remove points from the surface (but not change or erase the point object on which they were based), as well as add or remove triangle lines directly.

Minimize Flat Areas is a group of algorithms that can be used to minimize the number of flat areas created by contour data. **Raise/Lower Surface** enables you to raise and lower the entire surface by a set amount, and a **Smooth Surface** enables you to smooth surfaces using the **Natural Neighbor** or **Kriging** method. (Contour smoothing is handled through surface styles. These techniques smooth the actual surface geometry.)

3.2 Surface Properties

The *Definition* tab in the Surface Properties dialog box displays the **Build**, **Data**, and **Edit** operations for a surface. The *Operation Type* column is a record of the surface data addition and edits. Using the checkboxes, you can toggle off individual actions in the history and display the resulting changes to the surface. The entries can be toggled on or off. This helps to isolate possible errors or review features (such as surface slopes) that are greatly affected by the addition of a headwall or retaining wall.

You can change the order of items in the list of operations. Operations higher in the list are applied to the surface before items further down in the list. Open this dialog box by right-clicking on the surface name in the Toolspace, *Prospector* tab (or by selecting the surface in the drawing and right-clicking) and selecting **Surface Properties...**. It is also featured prominently in the contextual ribbon when the surface is selected. The dialog box is shown in Figure 3–8.

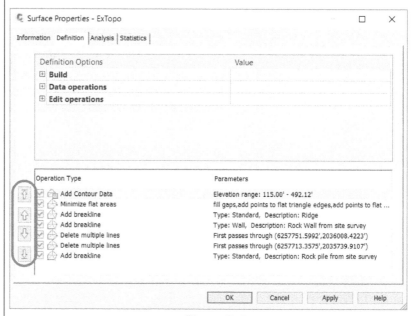

Figure 3–8

The *Information* tab enables you to rename the surface, edit the description, apply a surface object style, and render material, which controls how the surface displays in a rendered view or when the surface is exported to another (rendering) program.

The *Statistics* tab displays the current surface slope, elevation, and triangulation. It contains three areas:

- **General:** Provides an overall view of the surface. The **Minimum**, **Maximum**, and **Mean** elevations are the important entries in this area and provide the first hint of bad or incorrect data.

- **Extended:** Reports the **2D** and **3D** surface areas and **Minimum**, **Maximum**, and **Mean** slope values.

- **TIN:** Reviews the number of triangles, minimum and maximum triangle areas, and leg lengths in the surface.

The areas of triangles, along with the minimum and maximum triangle side lengths are indicators of data consistency. Generally, the longest triangles form around the perimeter of the surface. Limiting the length of triangle edges removes these types of triangles from the surface. You can delete these lines rather than try to set an optimum length, or you can create a boundary to prevent these types of triangles from being created.

When surfaces are created, they are assigned properties based on the *Build Options* area in the Edit Command Settings dialog box, as shown on the right in Figure 3–9. To open this dialog box, right-click on the **Create Surface** command and select **Edit Command Settings**, as shown on the left in Figure 3–9.

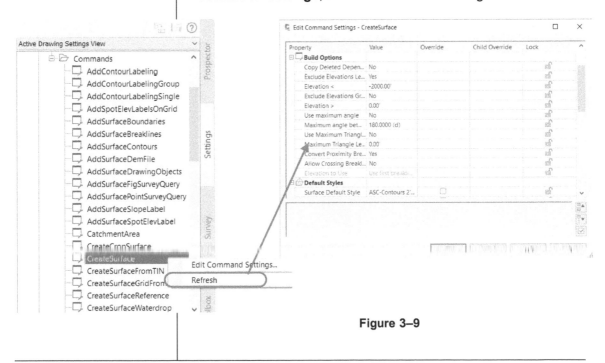

Figure 3–9

Surface Rebuilding

Some surface edits and point modifications can render a surface out of date. At that point, the surface is flagged as being out of date in the Toolspace, *Prospector* tab, as indicated by the **Drawing Item Modifier** icon shown in Figure 3–10.

Figure 3–10

When this occurs, you can right-click on the surface in the Toolspace, *Prospector* tab and select **Rebuild**. This updates the surface to reflect the recent changes. Alternatively, you can right-click on the surface in the Toolspace, *Prospector* tab and select **Rebuild-Automatic**, which updates the surface automatically without input from you. However, turning this option on increases the strain on the computer resources and graphics capabilities, depending on the surface size and complexity, as well as the computer hardware.

3.3 Contour Data

Surfaces can also be built directly from LIDAR or point clouds. This is explored in Appendix A: Additional Information.

Contour data is available from many sources. Large sites are often surveyed using aerial photogrammetry, which provides contour polylines and spot elevations. Contour data can also be obtained from other Civil Engineering applications.

Polylines with elevation can represent contours, which Autodesk Civil 3D can use to build a surface by triangulating between contours. The end of each triangle side connects to a vertex of two different contours.

When processing contours for surface data, the Autodesk Civil 3D software inspects the contour vertices for two conditions: too many data points representing similar data (e.g., 10 vertices on 15 units of contour length in an almost straight line), and not enough data points over the length of a contour.

You can set the values for these conditions in the Add Contour Data dialog box (as shown in Figure 3–11) when you add contour data.

Figure 3–11

Weeding Factors

The *weeding* process removes redundant vertices from contours. The first step in the weeding process is to inspect three adjacent contour vertices, whose overall distance is shorter than a user-specified distance (e.g., three vertices in less than 15 units of contour). When encountering this situation, the weeding process prompts you about the change in direction between the three vertices.

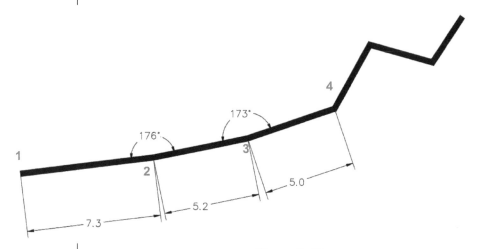

Figure 3–12

For example, in Figure 3–12 above, does the direction from vertex 1 to vertex 2 change more than four degrees when going from vertex 2 to vertex 3? If not, the vertices are almost in a straight line and are too close. The Autodesk Civil 3D software considers vertex 2 to be redundant and removes it from the surface data. This process repeats for the next three vertices. If the distance is under 15 units and the change of direction is less than four degrees, the next vertex 2 is removed from the data.

If a contour has three vertices in less than 15 units, and turns more than four degrees, vertex 2 is kept because the change in direction is significant. If there are more than 15 units between the three vertices, the Autodesk Civil 3D software moves on to the next group.

Therefore, the higher the number for distances and angles, the more vertices will be removed.

An important feature of weeding is not what it removes from the data, but what is left over. If not enough data remains, the numbers for the weeding factors should be set to lower values.

Supplementing Factors

When the Autodesk Civil 3D software inspects contour data, it uses supplementing factors to add vertices to the surface data. The first supplementing factor is the distance between contour vertices. When the distance between vertices is over 100 units, the Autodesk Civil 3D software adds a vertex to the data along the course of the contour as shown in Figure 3–13.

Figure 3–13

The second supplementing factor is a mid-ordinate distance for the curve segments of a contour. If the length of a line from the mid point of the chord length of the arc to perpendicular to the arc is more the desired distance, a new vertex is inserted at the midpoint of the arc and the process is repeated, as shown in Figure 3–14.

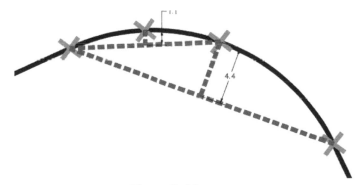

Figure 3–14

If curves are distributed throughout the contour data, a setting of 0.1 is a good starting point.

- All weeding and supplementing factors are user-specified.

- Weeding and supplementing does not modify the contours or polylines in a drawing, only their data.

- There is no *correct* setting for weeding and supplementing. Varying the values creates more or less surface data.

Contour Issues

You should be aware of two issues when working with contour data: bays and peninsulas within the contours and the lack of high and low point elevations. These two issues affect triangulation and the quality of a surface.

Bays and peninsulas within contours represent gullies or isolated high points on a surface. As long as there is data to work with, the Autodesk Civil 3D software builds a surface by triangulating between contours of different elevations. When the software cannot triangulate between different contours, the triangulation switches to connecting vertices on the same contour.

The **Minimize Flat Areas** command helps mitigate this situation by forcing the triangulation to target different contours, as shown in Figure 3–15. However, this method, similar to the swap edge method, does not correct every problem on a contour surface.

- To launch the **Minimize Flat Areas** command, in the Toolspace, *Prospector* tab, right-click on the *Edits* heading in the *Definition* collection of a surface and select the command.

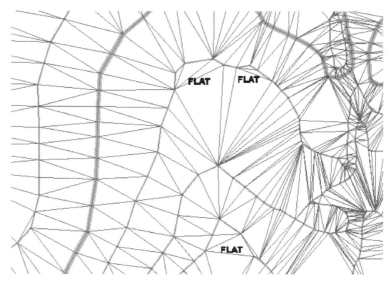

Figure 3–15

The second issue with contour data regards the loss of high and low points. Contours represent an elevation interval (120, 122, 123, etc.). However, the top of a hill could be 123.04 or 136.92 and the only contours present are for the elevations of 123 or 136. Spot elevations are required in the surface data to help correctly resolve the high and low spots of a surface.

- Flat spots and the loss of high and low points affect the calculation of volumes for earthworks, as shown in Figure 3–16.

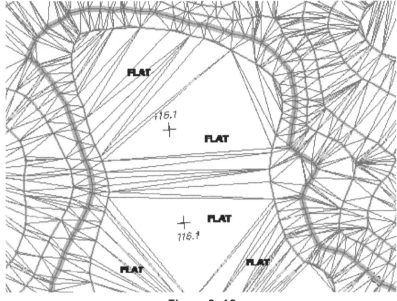

Figure 3–16

Minimizing Flat Triangle Strategies

By default, the Add Contour Data dialog box suggests using the **Minimize flat areas by:** options shown in Figure 3–17.

Figure 3–17

Together, these three methods attempt to detect and resolve peninsulas, bays, and other issues by adding additional points and filling in gaps based on surface trends. Generally, these provide the most expected results. The **Swapping edges** option is provided as a way of emulating how other terrain modeling software traditionally approached minimizing flat areas.

3.4 Other Surface Data

DEM Files

Digital Elevation Models (DEMs) are grid-based terrain models primarily used by GIS applications to represent large areas. Since they are large-scale and grid-based, they are generally only used in the Autodesk Civil 3D software for preliminary design and other approximate tasks.

Drawing Objects

AutoCAD points, text, blocks, and other objects can be used as surface data. Individual Autodesk Civil 3D point objects can also be selected using the **Drawing Objects** option. Selected objects need to have a valid elevation value.

- All data added as drawing objects is considered point data.

- You can add 3D lines and polyfaces using this method, but each end point is treated as if it were a point object. Linework is not treated as contours or breaklines. The Add Points From Drawing Objects dialog box is shown in Figure 3–18.

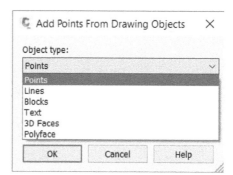

Figure 3–18

Point Files

Points in an ASCII point file can be used as surface data.

- You can use any import/export file format.

- This is an excellent way to create a large surface from a massive number of points, as it bypasses creating point objects, thereby reducing drawing overhead.

Point Groups

Using previously defined point groups in a surface definition enables you to isolate only the points on the ground to ensure that the tops of walls and invert elevations do not distort the surface, by not including these in the point group definition. This is a very common data type used for surfaces.

Point Survey Queries

Select points in a survey database can be used as surface data by creating a survey query. The point data is used, but point objects are not created.

- Dynamic references to the points provide a more seamless update if changes to the database or query are made.

- This is an excellent way to create a large surface from a massive number of points, as it bypasses creating point objects, thereby reducing drawing overhead.

- You can query the survey points required for creating a surface (similar to the point groups).

- Points from a survey query display under point groups in the surface definition.

Figure Survey Queries

Select figures in a survey database can be used as surface data. The figures are used as breaklines, but 3D polylines are not created in the drawing.

- Dynamic references to the figures provide a more seamless update if changes to the database or query are made.

- This is an excellent way to create a large surface from a massive number of figures, as it bypasses creating 3D polylines and turning them into breaklines, thereby reducing drawing overhead.

- Figures from a survey query display under breaklines in the surface definition.

Practice 3a

Creating an Existing Ground Surface

Practice Objectives

- Add contour data and point data to a surface that already exists in the drawing.
- Creating a Surface style

In this practice, you will define the surface with surface data. You will use this model to create existing ground contours and for reference during the design. You will begin the model with the provided contours and the previously created **Existing Ground** point group.

Task 1 - Create a surface and set properties.

Ensure that you open the indicated file rather than continuing to work from the last exercise. Otherwise you will be missing information in your surfaces.

1. Open **SUF1-A1.dwg** from the *C:\Civil 3D Projects\Working\ Surface* folder.

2. In the Toolspace, *Prospector* tab, select **Surfaces**, right-click, and select **Create Surface**.

3. In the Create Surface dialog box, set the following, as shown in Figure 3–19:

   - *Type*: **TIN surface**.
   - *Name:* **ExTopo**
   - *Description*: **Existing Topology**
   - *Style:* **ASC-Contours 2' and 10' (Background)**

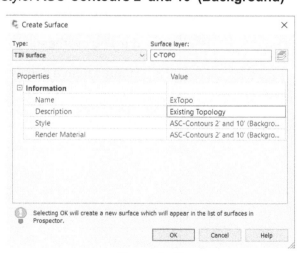

Figure 3–19

4. Click **OK** to accept the changes and close the dialog box.

5. Save the drawing.

Task 2 - Define a surface with contour data.

1. In the *Insert* tab>Block panel, click 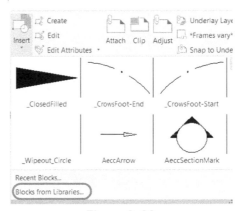 (Insert) and select **Blocks from Library**, as shown in Figure 3–20.

Figure 3–20

2. From the *C:\Civil 3D Projects\References\DWG\Existing* folder, select **Site-Contours.dwg**, as shown in Figure 3–21.

- Ensure that **Explode** is selected.
- Double-click on the **Site-Contours** image.

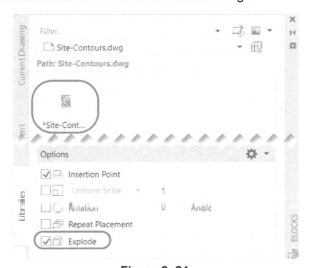

Figure 3–21

3. In the *Insert - Geographic Data* dialog box, confirm, that you want to prompt for insertion point, as shown in Figure 3–22.

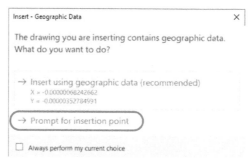

Figure 3–22

4. When prompted for an insertion point, type **0,0,0**.

5. Close the BLOCKS panel.

6. In the *Home* tab>Layers panel, click 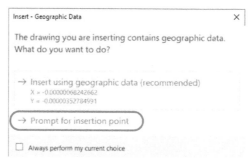 (Isolate). Do the following before selecting the layers:

   - Type **S** for **Settings**.
   - Select **Off** and then select **Off** again to ensure that **layiso** does not lock the layer by changing the settings to toggle off isolated layers.

7. Select one major and one minor contour from the **Site-Contours.dwg** to isolate the layers **A-TOPO-MAJR** and **A-TOPO-MINR** and press <Enter>.

8. Expand the *Surfaces* collection in the Toolspace, *Prospector* tab.

9. Expand the *ExTopo* surfaces collection and the *Definition* collection.

*If this setting is not changed, the **C-TOPO** layer will lock and the Autodesk Civil 3D software will not create the surface.*

10. Select the **Contours** data element, right-click, and select **Add…**, as shown in Figure 3–23.

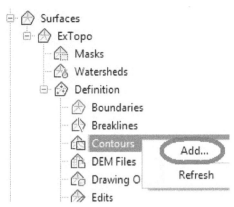

Figure 3–23

11. In the Add Contour Data dialog box, accept the defaults, as shown in Figure 3–24, and click **OK**.

Figure 3–24

12. When prompted to select contours, use the AutoCAD window or crossing selection method to select all of the AutoCAD contour objects on the screen, as shown in Figure 3–25. Press <Enter> to end the command.

Figure 3–25

13. The Autodesk Civil 3D software has created a surface. However, only the original two isolated contour layers display, the surface is not displayed. You need to restore the previous layer state. To do so, click  (Unisolate) in the *Home* tab>Layer panel as shown in Figure 3–26.

Figure 3–26

After freezing the original contours, if the contours for the new surface are not displayed, verify that the C-TOPO layer is not frozen.

14. Freeze the layers **A-TOPO-MAJR** and **A-TOPO-MINR** by clicking (Layer Freeze) and selecting the contours you selected when adding contours to the surface. This will clean up the drawing while ensuring that you do not accidentally modify the surface by changing any of the original contour polylines.

15. If you select the green surface boundary or any contour line, the *Tin Surface: ExTopo* contextual tab displays, as shown in Figure 3–27.

Figure 3–27

16. Press <Esc> to clear the selection. The *Tin Surface: ExTopo* contextual tab closes and reverts back to the previous tab you had opened, which is the *Home* tab.

17. Save the drawing.

Task 3 - Define surface with point data.

In examining the **ExTopo** surface more closely, note that although the internal site contours correctly reflect the surveyed point elevations, the original contours are out of date or have missing information in the area of the existing road, **Mission Avenue** (the road running east to west at the top of the site). However, you have a detailed survey of the road. Using this data, you will generate a surface.

1. Continue working with the drawing from the previous task or open **SUF1-A2.dwg**.

*If the points still display in the model, you might have to right-click on Point Groups and select **Update**.*

2. Although the point group that you use in this practice has been created, you should change the display order of the point groups to display them clearly. To do so, in the Toolspace, *Prospector* tab, right-click on *Point Groups* and select **Properties**. Move the **No display** point group to the top and then move the **ExRoad** point group above it.

3. In the Toolspace, *Prospector* tab, select the **Surfaces** collection, right-click, and select **Create Surface**.

4. In the Create Surface dialog box, select **TIN surface** for the surface type, type **ExRoad** for the surface name, type **Existing Road** for the description, and select **ASC-Contours 2' and 10' (Background)** for the style.

5. Click **OK** to accept the changes and close the dialog box.

6. Expand the *Surfaces* collection in the Toolspace, *Prospector* tab and expand the *ExRoad* collection.

7. Expand the *Definition* collection, select *Point Groups*, right-click, and select **Add…**.

8. In the Point Groups dialog box, select the **ExRoad** point group, as shown in Figure 3–28. Click **OK** to accept the changes and close the dialog box.

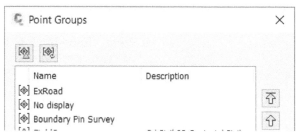

Figure 3–28

9. Save the drawing.

Task 4 - Create a surface contour style.

---

1. Since there is very little grade change along the road, the frequency of the contours is small, making the surface difficult to see. Expand the *Surfaces* collection, right-click **ExRoad** and select **Surface Properties**.

2. In the Surface Properties dialog box, in the *Information* tab, expand 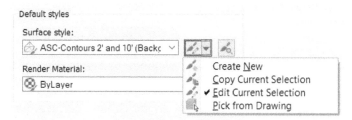 to the right of the *Surface style* field and select **Copy Current Selection**, as shown in Figure 3–29.

Figure 3–29

3. In the *Information* tab, type **ASC-Contours 0.5' and 2.5' (Background)** for the style name, as shown in Figure 3–30.

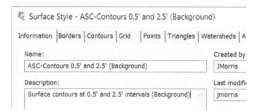

Figure 3–30

4. In the *Contours* tab, expand the *Contour Intervals* collection and type **0.5'** for the *Minor Interval* and **2.5'** for the *Major Interval*, as shown in Figure 3–31.

Figure 3–31

5. Click **OK** to accept and close the Edit Style dialog box, and click **OK** to close the Surface Properties dialog box.

6. Zoom into the existing road at the north end of the site and note the detail contours identifying the crown of the road.

7. Save the drawing.

3.5 Breaklines and Boundaries

A surface can include data from boundaries, breaklines, contours, Digital Elevation Model files (DEMs), drawing objects (AutoCAD points, individual Autodesk Civil 3D points, lines, 3D faces, etc.), and point files. The *Boundaries* collection displays above the *Breaklines* collection under the surface's *Definition* (in the Toolspace, *Prospector* tab), as shown in Figure 3–32. However, you should generally add boundaries after adding breaklines to a surface. If you use the Data Clip boundary type, any data that you add to the surface (point file, DEM file, or breakline) is only added to the area within the boundary. In that case, breaklines can be added to the surface after a Data Clip boundary type. Surface edit operations are not affected by the Data Clip boundary.

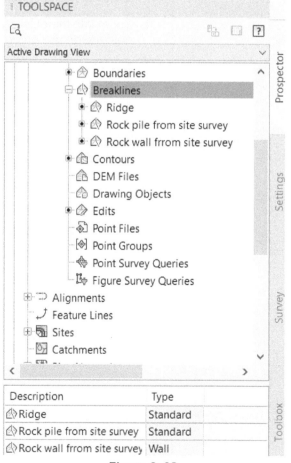

Figure 3–32

Breaklines

Breaklines affect surface triangulation and are important in point-based surfaces. Think of breaklines being a fold in a surface, much like a fold in a piece of paper. They ensure that terrain models are triangulated correctly along linear features, as shown in Figure 3–33.

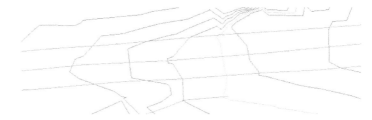

Surface before breaklines have been applied along the center line of a road.

Surface after breaklines have been applied along the center line of a road.

Figure 3–33

- When adding a breakline to a surface, the Autodesk Civil 3D software creates an entry under the *Breakline>Definition* collections, based on a description that you supply.

- When you define multiple breaklines at the same time, the Autodesk Civil 3D software creates a single entry under the *Breaklines* collection. However, they are listed separately in the Toolspace, *Prospector* tab's List View.

- Breaklines can be defined as one of four types:

  - **Standard**
  - **Proximity**
  - **Wall**
  - **Non-Destructive**

Standard Breaklines

A standard breakline is one that has valid elevations assigned at each vertex.

- Standard breaklines can be defined from 3D lines, 3D polylines, survey figures, or grading feature lines.

- The number of points generated along a breakline can be reduced by specifying a *Weeding* factor or increased by specifying a *Supplementing* factor, similar to weeding and supplementing factors for contour data.

- Curves in standard breaklines are approximated through the use of a mid-ordinate distance, similar to the way curved boundaries are resolved.

- When drawing 3D lines, polylines, or feature lines, you can use Autodesk Civil 3D's transparent commands. For example, using the **Point Object ('PO)** transparent command to select a point as a vertex of a 3D polyline prompts the Autodesk Civil 3D software to assign the point's elevation to the vertex of the polyline.

- Standard breaklines can also be defined from ASCII breakline data files (.FLT file extension).

Proximity Breaklines

Proximity breaklines do not need to have elevations at their vertices. A polyline at the zero elevation could be used as a proximity breakline. When a proximity breakline is defined, the Autodesk Civil 3D software automatically assigns vertex elevations from the nearest TIN data point, such as a nearby point object or contour line vertex.

- The Autodesk Civil 3D software can define proximity breaklines from 2D polylines or grading feature lines.

- The Autodesk Civil 3D software does not support curves in proximity breaklines. Arc segments are treated as if they were straight line segments.

- One of the default options in the surface *Build* area enables the conversion of all proximity (2D) breaklines into standard (3D) breaklines. After conversion, the breakline is listed as a standard breakline and has the same elevations as the point objects that are at each vertex.

Wall Breaklines

- A wall breakline can be used to represent both the top and bottom of a wall, curb, or other sheer face.

- Wall breaklines are defined by 3D lines, 3D polylines, or feature lines. When defining them from linework, the object itself is meant to define either the top or bottom of the wall.

- The other end of the wall (top or bottom) is defined interactively by entering the absolute elevations or height differences from the defining line.

- If a Wall breakline starts as a 2D polyline or feature line, it can contain curve segments.

- The number of points generated along a breakline can be reduced by specifying a *Weeding* factor or increased by specifying a *Supplementing* factor.

Survey Figures as Breaklines

Figures created by surveyors can be used as breaklines if a connection exists between the drawing and the survey database.

How To: Add Survey Figures as Breaklines

1. Open the survey database for editing.
2. In the Toolspace, *Survey* tab, expand the *Survey Data* collection and select **Figures**. The list of figures in the grid view displays at the bottom of the Toolspace.

3. Select the figures, right-click, and select **Create breaklines...**, as shown in Figure 3–34.

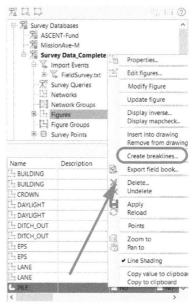

Figure 3–34

4. In the Create Breaklines dialog box, select the surface on which to place the breaklines, and then in the *Breakline* column, select **Yes** on to create the breaklines, as shown in Figure 3–35. Click **OK** to close the dialog box.

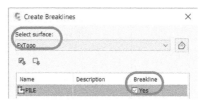

Figure 3–35

Boundaries

Boundaries provide interior or exterior limits to the surface triangulation. Boundaries are typically created from 2D closed polylines. There are four types of boundaries:

- **Outer**
- **Hide**
- **Show**
- **Data Clip**

An outer boundary should be one of the last items added to a surface, because adding data outside an existing boundary extends the surface past the boundary.

- An **Outer** boundary hides or excludes data outside its edge.

- A **Hide** boundary hides an interior portion of a surface to delineate features (such as water bodies and building footprints).

- A **Show** boundary displays a portion of a surface within a Hide boundary (such as to display an island in a pond).

- A **Data Clip** boundary acts as a filter on all data, including points, DEMs, and breaklines added to the surface after the creation of the Data Clip boundary. If a data clip boundary is used, any data added after it, that falls outside the data clip boundary, is ignored.

A boundary can contain arc segments. To better represent surface elevations around an arc, the Autodesk Civil 3D software uses a mid-ordinate value to calculate where the triangles interact with the boundary. The mid-ordinate value is the distance between the midpoint of the cord and the arc. The smaller the mid-ordinate value, the closer the surface data is to the original arc. An example is shown in Figure 3–36.

Figure 3–36

A boundary can limit a surface to the data within it. When you want to extend the triangulation exactly to a boundary line, select the **Non-destructive breakline** option in the Create Boundary dialog box. A non-destructive breakline fractures triangles at their intersection with the boundary. The resulting triangles preserve the original elevations of the surface at the boundary intersection as close as possible.

Non-destructive breaklines are rarely used in practice.

The example in Figure 3–37 shows the following:

1. The surface with a polyline is used as an outer boundary.
2. The boundary is applied without the **Non-destructive breakline** option. This is typically used when the boundary polyline is approximate and not meant to represent a hard edge. Triangles that lie under the boundary will be removed from the surface, resulting in a jagged edge.
3. The boundary is applied with the **Non-destructive breakline** option. Non-destructive breaklines are often used to create a specific termination limit for the surface (such as at a parcel boundary). Triangles that lie under the boundary will be trimmed back to the boundary, resulting in a smooth edge.

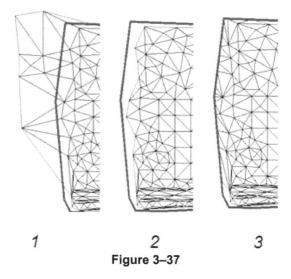

1 *2* *3*

Figure 3–37

Practice 3b

Add Additional Data to an Existing Ground Surface

Practice Objective

- Improve the accuracy of a surface by adding various breaklines, such as standard breaklines, wall breaklines, and breaklines from survey figures.

Task 1 - Add surface breaklines.

TIN lines are generally created using the shortest distance between points. To further define a surface, you might need to supplement it with breaklines of ridges, ditches, walls, etc., that accurately define the surface. These breaklines prevent the software from triangulating directly between points that are bisected by a breakline. The breakline becomes part of the triangulation between the two adjacent points.

1. Continue working with the drawing from the previous practice or open **SUF1-B.dwg**.

2. Select any part of the **ExTopo** surface in Model Space.

The contextual tab displays.

3. In the *Surface* contextual tab>Modify panel, select **Surface Properties**, as shown in Figure 3–38. The Surface Properties dialog box opens.

Figure 3–38

4. In the *Information* tab, expand the Surface style drop-down list and select **ASC-Contours and Triangles**, as shown in Figure 3–39. Click **OK** to close the dialog box.

Default styles

Surface style:

ASC-Contours and Triangles

Figure 3–39

Now that the triangulations display, you will examine how adding a feature line impacts the surface.

5. In the *View* tab>Named Views panel, expand the drop-down list and select **Surf-Breakline**. This zooms into the breakline that is located north of the existing road as shown in Figure 3–40.

Figure 3–40

The triangulation crosses the breakline.

6. Expand the *Current Drawing* collection in the Toolspace, *Prospector* tab and then expand the *Surfaces>ExTopo> Definition* collections. Select **Breaklines**, right-click, and select **Add**, as shown in Figure 3–41.

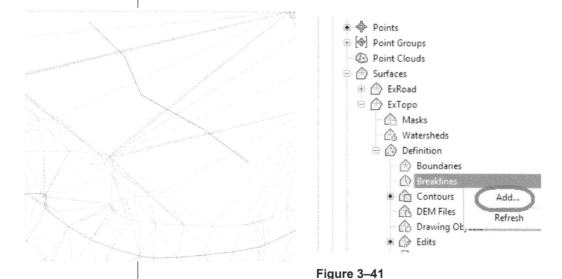

Figure 3–41

7. Type **Ridge** in the *Description* field, as shown in Figure 3–42. Accept all of the defaults and click **OK** to close the dialog box.

Figure 3–42

8. When prompted to select objects, select the red 3D polyline and press <Enter> to complete the command.

9. The surface should rebuild automatically. Note that the triangulation now takes the breakline into consideration, as shown in Figure 3–43.

*If the **ExTopo** surface is marked as out-of-date*

*, select the **ExTopo** surface, right-click, and select **Rebuild Automatic**.*

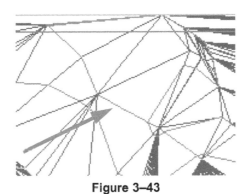

Figure 3–43

10. Save the drawing.

Task 2 - Set up the survey database.

In this practice, you will need to incorporate survey data into the surface. To do so, you must first establish a connection to the survey database. If you have not completed the practices in the Survey section, you will need to open the survey database **Survey Data_Complete** to open the connection.

In the Toolspace,

Survey tab, click 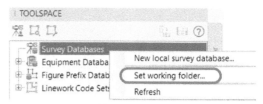 *in the Home tab>Palettes panel to toggle it on.*

1. If not already done, in the Toolspace, *Survey* tab, right-click on Survey Databases and select **Set working folder**, as shown in Figure 3–44.

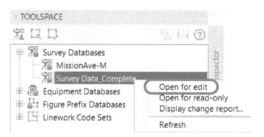

Figure 3–44

2. If need be, select the *Survey Databases* folder in the *C:\Civil 3D Projects\Survey Databases* folder, and click on the **Select Folder** button.

3. Select the survey database **Survey Data_Complete**, right-click, and select **Open for edit**, as shown in Figure 3–45. Do not double-click, this would open the survey database read-only.

Figure 3–45

4. In the Toolspace, *Survey* tab, expand the *Survey Data_Complete* collection and select **Figures**. The list of figures in the grid view displays at the bottom of the Toolspace.

5. Select the figure **Pile**, right-click, and select **Create breaklines...**, as shown in Figure 3–46.

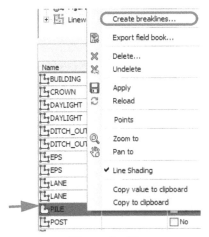

Figure 3–46

6. In the Create Breaklines dialog box, select **ExTopo** for the surface, and select the **Yes** option in the *Breakline* column to create breaklines, as shown in Figure 3–47. Click **OK** to close the dialog box.

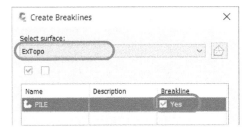

Figure 3–47

7. The Autodesk Civil 3D software will zoom in to the location of the breakline, and open the Add Breaklines dialog box. Type **Rock pile from site survey** in the *Description* field, and ensure that **Standard** is selected in the Type drop-down list, as shown in Figure 3–48. Click **OK** to close the dialog box.

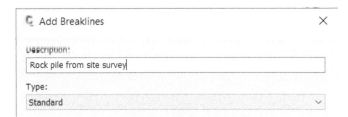

Figure 3–48

8. The Event Viewer vista in the Panorama opens. You have received a number of errors with crossing breaklines. You can zoom to the error by selecting **Zoom to** in the far right column. The reason for this error is that when building surfaces from contour-type objects, each of these objects becomes a breakline. By default, Civil 3D does not allow crossing breaklines. For now you need to clear these errors from the event log file.

9. Click **Action** in the Panorama and select **Clear All Events**, as shown in Figure 3–49.

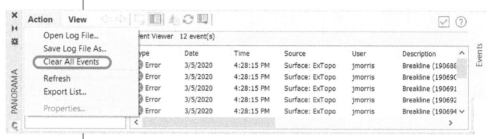

Figure 3–49

10. Close the Panorama by clicking ☑ (checkmark) in the dialog box.

11. In Model Space, select the **ExTopo** surface. The *Tin Surface: ExTopo* contextual tab displays. In the Modify panel, select **Surface Properties** as shown in Figure 3–50.

Figure 3–50

In practice, you should use this option with caution. Unless you use contours to build a surface, this option can produce unexpected results.

12. The Surface Properties - ExTopo dialog box opens. In the *Definition* tab, expand the *Build* collection and set the value of *Allow crossing breaklines* to **Yes**. Set the value for the *Elevation to use* field to **Use last breakline elevation at intersection**, as shown in Figure 3–51. When you have finished, click **OK**.

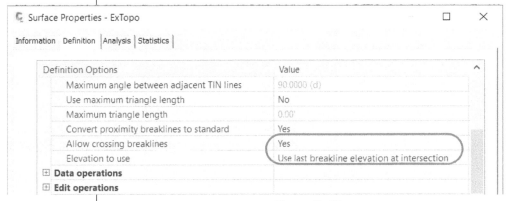

Figure 3–51

13. When prompted to *Rebuild the surface* or *Mark as out of Date*, select **Rebuild the surface**. When you review the surface contours, note that the surface has used the figure as a breakline.

14. Save the drawing.

Task 3 - Add a wall breakline.

In the task, you will add a wall breakline to the surface from figures that were created when the field books were imported.

1. Open the survey database **Survey Data_Complete**, if it is not already open.

2. In the Toolspace, *Survey* tab, expand the *Survey Data* collection and select **Figures**. Note the list of figures in the grid view at the bottom of the Toolspace.

3. Select the **Wall** figure, right-click, and select **Zoom to** or right-click and select **Create breaklines.**

4. In the Create Breaklines dialog box, select the **ExTopo** surface and select the **Yes** option in the *Breakline* column to create breaklines. Click **OK** to close the dialog box.

5. The Autodesk Civil 3D software zooms in a bit closer to the location of the breakline and opens the Add Breaklines dialog box. Type **Rock Wall from site survey** in the *Description* field, and ensure that **Wall** is selected in the Type drop-down list, as shown in Figure 3–52. Click **OK** to close the dialog box.

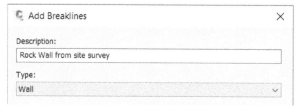

Figure 3–52

6. At the prompt to pick the offset side, select a point to the south of the wall break line, as shown in Figure 3–53.

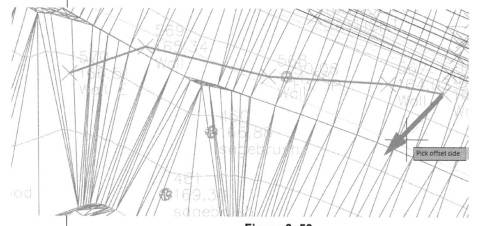

Figure 3–53

7. When prompted to select the option for the wall height, select the default **All** option because the wall has a constant height.

The wall has a constant height of 1.5 feet from the base.

8. When prompted for the elevation difference or elevation, type **1.5** and press <Enter>.

9. The Event Viewer vista opens again in the Panorama. Click **Action** in the Panorama and select **Clear All Events**, then close the Panorama by clicking ☑ (checkmark) in the dialog box.

10. Save the drawing.

3.6 Surface Editing

There are three ways of adjusting surfaces graphically: using lines, points, and area edit tools (such as **Minimize Flat Areas** and **Smooth Surface**). All of these tools are available by right-clicking on the *Edits* heading in a surface's *Definition* area (Toolspace, *Prospector* tab), as shown in Figure 3–54. These editing tools are also available through the contextual tab of the surface.

Figure 3–54

- The Autodesk Civil 3D software considers each graphical surface edit to be additional data that can be removed later.

- Most surface edits apply immediately. If the drawing item modifier icon displays (as shown in Figure 3–55), then an edit has rendered the surface out of date. When this happens, a surface should be rebuilt by right-clicking on the surface name in the Toolspace, *Prospector* tab and selecting **Rebuild**.

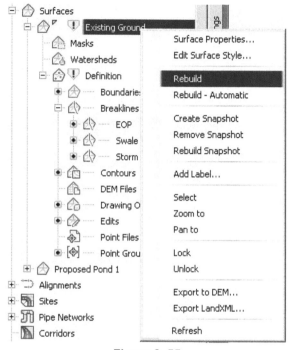

Figure 3–55

- To have a surface automatically rebuild as required, right-click on the surface name in the Toolspace, *Prospector* tab and select **Rebuild-Automatic**. However, toggling this option on increases the use of computer resources and graphics capabilities, depending on the complexity of the surface and your computer's hardware.

- To delete an edit from a surface permanently, remove it from the *Edits* list in Toolspace, *Prospector's* preview area or from the *Operations Type* list in the *Definition* tab in the Surface Properties dialog box through the right-click menu.

Line Edits

The line editing commands include **Add Line**, **Delete Line**, and **Swap Edge**. The **Add Line** and **Delete Line** commands add or remove triangle lines. The **Delete Line** command is often only applied around the outside edge of a surface to remove unwanted edge triangulation. Deleting lines in the interior of a surface causes both of the triangles next to the removed line to be deleted, leaving a hole in the surface that needs to be repaired by adding another line.

If you are considering deleting a line only to replace it with the opposite diagonal, such as the central line shown in Figure 3–56, using the **Swap Edge** command instead might be more efficient.

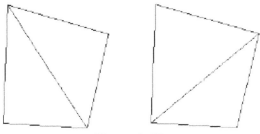

Figure 3–56

Adding an interior line that crosses many existing triangles swaps them where possible to adhere to the geometry represented by the added line. This method can be a good way of swapping multiple edges at the same time.

Point Edits

The Point editing commands can **Add**, **Delete**, **Modify**, or **Move** surface points. They do not affect point objects in the drawing, but rather the surface points created from them. Surface points can be adjusted or deleted as required.

When an Autodesk Civil 3D point object is adjusted (e.g., moved), the surface containing that point data might not be identified as being out of date nor update automatically. In this situation, you should rebuild the surface.

Simplify Surface

As the collection methods of surface data continue to evolve, yielding significantly larger data sets, the drawing file size increases in proportion to the surface data contained in the drawing. The Autodesk Civil 3D software has a limit of 2.5 million vertices for a surface. Once it exceeds this limit, the software prompts you to store surface data to an external file with an .mms extension. The resulting external surface files can be quite large. To avoid this, you can simplify your surface using the Simplify Surface wizard. Extra points can be removed from a surface without compromising its accuracy. Points that you might want to remove include points that are in an external point file or database, or redundant points in areas of high data concentration where the value of this extra information is minimal. There are two simplification methods available.

- **Edge Contraction:** This method simplifies the surface by using existing triangle edges. It contracts triangle edges to single points by removing one point. The location of the point to which an edge is contracted is selected so that the change to the surface is minimal.

- **Point Removal:** This method simplifies the surface by removing existing surface points. More points are removed from denser areas of the surface.

When you simplify a surface, you specify which regions of the surface the operation should address. The region options include using the existing surface border, or specifying a window or polygon. The **Pick in Drawing** icon enables you to select the region from the drawing. If a closed polyline exists in the drawing that you want to use as the region boundary, you can select the **Select objects** option and then use the **Pick in Drawing** icon to select the boundary. Curves in the boundary are approximated by line segments. The line segment generation is governed by a *Mid Ordinate Distance* value that you determine.

Once you have selected the region, the dialog box displays the *Total Points Selected In Region* value. You can refine the surface reduction options by setting a percentage of points to remove, the maximum change in elevation, or the maximum edge contraction error.

Smooth Contours

Although not a true surface edit, Autodesk Civil 3D surface contours can be smoothed to reduce their jagged appearance using the Surface Object Style settings. There are two approaches to this: the *Add Vertices* method and the *Spline Curve* method. The *Add Vertices* method enables you to select a relative smoothness from the slider bar at the bottom of the Surface Style dialog box, as shown in Figure 3–57.

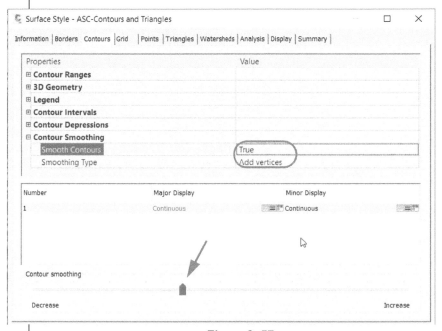

Figure 3–57

The *Spline Curve* method generates very smooth contours, but the contours are more liberally interpolated and might overlap where surface points are close together. This approach is best applied to surfaces with relatively few data points or in areas of low relief, as shown in Figure 3–58.

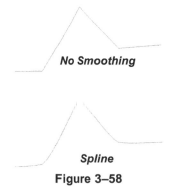

No Smoothing

Spline

Figure 3–58

Smooth Surface

The Smooth Surface edit introduces new, interpolated elevations between surface data. It is used to create a more realistic-looking terrain model, though not necessarily a more accurate one. Generally, surface smoothing works best with point-based surface data.

The Autodesk Civil 3D software has two smoothing methods: *Natural Neighbor* and *Kriging*.

- *Natural Neighbor* interpolates a grid of additional data points that produce a smoother overall terrain model.

- *Kriging* reads surface trends to add additional data in sparse areas.

Surface smoothing is applied by right-clicking on the *Edits* collection under a surface's *Definition* and selecting **Smooth Surface**. The Smooth Surface dialog box and example of surface smoothing are shown in Figure 3–59.

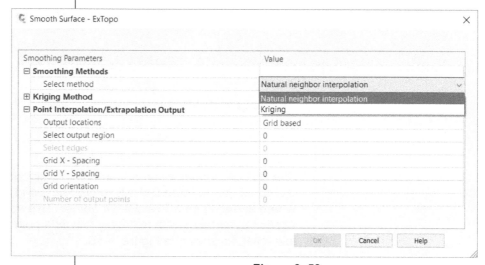

Figure 3–59

Copy Surface

The Autodesk Civil 3D software does not have a copy surface command, but surface objects can be copied using the AutoCAD **Copy** command (**Modify>Copy**). When copying surface objects, select the same base and then a second point to ensure that the surface is not moved during the copy. Another option is not to specify a base point, but simply give it a Displacement distance of 0,0,0, which means there is no displacement.

After a copy, a duplicate surface is created and displays in the Toolspace, *Prospector* tab. The copy has the same name as the original followed with a number in parenthesis, such as (1). These copied surfaces can be renamed as required. Surface copies are independent of each other and can be edited independently.

Surface Paste

The **Surface Paste** command enables the Autodesk Civil 3D software to combine multiple surfaces into a single surface. You might want to paste into a copy of a surface if you want to keep the original unmodified. For example, a finished condition surface is needed that includes a proposed surface (*Proposed*) along with the existing ground (EG). In this situation, you would first create a new surface and name it **Finished Ground**. In the *Surfaces* collection in the Toolspace, *Prospector* tab, right-click on the Finished Ground surface's *Edit* collection and select **Paste** to merge in the **Existing ground (EG)** and **Proposed** surfaces.

Once the command has executed, the surface's **EG** and **Proposed** surfaces are left unchanged, and the **Finished Ground** surface represents a combination of the two. If you did not create the **Finished Ground** surface, but pasted the **Proposed** surface into the **EG** surface, you would not have the original **EG** surface for reference in profiles and other places (unless you copied the EG surface as explained above). If surfaces are pasted in the wrong order, the order can be rearranged using the *Definition* tab in the Surface Properties dialog box.

Surfaces remain dynamically linked after pasting. Therefore, if the **Proposed** surface changes, the **Finished Ground** surface updates to display the change, when the **Finished Ground** surface is set to Rebuild Automatically.

Raise/Lower Surface

The **Raise/Lower Surface** command adds or subtracts a specified elevation value. This adjustment is applied to the entire surface. It is useful for modeling soil removal and changing a surface's datum elevation.

Adjusting Surfaces Through Surface Properties

In addition to the graphical edit methods, you can adjust surfaces by changing their surface properties. Surface property adjustments include setting a *Maximum triangle length* or *Exclude elevations* greater or less than certain values. You can also enable or disable the effects of certain surface data (such as breaklines and boundaries) by disabling them in the dialog box.

To locate these options (as shown in Figure 3–60), in the Surface Properties panel, select the *Definition* tab and expand the **Build** branch.

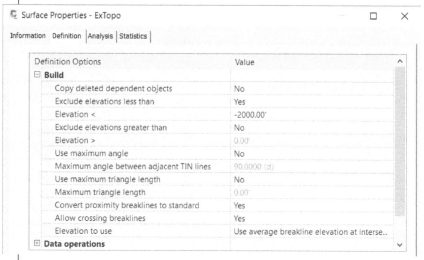

Figure 3–60

Copy Deleted Dependent Objects

If dependent objects, such as polylines (used for contour definitions), breaklines, or any AutoCAD objects (used to define the surface), are deleted from the drawing, this will copy the definition of those objects into the surface object. The surface will remain unaffected.

However, if such dependent objects are removed from the drawing without this option enabled, the surface will lose the definition those objects had provided and update to reflect the removal of these objects it was dependent on.

3.7 Surface Analysis Tools

Viewing a Surface in 3D

AutoCAD's default view, the overhead or plan view, is not the only way to view a surface. The AutoCAD **3D Orbit** command and the Autodesk Civil 3D **Object Viewer** tilt the coordinate space to display a 3D surface model. How the surface displays is dependent on the assigned style. You can view a surface in 3D using the Object Viewer or directly in the drawing window using the **3D Orbit** command. Both have similar navigation controls, but the Object Viewer enables you to review only your surface in 3D without changing your current view.

Both methods can display a wireframe (3D Wireframe and 3D Hidden), conceptual, or realistic view. By default, a Conceptual display is a cartoon-like rendering without edge lines, while a Realistic display has material styles with edge lines. Both viewing methods use the AutoCAD ViewCube, which uses labels and a compass to indicate the direction from which you are viewing a model.

The Object Viewer method is shown in Figure 3–61.

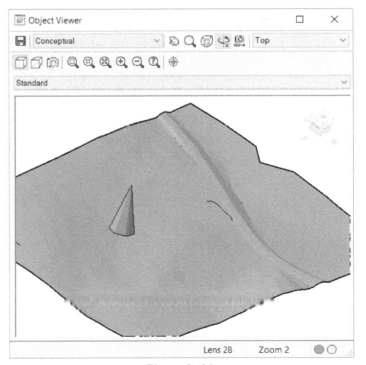

Figure 3–61

Surface Preview in the Prospector

The Prospector lists all surfaces in the active drawing in its tree branch. When you select the **Surfaces** main branch, all surfaces in the drawing are listed below in the Preview section. This is quite handy because you can change the name, description, and surface styles of the surfaces in this view, as shown on the left in Figure 3–62.

Figure 3–62

However, by default, Civil 3D will not preview the individual surfaces when they are selected in the branch, as shown on the right in Figure 3–62.

In order to see a preview in the Preview section, first you need to enable the preview for the entire Prospector by clicking on the

(Click here to toggle the use of item previews) toggle at the top left of the Prospector. Then, right-click on the **Surface** branch and select **Show Preview**, as shown in Figure 3–63.

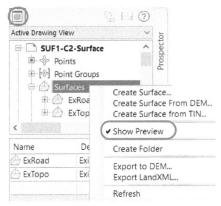

Figure 3–63

When both of these are set, you can select an individual surface in the Surface branch of the Prospector to see a preview. This is actually a mini version of the Object View described earlier, with most of the Object Viewer's capabilities available through the right-click menu within the Preview section, as shown in Figure 3–64.

Figure 3–64

Quick Profile

Understanding the affect of breaklines and other data on a surface is critical to generating an accurate surface. The **Analyze>Ground Data>Quick Profile** command enables you to produce an instant surface profile with minimal effort. It is also accessible through the **Home>Profile** drop-down menu.

A *Quick Profile* is a temporary object, which disappears from the drawing when you save or exit. If you need a more permanent graphic, you should create an alignment and profile.

Quick Profiles can be created along lines, arcs, polylines, lot lines, feature lines, or survey figures, or by selecting points. In addition to the command being located in the *Analyze* tab, you can select one of the previously mentioned objects, right-click, and select **Quick Profile**. Two examples of the Quick Profile are shown in Figure 3–65.

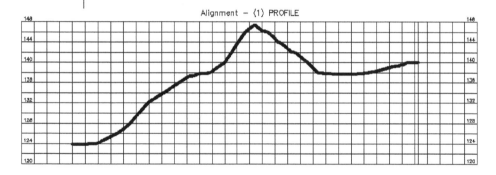

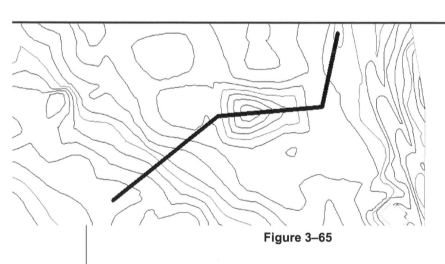

Figure 3–65

Practice 3c

Surface Edits

Practice Objective

- Edit a surface using definition options in the surface properties and commands found in the Toolspace.

In this practice, you will refine a previously created surface. The **ExTopo** surface has some triangulations that are not valid. You will eliminate these TIN lines using three methods: you will set options for the surface properties, delete TIN lines (triangle edges), and add a boundary to the surface. Each of these methods has advantages and disadvantages and should be used appropriately.

Task 1 - Copy deleted dependent objects.

1. Continue working with the drawing from the previous practice or open **SUF1-C1.dwg** from the *C:\Civil 3D Projects\Working\ Surface* folder.

2. In the *View* tab>Named Views panel, select the preset view **Surface-Edit**.

Ensure that the ExTopo surface is using the Contours and Triangles surface style.

3. In Model Space, select the **ExTopo** surface. The *Tin Surface ExTopo* contextual tab will display. In the *Modify* panel, select **Surface Properties**, as shown in Figure 3–66.

Figure 3–66

4. The Surface Properties dialog box opens. Select the *Definition* tab and expand the **Build** options in the *Definition Options* area.

5. Set the *Copy deleted dependent objects* value to **Yes**, as shown in Figure 3–67. Click **OK** to close the dialog box and accept the changes.

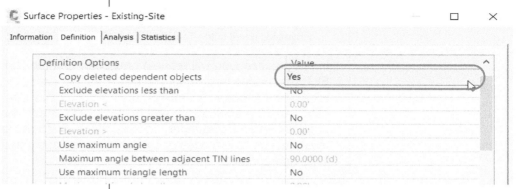

Figure 3–67

6. When prompted to *Rebuild the surface* or *Mark the surface as out-of-date*, select **Rebuild the surface**.

7. The Event Viewer vista opens again in the Panorama. Click **Action** in the Panorama and select **Clear All Events**, then close the Panorama in the dialog box.

8. Save the drawing.

Task 2 - Delete lines.

Some triangles, along the eastern edge of the surface, need to be removed.

1. Figure 3–68 shows the lines that you will be deleting.

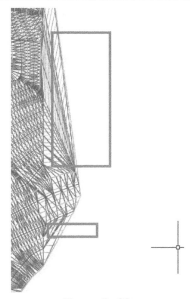

Figure 3–68

2. In Model Space, select the **ExTopo** surface. The *Tin Surface ExTopo* contextual tab will display. In the *Modify* panel,

expand the ⬦ (Edit Surface) drop-down list, and select **Delete Line**, as shown in Figure 3–69.

Figure 3–69

3. Select each of the required TIN lines in Model Space, as shown in Figure 3–70. When you have finished, press <Enter> to end the selection and press <Enter> to end the command.

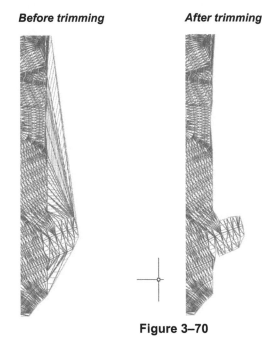

Before trimming   **After trimming**

Figure 3–70

4. Save the drawing.

Task 3 - Add a boundary.

The **Delete Line** command can be effective, but might not efficiently clean up the edges of large surfaces. A surface boundary is useful if you have a well-defined boundary.

1. If necessary, in the *View* tab>Named Views panel, select the preset view **Surface-Edit**.

2. Turn on the **A-SITE-BOUNDARY** layer, which contains a red polyline you will use to define the border of the surface.

3. In Model Space, select the **ExTopo** surface. The *Tin Surface ExTopo* contextual tab will display. In the *Modify* panel, click (Add Data), expand the drop-down list, and select **Boundaries**, as shown in Figure 3–71.

Figure 3–71

4. The Add Boundaries dialog box opens, as shown in Figure 3–72. Type **Limits** in the *Name* field, and select **Outer** in the Type drop-down list. Select the **Non-destructive breakline** option, because you do want to trim to this polyline shape. Otherwise, the dialog box options will erase all of the triangle lines that cross or are beyond the boundary. Click **OK** to accept the changes and close the dialog box.

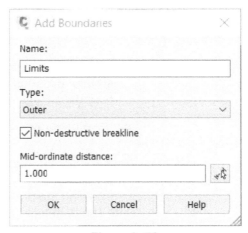

Figure 3–72

You might have to regen the screen to display the boundary.

5. When prompted to select an object, select the red polyline that represents the boundary, as shown in Figure 3–73.

Figure 3–73

6. Examine how this boundary affected the surface. The boundary only trimmed the surface to the picked rectangle, but it did not extend the surface to the rectangle. This boundary is a dynamic part of the **ExTopo** surface.

7. Select the boundary line and move the grips. Note in the Prospector that the **ExTopo** surface is marked as being *Out of Date.* If necessary, right-click on the **ExTopo** surface and set it to *Rebuild - Automatic*, as shown in Figure 3–74.

Figure 3–74

8. Now as you change the polyline defining the boundary, the surface expands or contracts to match the change in the boundary. Restore the polyline to its original position.

9. Save the drawing.

Task 4 - Set the elevation range.

In reviewing the drawing, you need to address an error in the site. The original topographical contour file contains an invalid piece of data that has transferred to the surface.

1. Continue working with the drawing from the previous task or open **SUF1-C2.dwg**.

2. Select the preset view **Surf Elev Edit**.

3. In Model Space, as shown on the left in Figure 3–75, select the **ExTopo** surface, right-click, and select **Object Viewer**.

4. In the Object Viewer, click and drag the view, as shown on the right in Figure 3–75, to rotate the 3D view to identify the issue. Change the Visual Style to **Conceptual** using the drop-down list in the top left corner.

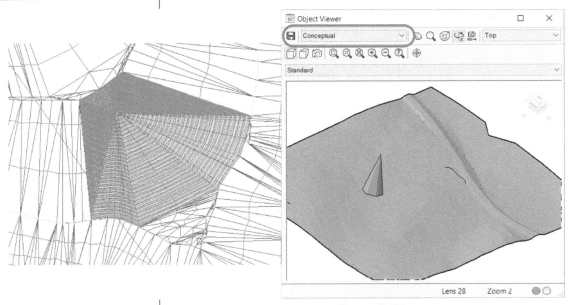

Figure 3–75

5. Close the Object Viewer by selecting **X** in the top right corner of the dialog box.

6. With the **ExTopo** surface still selected, select **Surface Properties** in the *Tin Surface ExTopo* contextual tab. The Surface Properties dialog box opens.

7. Select the *Statistics* tab and expand the value list in the *General* area.

8. When you review the site conditions, note that the site ranges from an elevation of roughly 100' to 330'. However, the statistics indicate that the surface ranges from an elevation of 115' to 492.12', as shown in Figure 3–76.

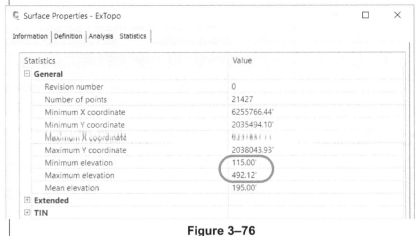

Figure 3–76

9. To correct the surface, select the *Definition* tab. Expand *Build* properties and set the *Exclude elevation less than* value to **Yes**. Set the *Elevation <* value to **100'**, the *Exclude elevation greater than* value to **Yes**, and the *Elevation >* value to **330'**, as shown in Figure 3–77.

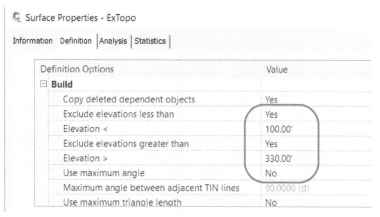

Figure 3–77

10. Click **OK** to accept the changes and close the dialog box.

All points that are above an elevation of 330' are removed and the error is fixed.

11. When prompted to *Rebuild the surface* or *Mark the surface as out-of-date*, select **Rebuild the Surface**.

12. The Event Viewer vista opens again in the Panorama. Click **Action** in the Panorama and select **Clear All Events**, then close the Panorama in the dialog box.

13. Save the drawing.

Task 5 - Review edits in the Toolspace, *Prospector* tab and in the Surface Properties dialog box.

The history of all of the changes made to a surface is saved in the drawing. You can apply and remove these changes selectively to the surface.

1. Select the preset view **Surface-Edit**.

2. In the Toolspace, *Prospector* tab, expand the *Surfaces* collection and select the **ExTopo** surface. Right-click and select **Surface Properties**. In the Surface Properties dialog box, clear the **Add boundary** *Operation Type* (as shown in Figure 3–78), and click **Apply**.

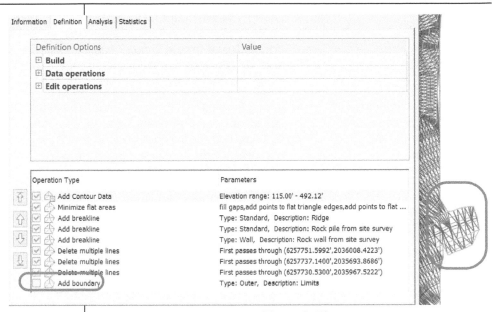

Figure 3–78

3. When prompted, select **Rebuild the Surface** in the Warning dialog box that opens. The boundary is ignored.

4. The Event Viewer vista opens again in the Panorama. Click **Action** in the Panorama and select **Clear All Events**, then close the Panorama in the dialog box.

The boundary is once again used in the surface definition.

5. Re-select the **Add boundary** *Operation Type* and click **Apply**. When prompted, select **Rebuild the Surface** in the Warning dialog box that opens, and dismiss the Panorama that appears.

6. Save the drawing.

Task 6 - Create a composite surface.

In the preceding tasks, you created a surface from available contour data. However, the data around the existing road, **Mission Avenue** (the road running east to west at the top of the site), was inaccurate, so you surveyed the road and created a surface. You need to create a composite surface that represents the site condition combined with the road.

1. Select the preset view **Survey Main**.

2. In the Toolspace, *Prospector* tab, right-click on the *Surfaces* collection and select **Create Surface**.

3. Select **TIN surface** for the surface *Type*. Type **Existing-Site** for the surface name and **Composite surface of ExTopo and ExRoad** for the *Description*. Select **ASC-Contours 2' and 10' (Background)** for the surface *Style*. Click **OK** to close the dialog box and create a surface.

You may need to widen the Toolspace panel to be able to select the Style column.

4. In the Toolspace, *Prospector* tab, select the *Surfaces* collection. In the preview list area, select the **ExRoad** and **ExTopo** surfaces. Right-click on the *Style* column heading and select **Edit**, as shown in Figure 3–79.

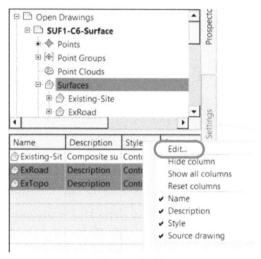

Figure 3–79

5. Set the surface style to **_No Display** and click **OK** to accept the changes and close the dialog box.

6. In the Toolspace, *Prospector* tab, expand the *Surfaces> Existing-Site>Definition* collections for that surface and select **Edits**. Right-click and select **Paste Surface...**, as shown in Figure 3–80.

Figure 3–80

To select both surfaces, hold <Ctrl> when selecting the second surface.

7. In the Select Surface to Paste dialog box, select the **Ex Topo** and **Ex Road** surfaces, as shown in Figure 3–81. Once selected, click **OK** to close the dialog box.

Figure 3–81

Note that the **ExRoad** surface was pasted first, followed by the **ExTopo** surface. In the area of overlap along the road, the **ExTopo** surface data will take precedence. This is not the required result.

8. In Model Space, select the **Existing-Site** surface from the surfaces listed in the *Surfaces* collection in the Toolspace, *Prospector* tab. The contextual tab for the surface object will display. Select **Surface Properties** in the ribbon panel. The Surface Properties - Existing Site dialog box opens. In the *Definition* tab, note the order of the paste operations, as shown in Figure 3–82.

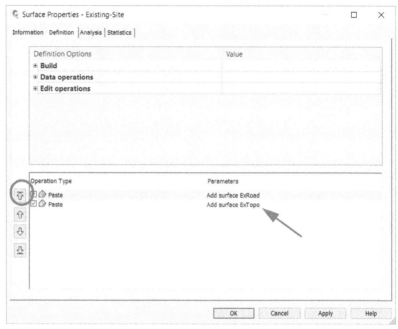

Figure 3–82

9. Select the **Paste** operation with the value **Add surface ExTopo** and move it to the top of the list by clicking ⬆.

10. Click **Apply**. When prompted to *Rebuild the surface* or *Mark the surface as out-of-date*, select **Rebuild the Surface**.

11. Click **OK** to exit the dialog box.

As a consequence of the Autodesk Civil 3D software's dynamic abilities, any changes to either the **ExTopo** or **ExRoad** surface will be reflected in the **Existing-Site** surface.

12. Save the drawing.

The Event Viewer in the Panorama is no longer triggered since you are now rebuilding a different surface and there are no alerts for the Existing-Site surface.

3.8 Surface Labels

Surface labels can be used to label contour elevations, slope values, spot elevations, and watershed delineations. Label values update when the surface changes.

To create surface labels, in the *Annotate* tab>Labels & Tables panel, expand Add Labels and select **Surface** to access the surface label flyout menu, as shown in Figure 3–83.

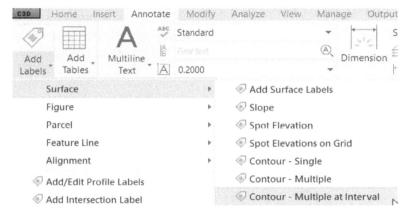

Figure 3–83

You can also click  (Add Labels) to open the Add Labels dialog box, as shown in Figure 3–84. This dialog box enables you to select the feature and label type while being able to control the label style on the fly.

Figure 3–84

Contour Labels

Contour labels can be created individually, as multiples along a linear path, or as multiples along a linear path with repeated labels at a set interval. Multiple contours are aligned along an object called a *Contour Label Line*, which can be repositioned as needed, and in turn updates the position of its labels. These label lines have a selectable property that can make them visible only when an attached label is selected. If they are left visible, they should be placed on a non-plotting layer.

Spot and Slope Labels

Spot elevation and slope labels can be created as needed to annotate a surface. These are dynamic surface labels and not point objects, although they might look similar to points. Slopes can be measured at a single point or interpolated between two points.

3.9 Surface Volume Calculations

You can generate volume calculations in the Autodesk Civil 3D software in many ways. Surface-to-surface calculations are often used to compare an existing ground surface to a proposed surface to determine cut and fill quantities. In the Autodesk Civil 3D software, quantities can be adjusted by an expansion (cut) or a compaction (fill) factor. Surfaces representing different soil strata can be compared to each other to determine the volume between the soil layers. There are multiple ways of comparing surfaces to each other in the Autodesk Civil 3D software.

Volumes Dashboard

In the *Analyze* tab>Volumes and Materials panel, click

(Volumes Dashboard).

The Volumes Dashboard creates a volume surface based on a graphical subtraction of one surface from the other, as shown in Figure 3–85.

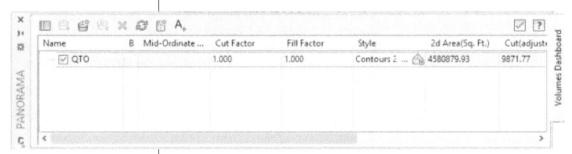

Figure 3–85

The *Net Graph* column color displays in red if the surface difference results in a net cut, and green if it is a net fill. You can have multiple volume entries listed if you are comparing multiple surfaces. If any surfaces change, return to this vista and click

(Recompute Volumes) to update the calculations. Alternatively, you can add another volume entry. Select the same two surfaces and compare before and after volume calculations.

Bounded Volumes

The area to calculate cut and fill can be limited by clicking

(Add Bounded Volume). This limits the calculations to the area defined by a polyline, polygon, or parcel.

Volume Reports

The dashboard's cut/fill summary contents can be placed directly into the drawing by clicking A_+ (Insert Cut/Fill Summary) inside the Volumes Dashboard. In addition, you can create a volume report from the dashboard contents to include in specifications or other project documents by clicking (Generate Volume Report) inside the Volumes Dashboard.

Grid Volume or TIN Volume Surface

This method enables you to assign the surfaces you want to compare as object properties of a volume surface. The volume between the surfaces is calculated and included in the volume surface object properties. The TIN surface calculation is the same one conducted in the Volumes Dashboard. The Grid surface calculation is based on a grid of points interpolated from both surfaces, rather than all of the surface points of both. Grid surfaces tend to be less accurate, but faster to calculate and easier to prove by manual methods.

A grid of spot elevation labels that list the elevation differences between two surfaces can be generated from either a Grid Volume surface or TIN Volume surface. Once the volume surface is established, create the labels. In the *Annotate* tab>Labels & Tables panel, expand **Add Labels**, expand **Surface**, and select **Spot Elevations on Grid**, as shown in Figure 3–86.

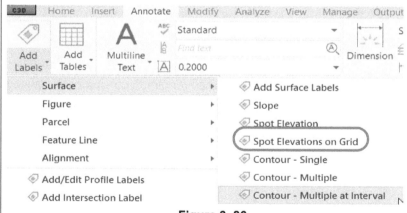

Figure 3–86

3.10 Surface Analysis Display

The Autodesk Civil 3D software can calculate and display many different surface analyses, including:

- **Contours:** This analysis can display contours differently based on their elevation ranges.

- **Directions:** This analysis can render surface triangles differently depending on which direction they face.

- **Elevations:** This analysis can render surface triangles differently depending on their elevation ranges.

- **Slopes:** This analysis can render surface triangles differently depending on their slope ranges.

- **Slope Arrows:** This analysis creates a dynamic slope arrow that points downslope for each triangle, colorized by slope range.

- **User-Defined Contours:** This analysis can display user-defined contours differently based on their elevation ranges.

- **Watersheds:** This analysis can calculate watershed areas, and render them according to area type. The AutoCAD Civil 3D watershed analysis usually results in a very large number of individual watersheds. Although a **Catchment Areas** command is available to assist in drawing the catchment areas, it is still up to the engineers to draw their own conclusions on how these should be merged together into catchment areas.

The above analyses are calculated on demand for each surface and their results are stored under the surface's Surface Properties.

In addition, the following separate utilities might be helpful when analyzing surfaces:

- **Check for Contour Problems:** Used to locate problems with the contour data, including crossing or overlapping contours. To access this command, in the *Surface* tab>expanded

  Analyze panel, select **Check for Contour Problems**, as shown in Figure 3–87.

Figure 3–87

- **Resolve Crossing Breaklines:** Identifies and fixes any breaklines that create an invalid condition when two elevations exist at the intersection point of two breaklines. The breaklines can be found in the drawing, in a survey figure, or in the survey database. To access this command, in the *Surface* tab>Analyze panel, click (Resolve Crossing Breaklines).

- **Water Drop:** Draws a 2D or 3D polyline indicating the expected flow path of water across the surface from a given starting point. To access this command, in the *Surface* tab> Analyze panel, click (Water Drop).

- **Catchment Area:** Draws a 2D or 3D polyline indicating the catchment boundary and catchment point marker for a surface drainage area. To access this command, in the *Surface* tab>Analyze panel, click (Catchment Area). You should use this command in conjunction with the **Water Drop** command to determine an accurate placement of catchment regions and points.

- **Visibility Check>Zone of Visual Influence:** Analyzes the line of sight for 360 degrees around a single point. To access this command, in the *Surface* tab>Analyze panel, click

  (Visibility Check>Zone of Visual influence). This command is good for analyzing if towers, buildings, and other objects can be seen within a certain radius.

- **Minimum Distance Between Surfaces:** Identifies the (X,Y) location where two overlapping surfaces are the closest elevation. To access this command, in the *Surface* tab>

  Analyze panel, click (Minimum Distance Between Surfaces). If there is more than one location with the shortest distance between the two surfaces (because it is flat), then the location might be represented by a series of points, a line, or a closed polyline.

- **Stage Storage:** Calculates volumes of a basin from a surface, using either a surface or polylines to define the basin. To access this command, in the *Surface* tab>Analyze

  panel, click (Stage Storage). Either the *Average End Area* or the *Conic Approximation* method, or both are used to calculate volumes for the stage storage table.

Analysis Settings

You apply a surface analysis using the *Analysis* tab in the Surface Properties dialog box. In this tab, you can select the number of ranges and a legend table to be used. All of the remaining analysis settings are located in the *Surface Object* style, including whether to display in 2D or 3D, the color scheme, elevations, range groupings, etc. If you want to change the number of ranges or the range values, use the settings in this tab at any time.

Analysis Data Display

Overall visibility, layer, linetype, and related controls for analysis elements are managed using the *Display* tab in the Object Style dialog box, as shown in Figure 3–88. The component entries for *Slopes, Slope Arrows, Watersheds*, etc., are displayed. These can be set to display different settings and combinations of elements in 2D and 3D.

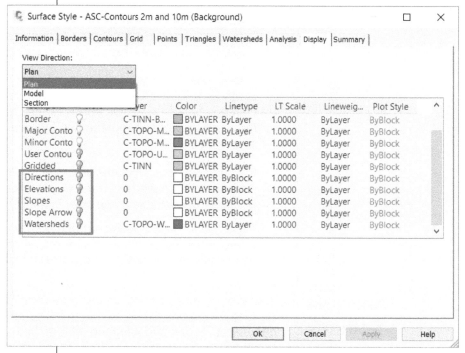

Figure 3–88

Practice 3d

Surface Labeling and Analysis

Practice Objective

- Communicate information about the surface by labeling and analyzing it.

Task 1 - Add surface labels.

1. Continue working with the drawing from the previous practice or open **SUF1-D.dwg** from the *C:\Civil 3D Projects\Working\Surface* folder.

2. Select the preset view **Surface Label**.

3. Select the **Existing-Site** surface in Model Space. In the *Surface* contextual tab>Labels & Tables panel, expand Add Labels and select the **Contour - Multiple**, as shown in Figure 3–89.

Figure 3–89

4. When prompted to select the first point, specify any point. When prompted for the next point, select a second and third point that creates a line intersecting all of the contours that you want to label, as shown in Figure 3–90. Press **<Enter>** when done.

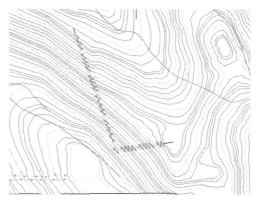

Figure 3–90

5. Move and reorient the contour label line. The labels update.

6. The *Display Contour Label Line* property can be set to only be visible when contour labels are selected. To change the visibility property, select the contour label line in Model Space and select **Properties** in the *Label* contextual tab>General Tools panel. In the Properties dialog box, set the *Display Contour Label Line* property and the *Display Minor Contour Labels* property to **False,** as shown in Figure 3–91.

Figure 3–91

Once the grips disappear, the line is no longer displayed. Select a contour label to have the contour label line temporarily display for editing.

7. Close the Properties dialog box and press **<Esc>** to cancel your selection.

8. To have all of the future contour label lines behave this way in this drawing, select the *Settings* tab in the Toolspace. Select **Surface**, right-click, and select **Edit Feature Settings...**,as shown in Figure 3–92.

Figure 3–92

9. In the Edit Feature Settings dialog box, expand *Contour Labeling Defaults* and set the *Display Contour Label Line* property to **False** and change *Surface Contour Label Style Minor* to **<none>**, as shown in Figure 3–93. Click **OK** to accept the changes and close the dialog box.

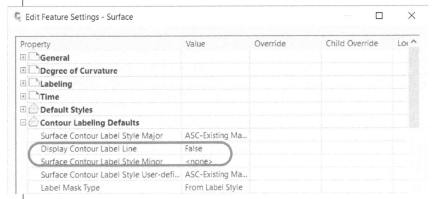

Figure 3–93

10. Select the **Existing-Site** surface again in Model Space. In the *Surface* contextual tab>Labels & Tables panel, expand Add Labels and select **Contour - Multiple**.

11. Select two points that will draw a line across some contours and press **<Enter>** when done. The contour label line and minor contour labels do not display.

12. Select the **Existing-Site** surface in Model Space. In the *Surface* contextual tab>Labels & Tables panel, expand Add Labels and select **Slope**.

13. To accept the prompt for the default One-point label, press **<Enter>**, and select a point in Model Space within the surface boundary. The Autodesk Civil 3D software will place the slope value at that point. When you finish placing the labels, press **<Enter>** to exit the command.

14. (Optional) Using the processes, experiment with labeling the surface with spot elevations and two point slopes. Note that you will be able to copy a label and place it at a different location. As the labels are dynamic, the values will change to reflect the surface information at the location of the label.

Task 2 - Perform a slope analysis.

1. Select the preset view **Survey Main**.

2. Select the **Existing-Site** surface in Model Space. In the *Surface* contextual tab>Modify panel, select **Surface Properties**.

3. In the *Information* tab in the Surface Properties dialog box, select **ASC-Slope Banding (2D)** as the surface style.

4. In the *Analysis* tab, select **Slopes** for the *Analysis type* and select **4** for the number of ranges to use. Click 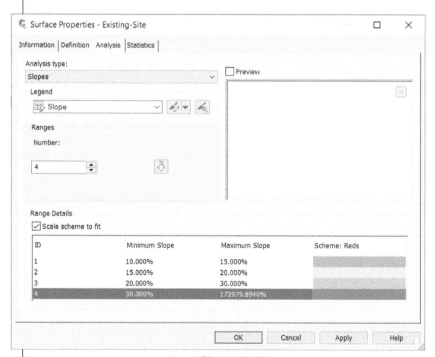 (Run Analysis).

The Autodesk Civil 3D software calculates a range of values to fit within the specified number of ranges.

5. Change the range values for Range 4 of the *Minimum Slope* to 30.0% (leaving the *Maximum Slope* as is), Range 3 from 20% to 30%, Range 2 from 15% to 20% and Range 1 from 10% to 15%, as shown in Figure 3–94.

Figure 3–94

6. Change the range of colors for the slope range from light
    green to yellow to orange to red as shown above in
    Figure 3–94. To change the color, click on it to open the
    Select Color dialog box, as shown in Figure 3–95, and select
    the required color. Click **OK** to close the dialog box.

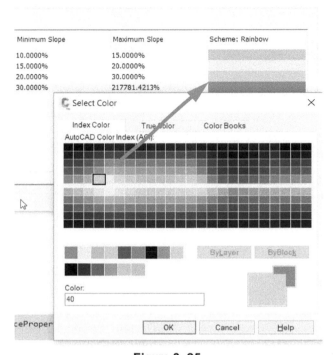

Figure 3–95

7. Click **OK** to close the dialog box and apply the changes.
    Press **<Esc>** to exit the surface selection.

8. Review the area that you want to develop. The slope ranges
    will be an issue.

9. You need to create a slope values table. Select the
    Existing-Site surface in Model Space. In the *Surface*
    contextual tab>Labels & Tables panel, select **Add Legend**.

10. Select **Slopes** from the command options, and then select
    Dynamic for a dynamic table.

11. When prompted for the top corner of the table (top left), select a location in an open area to the right of the surface, as shown in Figure 3–96. Press <Esc> to exit the selection.

Slopes Table				
Number	Minimum Slope	Maximum Slope	Area	Color
1	10.00%	15.00%	1116953.11	
2	15.00%	20.00%	585352.95	
3	20.00%	30.00%	155916.74	
4	30.00%	217781.42%	185938.85	

Figure 3–96

Because this table is dynamic, any changes made to the surface or to the ranges in the analysis will update the table automatically.

12. (Optional) Open the Surface Properties dialog box (Steps 3 to 7) and change the number of slope ranges or the values. The Model Space Legend table will be updated.

13. Save the drawing.

14. (Optional) Save the drawing as **<Your Initials>-Surface-Complete.dwg** in the *C:\Civil 3D Projects\References\DWG\Existing* folder.

15. Update the relative paths of the referenced drawings in the alert box.

Chapter Review Questions

1. Put the following steps in the order suggested for building a surface.

Step	Answer
a. Add Breaklines, assign more data, modify the data, or edit the surface, as required.	
b. Assign data to a surface.	
c. Accumulate data.	
d. Evaluate the resulting surface.	

2. What controls how an Autodesk Civil 3D surface displays (whether it displays contours, TIN lines, or an analysis)?

   a. Surface Style

   b. Surface Definition

   c. AutoCAD Layers

   d. Surface Boundary

3. Where would you set the lowest and highest acceptable elevations for a surface?

   a. In the Create Surface dialog box when you are first creating the surface.

   b. In the *Definition* tab in the Surface Properties dialog box.

   c. In the *Analysis* tab in the Surface Properties dialog box.

   d. Under Edits within the surface definition.

4. Select which type of breakline this statement defines: *This type of breakline is a 3D polyline or Feature Line. It does not need a point object at each vertex because each has its own elevation.*

   a. Non-Destructive

   b. Proximity

   c. Wall

   d. Standard

5. A Quick Profile disappears when you save or exit a drawing.

   a. True

   b. False

6. What are the types of edits that can be done to a surface? (Select all that apply.)

   a. Line Edits

   b. Point Edits

   c. Simplify Surface

   d. Grip Edit

7. How do you remove an edit from a surface? (Select all that apply.)

   a. Clear it in the Operations Type list in the Surface Properties in the *Definition* tab.

   b. Remove it from the Edits list in the Prospector's Preview.

   c. Select it and press <Delete>.

   d. Delete it from the Operations Type list of the Surface Properties in the *Definition* tab.

8. Which type of boundary would you use to ensure that any data that you add to a surface is ignored if it falls outside that boundary?

   a. Hide

   b. Show

   c. Data Clip

   d. Outer

9. Which of the following is not a surface label that is available out of the box in the Autodesk Civil 3D software?

   a. Contour Labels

   b. Spot Elevation Labels

   c. Slope Labels

   d. Cut/Fill Labels

10. How do you calculate the volume between two surfaces in a specific parcel?

a. Bounded Volumes

b. Grid Volume Surface

c. TIN Volume Surface

d. Show Cut/Fill Labels in a grid pattern

11. Which of the following is not a surface analysis that you can run in the Autodesk Civil 3D software?

a. Slope Analysis

b. Visibility Check

c. Runoff Coefficient Analysis

d. Water Drop

12. Which of the following are vertical definition options when creating a solid surface from a TIN surface? (Select all that apply.)

a. Kriging interpolation

b. Depth

c. Fixed elevation

d. Surface

Command Summary

Button	Command	Location
	Add Data	• **Contextual Ribbon:** *Surface* tab> Modify panel
	Catchment Area	• **Contextual Ribbon:** *Surface* tab> Analyze panel
		• **Command Prompt:** Catchment Area
	Create Surface	• **Ribbon:** *Home* tab>Create Ground Data panel
		• **Command Prompt:** CreateSurface
	Create Surface from point clouds	• **Contextual Ribbon:** *Point Cloud* tab> Civil3D panel
	Edit Surface	• **Contextual Ribbon:** *Surface* tab> Modify panel
	Resolve Crossing Breaklines	• **Contextual Ribbon:** *Surface* tab> Analyze panel
		• **Command Prompt:** BreaklineTool
	Surface Properties	• **Contextual Ribbon:** *Surface* tab> Modify panel
		• **Command Prompt:** EditSurfaceProperties
	Volumes Dashboard	• **Ribbon:** *Analyze* tab>Volumes and Materials panel
		• **Contextual Ribbon:** *Surface* tab> Analyze panel
		• **Command Prompt:** VolumesDashboard
	Water Drop	• **Contextual Ribbon:** *Surface* tab> Analyze panel
		• **Command Prompt:** CreateSurfaceWaterdrop

Project Management

In this chapter, you will learn about the various project structures that can be used inside of an Autodesk® Civil 3D® project. Then, you will create a new project and learn how to move between different projects. Using data shortcuts, you will practice creating references to AEC objects to share design data, which ensures that you always have the most up-to-date design data in the current model.

Learning Objectives in This Chapter

- Examine a Civil 3D drawing template.
- Control and distribute Civil 3D styles and settings.
- Use online maps.
- List the three different ways in which Autodesk Civil 3D project drawings can be organized.
- List the ways in which teams can collaborate with each other and share design information in the Autodesk Civil 3D software.
- Share design information with other members of the design team using data shortcuts.

4.1 Design Development

By now, you have gathered and processed the information to show existing conditions. You've created surface from survey and contour data and are now ready to begin the design on developing the site.

For more information on Externally Referenced (XREF) files, see the AutoCAD: Fundamentals guide (published by ASCENT) or Autodesk Help.

A Data Shortcut has been created for the Existing-Site surface, and there are AutoCAD drawings outlining the proposed design. To expedite the process, these have been referenced into the practice files going forward.

The drawings have been externally referenced through the **XREF** command. Autodesk Civil 3D, by default, fades these referenced drawings by 50%, making them quite faint, as shown in Figure 4–1.

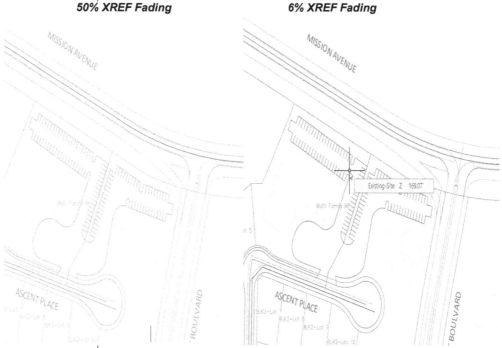

50% XREF Fading   **6% XREF Fading**

Figure 4–1

The left side is the default fade of 50%, the right has been adjusted to a fade of 6%. This can be adjusted in the AutoCAD Options, on the *Display* tab.

4.2 Templates

A drawing template (.DWT extension) contains all blocks, Paper Space title sheets, settings, layers, Autodesk Civil 3D styles, and content-specific settings for a new drawing.

Creating Template Files

To use the Autodesk Civil 3D software efficiently and effectively, you need to configure styles and settings to control the object display. All of these styles and settings affect the final delivered product and enable you to deliver a product with consistent CAD standards. Once all of the styles required for a set of drawings have been created, saving the file as a template enables you to use the same styles over and over in various projects. To create a template file, use the **Save As** command and in the Save As dialog box, change the *File of Type* to **DWT**. After giving it a name, the Template Options dialog box opens as shown in Figure 4–2. It enables you to enter a description, set the measurement units, and save new layers as reconciled or unreconciled.

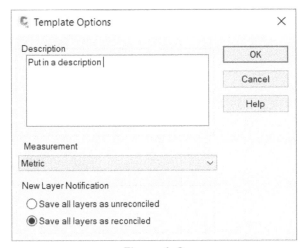

Figure 4–2

Hint: Default Coordinate System

If you work primarily within one coordinate system, set that coordinate system as your default template to ensure that all drawings will be set up with the same coordinate system. Enter a message in the template to this effect.

4.3 Managing Styles

There are three methods of managing styles in a drawing: **Import**, **Purge**, and **Reference**. These commands are located in the *Manage* tab>Styles panel.

Import

The **Import** styles command ( ) enables you to import the styles from a source drawing into the current drawing. The Import Civil 3D Styles dialog box opens, as shown in Figure 4–3. It lists the styles that are available for import and also displays the style differences between the source and the current drawing. Each style collection lists three subcategories: styles to be added, styles to be deleted, and styles to be updated. When you use the **Import** command, the styles in the design file are overwritten. However, if the styles change in the DWG or DWT source file that you imported, the styles in the design file do not automatically update.

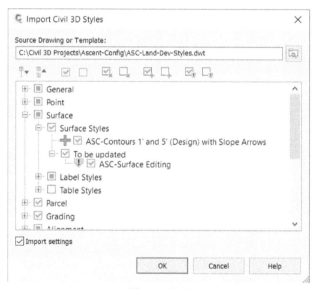

Figure 4–3

Drag and Drop Method

Another method for importing styles is by the Drag and Drop method. This is the preferred method when only a few specific styles need to be imported into your current drawing. The steps are as follows:

1. Ensure that both the source drawing (where the style resides) and the destination drawing (where you want to import the style into) are open in Civil 3D.
2. In the Toolspace of destination drawing, go to the *Settings* tab and set your display option to **Master View,** as shown in Figure 4–4.

Figure 4–4

3. On the *Settings* tab, note that your current drawing is in bold. Click on the Minus symbol (-) next to the drawing name to collapse its branch, revealing the other drawing you have open.
4. If required, click on the Plus symbol (+) of the drawing which contains the styles you need to expand the branch.
5. Browse to the style you require, and click and drag it into your current drawing by dragging it into the drawing area, as shown in Figure 4–5.

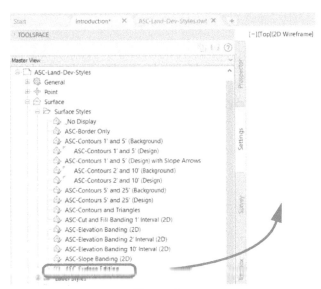

Figure 4–5

6. Repeat these steps, for other styles you wish to import, on an individual basis.

Purge

The **Purge** styles command ( ) enables you to purge all of the selected unused styles in a drawing. Typically, you will need to run this command more than once as there are some styles that are used as parents to other styles. The purging information displays in the Style Purge Confirmation dialog box, as shown in Figure 4–6. The Command Line prompts you when there are no unused styles in the drawing.

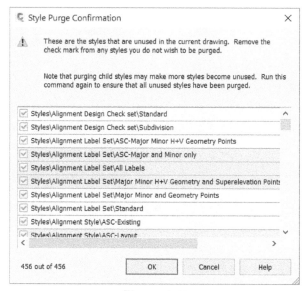

Figure 4–6

Reference

The **Reference** styles command ( ) enables you to attach one or more DWG or DWT files to your design file. Styles that are in the attached files override styles with the same name in the design drawing. If the styles in the attached DWG or DWT file change, the styles in the design file also change. Using the **Reference** styles command enables you to maintain a consistent style across multiple drawings, and can be used to implement and maintain a company-wide CAD standard. Figure 4–7 shows the Attach Referenced Template dialog box.

- When multiple style templates are attached, you can set the priority using the arrows on the right of the Attach Referenced Template dialog box.

- You can choose which objects are to be referenced from the attached template by clicking on the

  Double Down Arrow symbol ( ) in the lower right corner.

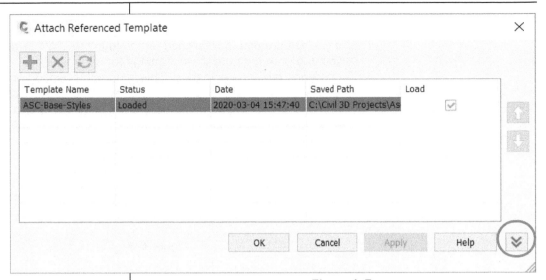

Figure 4–7

- In the expanded window are multiple tabs where you can drill down to the various components within the reference template and check on or off which ones are to be loaded. If you select an individual component, its settings are displayed in the right panel in read-only mode, as shown in Figure 4–8.

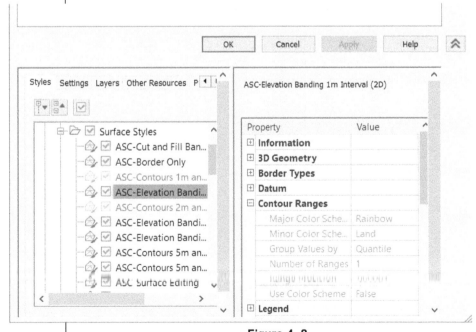

Figure 4–8

Hint: Reference Template Default

If you are creating a reference template in the DWT format, you can pre-configure these settings for each time the reference template is loaded. This is done by clicking on the icon in the *Manage* tab>Styles panel, as shown in Figure 4–9. The **Set Reference Template Defaults** icon is only available when you are working in the drawing template file (*.DWT).

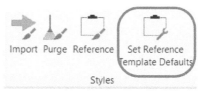

Figure 4–9

4.4 Styles in Depth

Styles are central to the Autodesk Civil 3D software. Their flexibility enables an Office or Company to create a unique *look* for their drawings. By changing the assigned style, you can change the composition of a profile view as shown in Figure 4–10.

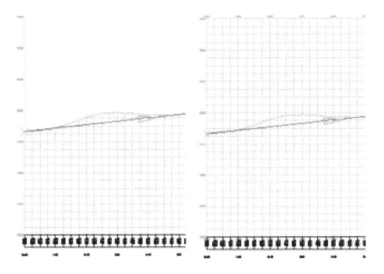

Figure 4–10

In the Toolspace, *Settings* tab, an object type branch identifies each style type and lists its styles below each heading. An example is shown in Figure 4–11.

Figure 4–11

Object Styles

Object Styles stylize an object's data for display and print. To edit a style, in the Toolspace, *Settings* tab, right-click on the style and select **Edit**. Much of the work for the object styles is done in the *Display* tab. For certain objects, other tabs might need to be modified.

For example, in the Surface Style dialog box, the *Display* tab enables you to toggle on or off triangles, borders, contours, and other items, as well as define the layer, color, linetype, etc. that are assigned, as shown in Figure 4–12. The *Contours* tab sets the contour interval, smoothing, and other settings, as shown in Figure 4–13.

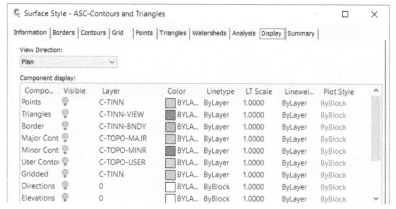

Figure 4–12

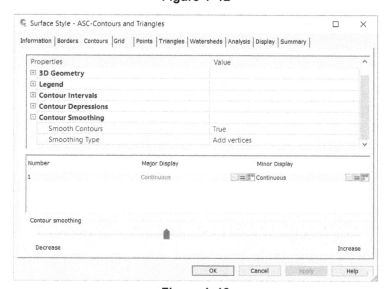

Figure 4–13

From the default Autodesk Civil 3D template, the respective Parcel Style dialog box for Open Space, Road, or Single Family, (as shown in Figure 4–14), define how each displays their segments and hatching by assigning different layers for the components. The other tabs are rarely used for the Parcel styles.

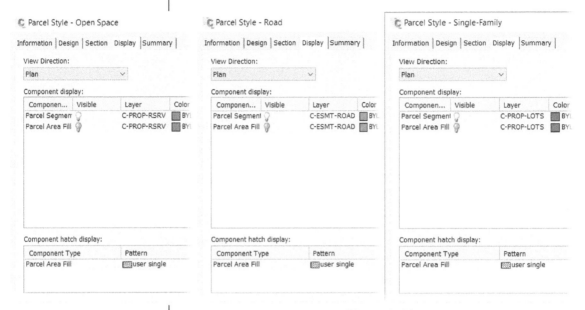

Figure 4–14

An object style represents a specific task, view, type, or stage in a process. For example, a surface style for developing a surface, reviewing surface properties, or documenting surface elevations as contours for a submission. For Parcels, styles represent a type such as open space, commercial, easement, single family, etc. One style can cause an object to look different in various views. For instance, you might want to display both the point and the label in the plan view but only the point marker in a model (3D view). As shown in Figure 4–15, there are four view directions to consider when creating an object style.

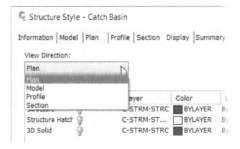

Figure 4–15

4.5 Online Maps Service

If a drawing template is already set up with a coordinate zone, the Geolocation tab will show up when using that template.

Once a coordinate zone is assigned to a drawing, a new tab appears in the ribbons to the far right, named *Geolocation,* as shown in Figure 4–16.

Figure 4–16

This service is only available if you have an Autodesk account and you are signed in. To sign in, go to the upper right area of the Civil 3D application, as shown in Figure 4–17.

Figure 4–17

The online maps are geolocated — meaning, they have coordinates and therefore they "know where they belong". Since the Civil 3D drawing is set up with a coordinate zone, it too knows where it belongs. The Online Map Service will access maps in various styles and dynamically reference them in your drawing. They have the following characteristics:

• The map is temporary (there are options to "capture" a map).

• The map displays behind all other objects in the drawing, thus no need for changing display orders.

• The map covers a large area (in fact, it covers the extents of the coordinate zone assigned to the drawing).

• Since the map is temporary, you cannot plot the map.

The first time you access the online maps, you are greeted with a splash screen outlining the "fine print" along with a link to the **Terms of Service**. You need to accept these by clicking on the **Yes** button in order to use this service, as shown in Figure 4–18.

*If you did check the box and selected the **Remember my choice** option, the way to restore the splash screen is through the Systems tab in the Options dialog box, where you can change the Hidden Messages setting.*

Select the **Remember my choice** option to avoid seeing this splash screen in the future.

Figure 4–18

Map Styles

In the Map drop-down list of the *Online Map* panel are four choices for map styles, as shown in Figure 4–19.

Figure 4–19

- **Map Aerial**: Displays the map as a satellite image.

- **Map Road**: Displays the map as a vector image similar to road maps.

- **Map Hybrid:** Displays the Map as a satellite image with the vector data draped over.

- **Map Off**: Displays no map. If the maps are displayed in multiple viewports, then, each viewport can have a different map style.

Practice 4a

Autodesk Civil 3D Styles

Practice Objectives

- Examine a drawing template.
- Create an object and label style to be used in the drawing.
- Import object and label styles to be used in the drawing and purge any styles not being used.

In this practice, you will create Autodesk Civil 3D styles, import styles, and purge styles for both objects and labels.

Task 1 - Examine a drawing template.

Change the Files of Type to Drawing Template (.DWT) to be able to select the template files. Then, you will need to browse to the appropriate folder again.*

1. Open the **ASC-C3D (CA83-VIF) NCS.dwt** template file from the *C:\Civil 3D Projects\Ascent-Config* folder.

2. Note the message explaining the coordinate system the template is set to.

3. Check if the *Geolocation* tab (highlighted in blue) on the far right is available, since there is coordinate system assigned, as shown in Figure 4–20.

Figure 4–20

You need an Autodesk account and you need to be signed in, to use online maps. To sign in, go to the upper right area of the Civil 3D application.

4. In the **Map** drop-down list in the *Online Map* panel, select the *Map Book* as the map style, as shown in Figure 4–21.

Figure 4–21

5. If the *Geolocation - Online Map Data* alert box opens, click **Yes** to accept the terms and proceed. Note that you can prevent this message from appearing by checking the **Remember my choice** checkbox.

6. Note that the map is not limited to your drawing area. As you zoom out, the image resamples itself. As you zoom in, more detail becomes available.

7. Select the *Manage* tab, Styles panel as shown in Figure 4–22. The *Set Reference Template Defaults* icon is only available when you are working in the drawing template file (*.DWT). Do not invoke this command.

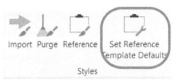

Figure 4–22

8. Click on the **Reference** styles command ( ) and notice the reference template file which is attached. Select the *ASC-Base-Styles* template in the list.

This is the same as picking the Set Reference Template Defaults in the previous step.

9. Select the **ASC-Base Styles** template, then click on the double down arrow symbol ( ) in the lower right corner to examine which styles and settings will be used for new drawings. When you drill down through the tree on the lower left panel, you can inspect each style and choose to load it or not by checking the checkbox, as shown in Figure 4–23.

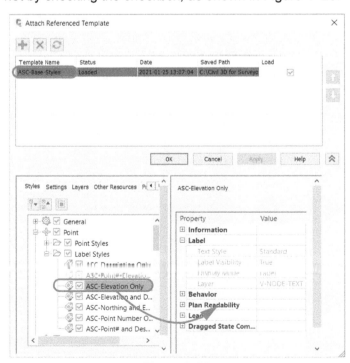

Figure 4–23

10. Close the file without saving it.

Task 2 - Create an object style.

1. Open the **ASC-Land-Dev-Styles.dwt** template file from the *C:\Civil 3D Projects\Ascent-Config* folder.

2. This is a style reference template specifically for Land Development use. It is intended to be attached to Land Development drawings.

3. Select the Toolspace, *Settings* tab to make it active.

The tabs are listed vertically along the right side of the Toolspace.

4. Click the **+** sign next to Parcel, and then click the **+** sign next to Parcel Styles. Five parcel styles are already in the drawing, but a new one needs to be created to designate blocks.

5. Right-click on Parcel Styles and select **New**. In the *Information* tab, type **ASC-Blocks** in the *Name* field.

6. In the *Display* tab, highlight both the Parcel Segment and Parcel Area Fill (press <Shift> to select both), and click **0** under the *Layer* column.

7. In the Layer Selection dialog box, click **New** to create a new layer. Name the layer **C-PROP-BLOK** and set its *color* to **blue**, as shown in Figure 4–24.

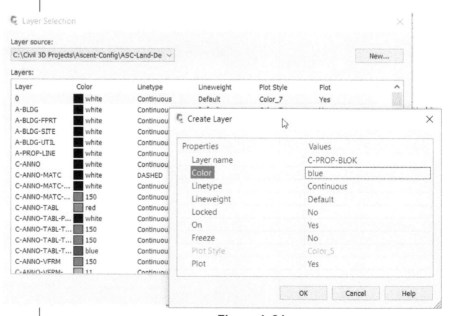

Figure 4–24

8. Click **OK** to exit the Create Layer dialog box.

9. In the Layer Selection dialog box, select the new **C-PROP-BLOK** layer and click **OK** to exit the Layer Selection dialog box.

10. Verify that the light bulb is on for the Parcel Segment visibility and off for the Parcel Area Fill visibility, as shown in Figure 4–25.

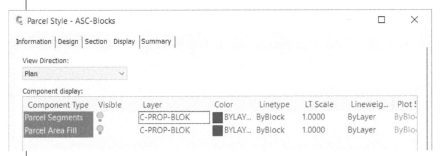

Figure 4–25

11. Click **OK** to exit the Parcel Style dialog box.

12. Save the template drawing but do not close it.

Task 3 - Drag and drop styles.

---

1. Open **Introduction.dwg** from the *C:\Civil 3D Projects\ References\DWG* folder.

2. Note the tabs across the top of the drawing area, one for each file you have open.

3. Go to the *Settings* tab and set your display option to **Master View,** as shown in Figure 4–26.

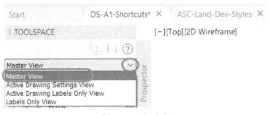

Figure 4–26

Change the Files of Type to Drawing (*.DWG) to be able to select the drawing files. Then, you will need to browse to the appropriate folder.

4. On the *Settings* tab, note that **Introduction** (your active drawing) is in bold. Click on the Minus symbol (-) next to the drawing name to collapse its branch.

---

5. If required, click on the Plus symbol (+) next to the
ASC-Land-Dev-Styles drawing, to expand the branch.

6. Browse to *Surface\Surface Style* and select the
ASC-Surface Editing style.

7. Click and drag it into your current drawing by dragging it into
the drawing area, as shown in Figure 4–27.

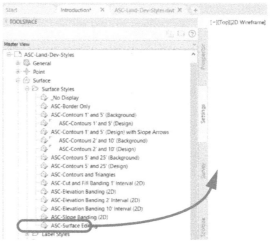

Figure 4–27

8. Expand the branch of the **Introduction** drawing and verify
that the new **ASC-Surface Editing** style is listed under
Surface\Surface Style.

9. Change the surface style to *ASC-Surface Editing* style, by
changing the surface properties. Note the point markers,
triangles and slope arrows shown in Figure 4–28.

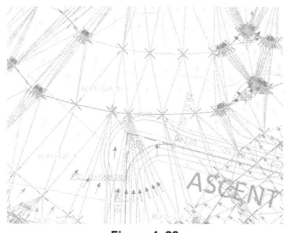

Figure 4–28

10. Save the **Introduction** drawing but don't close it.

11. Make the **ASC-Land-Dev-Styles.dwt** current (by clicking on its tab across the top).

12. Browse to *Surface\Surface Style* and select the **ASC-Surface Editing** style. Right click and pick **Edit**.

13. On the *Information* tab, put your name under Created by:, as shown in Figure 4–29.

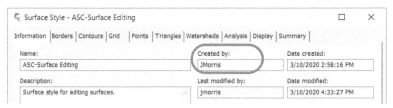

Figure 4–29

14. Click **OK** to close the Surface Style editor.

15. Save and close the **ASC-Land-Dev-Styles.dwt,**

16. Note that this file now has been updated *after* you imported the styles in the previous step.

Task 4 - Import styles.

---

1. Continue working on the **Introduction** drawing.

2. In the *Manage* tab>Styles panel, click (Import).

3. Select and open the **ASC-Land-Dev-Styles.dwt** file from the *C:\Civil 3D Projects\Ascent-Config* folder.

4. Expand *Surface Styles* and note that **ASC-Contours 1' and 5' (Design) with Slope Arrows** must be added and **ASC-Surface Editing** must be updated, as shown in Figure 4–30.

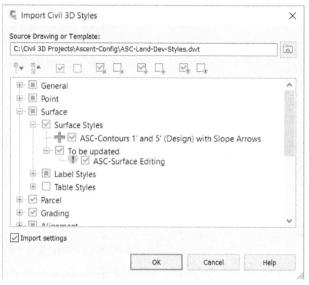

Figure 4–30

5. The **ASC-Surface Editing** appears in the list because you edited this style after you imported it.

6. Click **OK** in the Warning dialog box regarding overwriting duplicate styles. Click **OK** in the Message dialog box.

7. Change the surface style of the **Existing-Site** surface to the newly imported **ASC-Contours 1' and 5' (Design) with Slope Arrows** style by changing the surface properties. Note the slope arrows shown in Figure 4–31.

Figure 4–31

8. Save the drawing, but do not close it.

Task 5 - Purge styles.

1. In the *Manage* tab>Styles panel, click  (Purge).

2. In the Style Purge Confirmation dialog box, browse up and down to see all the styles that are marked for purging. Also, note the total in the lower left corner. Leave all checked and click **OK**.

3. You will need to repeat this command since there are nested styles. The simplest way to do that is simply hit <Enter> (to repeat the last command), and <Enter> again to proceed with the purge.

4. Keep repeating the **Purge** command until all is purged. Keep an eye on the total count in the lower left corner as you proceed.

5. Save the drawing.

Task 6 - Attach a styles template.

1. In the *Manage* tab>Styles panel, click 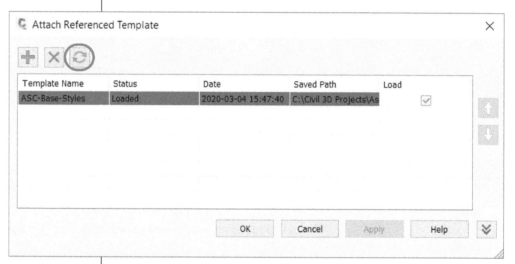 (Reference).

2. In the Attach Referenced Template dialog box, click ✛ (Attach New Template).

3. In the *C:\Civil 3D Projects\Ascent-Config* folder, select the **ASC-Base-Styles.dwt** file and then click **Open**.

4. In the Attach Referenced Template dialog box, shown in Figure 4–32, click (Check Template Status).

Figure 4–32

5. Save and close the drawing.

4.6 Autodesk Civil 3D Projects

There are multiple ways of organizing Autodesk Civil 3D project drawings. Three of the most common approaches are as follows:

Single-Design Drawing Projects

Since Autodesk Civil 3D surfaces, alignments, and other AEC objects can be entirely drawing-based, you can have a single drawing file act as the repository for all design data. Realistically, this might only be feasible for smaller projects and/or those worked on by only one person. The only external data might be survey databases, and externally referenced (XREF) drawings.

Multiple Drawings Sharing Data Using Shortcuts

This approach permits multiple existing conditions and design drawings to share data. For example, a surface could exist in one drawing and an alignment in another. A third could contain a surface profile based on the alignment and terrain model, and all could be kept in sync with each other using Data Shortcuts. This approach is usually preferable to the single-drawing approach, because it permits more than one user to work on the project at the same time (in the different design drawings) and keeps the drawings at more manageable sizes. Using data shortcuts is essential in larger projects to ensure that the regeneration time for drawings is at an acceptable speed. This approach does not create any external project data other than survey databases and XML data files that are used to share data between drawings.

Once an object has been referenced into the drawing and the drawing has been saved, the object is saved in the drawing. Therefore, it only needs access to the source drawing for validation and synchronization purposes if the source object changes. This makes it easy to share drawings with others because it ensures that the referenced objects display even if the source drawings are not available.

Shortcuts tend to be efficient for projects with a small number of drawings and project team members. Since the XML data files that connect drawings must be managed manually, keeping a large number of drawings and/or people in sync with shortcuts can be cumbersome. It is recommended that your BIM Manager establishes procedures to ensure that data is not unintentionally deleted or changed. These procedures need to be properly documented.

Autodesk Docs Design Collaboration

The Autodesk Docs cloud software enables Civil 3D to share External Reference Files (XREFs) and Data Shortcuts (DREFs) to be stored and shared within a project in a Autodesk Docs Hub. This allows you to collaborate your Civil 3D design through these references in the cloud with anyone anywhere.

Autodesk Docs makes extensive use of the Autodesk Desktop Connector, which serves as a traffic director between the Autodesk Docs project files in the cloud and the local caches on your hard drive.

When opening an Autodesk Docs based drawing for the first time (or after a long interlude), the Desktop Connector checks the local cache of the drawings and reference files to see if they are up to date. If not, the Desktop Connector downloads a fresh copy of the files. This can take some time, depending on the file sizes, your download speeds, and the traffic in the Autodesk Docs cloud.

Multiple Drawings Sharing Data with Autodesk Vault

The Autodesk® Vault software is a data and document management system (ADMS). It is used in conjunction with other Autodesk® applications in different industries. When working with the Autodesk Vault software, all project drawings, survey databases, and references are managed and stored inside an SQL-managed database. Autodesk Vault consists of user-level access permissions, drawing check-in/out, project templates, automated backups, data versioning, etc. These benefits are offset by the additional time required to manage and administer the database, and in some cases purchasing additional hardware and software. If you work on large projects with multiple design drawings or have many team members (more than 10), you might find that the Autodesk® Vault is the best way to keep those projects organized.

4.7 Sharing Data

In the Autodesk Civil 3D workflow, you can use two methods of project collaboration to share Autodesk Civil 3D design data: Data Shortcuts (local based or through Autodesk Docs) and Vault references.

Autodesk Vault and Data Shortcuts can be used to share design data between drawing files in the same project, such as alignment definitions, profiles, corridors, surfaces, pipe networks, pressure networks, sample line groups, and View Frame Groups. They do not permit the sharing of profile views, assemblies, or other Autodesk Civil 3D objects. Drawing sets using shortcuts typically use XREFs and reference other line work and annotations between drawings. Whether using Vault Shortcuts or Data Shortcuts, the process is similar.

The example in Figure 4–33 shows the sharing of data in a project collaboration environment. The data is divided into three distinctive levels. Using either Data Shortcuts or Autodesk Vault, these levels can be accessed and contributed to, on a local or remote server or across a WAN.

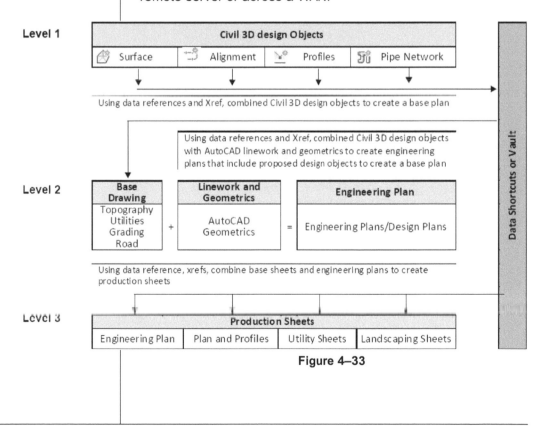

Figure 4–33

4.8 Using Data Shortcuts for Project Management

Data Shortcuts can be used to share design data between drawing files through the use of XML files. Using Data Shortcuts is similar to using the Autodesk Vault software, but does not provide the protection of your data or the tracking of versions the way the Autodesk Vault software does.

Data Shortcuts are managed using the Toolspace, *Prospector* tab, under the *Data Shortcuts* collection or in the *Manage* tab>Data Shortcuts panel, as shown in Figure 4–34. The shortcuts are stored in XML files in one or more working folders that you create. They can use the same folder structure as the Autodesk Vault software. This method simplifies the transition to using the Autodesk Vault software at a future time.

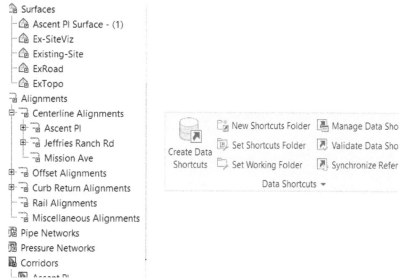

Figure 4–34

When the data shortcuts reside in an Autodesk Docs project in the cloud, it is designated as such in the Toolspace, *Prospector* tab with a small cloud symbol and a path pointing to the Autodesk Docs project, as shown in Figure 4–35.

Figure 4–35

Similarly, when you are working in a drawing that resides in an Autodesk Docs project, in the Toolspace, *Prospector* tab, the drawing has a cloud symbol as a prefix, as shown in Figure 4–36.

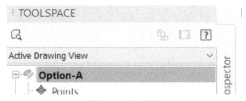

Figure 4–36

Whether using the Autodesk Vault software or Data Shortcuts (local based or through Autodesk Docs), the intelligent Autodesk Civil 3D object design data can be consumed and used on different levels. However, this referenced data only can be edited in the drawing that contains the original object. As referenced data can be assigned a different style than those in the source drawing, you can separate the design phase (where drawing presentation is not critical) from the drafting phase (where drawing presentation is paramount). Therefore, after the styles have been applied at the drafting phase, any changes to the design have minimal visual impact on the completed drawings.

Changing the name of a drawing file that provides Data Shortcuts or the shortcut XML file itself invalidates the shortcut. In the *Manage* tab, there is a Data Shortcut Manager that is used to correct such issues. It is used to repair references broken through renamed drawings or re-pathing drawings containing the Civil 3D objects.

Update Notification

If the shortcut objects are modified and the source drawing is saved, any drawings that reference those objects are updated when opened. If the drawings consuming the data referenced in the shortcuts are open at the time of the edit, a message displays to warn you of the changes, as shown in Figure 4–37.

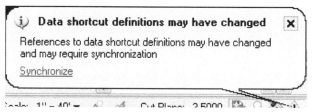

Figure 4–37

The following modifier icons help you to determine the state of many Autodesk Civil 3D objects.

▽	The object is referenced by another object. In the Toolspace, Settings tab this also indicates that a style is in use in the current drawing.
⤴	The object is being referenced from another drawing file (such as through a shortcut or Autodesk Vault reference).
⚠	The object is out of date and needs to be rebuilt, or is violating specified design constraints.
◣	A Vault project object (such as a point or surface) has been modified since it was included in the current drawing.
◢	You have modified a Vault project object in your current drawing and those modifications have not yet been updated to the project.

Figure 4–38 shows how the modifier icons are used with an Autodesk Civil 3D object as it displays in the Toolspace, *Prospector* tab.

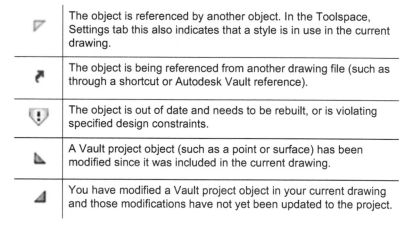

Figure 4–38

To update the shortcut data, select **Synchronize** in the balloon message or right-click on the object in the Toolspace, *Prospector* tab and select **Synchronize**.

Autodesk Docs Notification

In the current release of Autodesk Docs, there is no standard Civil 3D notification indicating that the Data Shortcuts have changed. For that, you need to go to the *Collaborate* tab and click ⟳ (Check Reference Status). It will examine if any of the referenced data items have changed and need updating.

Removing and Promoting Shortcuts

Shortcut data can be removed from the Shortcut tree in the Toolspace, *Prospector* tab by right-clicking on it and selecting **Remove**, but this does not remove the data from the drawing. To do so, right-click on the object in the Toolspace, *Prospector* tab and select **Delete**. This removes the shortcut data from the current list, so that the item is not included if a Data Shortcut XML file is exported from the current drawing.

You can also promote shortcuts, which converts the referenced shortcut into a local copy without any further connection to the original. You can promote objects by right-clicking on them in the Toolspace, *Prospector* tab and selecting **Promote**.

Data Shortcut Workflow

Whenever Civil 3D is searching for folders, you can use the Autodesk Desktop Connector to browse to the local cache folders of files that reside in an Autodesk Docs project.

1. In the Toolspace, *Prospector* tab, right-click on Data Shortcuts and select **Set the Working Folder…**
2. In the Toolspace, *Prospector* tab, right-click on Data Shortcuts and select **New Data Shortcuts Folder…** to create a new project folder for all of your drawings.
3. Create or import the data that you want to share in the source drawing and save it in the current working folder under the correct project folder.
4. In the Toolspace, *Prospector* tab, right-click on Data Shortcuts and select **Associate Project to Current Drawing**.
5. In the Toolspace, *Prospector* tab, right-click on Data Shortcuts and select **Create Data Shortcuts**.
6. Select all of the items that you want to share, such as surfaces, alignments, profiles, etc., and click **OK**.
7. Save the source drawing (and close, as required).
8. Create and save a new drawing or open an existing drawing to receive the shortcut data. Expand the *Data Shortcuts* collection and the relevant object trees (*Surfaces*, *Alignments*, *Pipe Networks*, *View Frame Groups, etc.*).
9. Highlight an item to be referenced, right-click and select **Create Reference…**. Repeat, for all of the objects, as required. You are prompted for the styles and other settings that are required to display the object in the current drawing.

10. You might also want to add an XREF to the source drawing if there is additional AutoCAD® objects that you want to display in the downstream drawing.

11. The Autodesk Civil 3D tools for Data Shortcuts are located in the *Manage* tab (as shown in Figure 4–39), and in the Toolspace, *Prospector* tab.

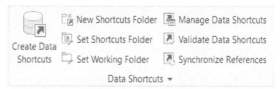

Figure 4–39

Workflow Details

- **Set Working Folder:** Sets a new working folder as the location in which to store the Data Shortcut project. The default working folder for Data Shortcut projects is *C:\Users\Public\Documents\Autodesk\Civil 3D Projects*.

- Obviously, in a shared working environment, the working folder needs to be accessible by all project team members. Often working folders are named for the year of the project, or perhaps the major clients for the project.

- For project team members who reside outside of your firewall, consider setting up an Autodesk Docs project for design collaboration and file referencing.

- The default working folder is also used for Autodesk Vault projects and local (non-Vault) Survey projects. If you work with the Autodesk Vault software, local Survey, and Data Shortcut projects, you should have separate working folders for each project type for ease of management.

- **New Shortcuts Folder:** Creates a new folder for storing a set of related project drawings and Data Shortcuts.

- **Create Data Shortcuts:** Creates Data Shortcuts from the active drawing.

Data Shortcuts are stored in the *_Shortcuts* folder for the active project and used to create data references to source objects in other drawings. Each Data Shortcut is stored in a separate XML file.

Advantages of Data Shortcuts

- Data Shortcuts provide a simple mechanism for sharing object data, without the added system administration needs of the Autodesk Vault software.

- Data Shortcuts offer access to an object's intelligent data while ensuring that this referenced data can only be changed in the source drawing.

- Referenced objects can have styles and labels that differ from the source drawing.

- When you open a drawing containing revised referenced data, the referenced objects are updated automatically.

- During a drawing session, if the referenced data has been revised, you are notified in the *Communication Center* and in the Toolspace, *Prospector* tab.

- When Data Shortcuts reside in an Autodesk Docs project, design collaboration and file referencing can be done beyond the firewall of your organization.

Limitations of Data Shortcuts

- Data Shortcuts cannot provide data versioning.

- Data Shortcuts do not provide security or data integrity controls.

- Unlike the Autodesk Vault software, Data Shortcuts do not provide a secure mechanism for sharing point data or survey data.

- Maintaining links between references and their source objects requires fairly stable names. However, most broken references can be repaired using the tools in the Autodesk Civil 3D software.

Practice 4b

Starting a Project

Practice Objective

- Create a new data shortcut project with the correct working folder for the project being worked on.

In this practice, you will walk through the steps of creating project-based Data Shortcuts folders.

Task 1 - Set the working folder.

In this task, you will set up a new working folder as the location in which to store Data Shortcut projects. The default working folder for Data Shortcut projects is *C:\Users\Public\Documents\ Autodesk\Civil 3D Projects*.

1. Open **DS-A1-Shortcuts.dwg** from the *C:\Civil 3D Projects\Data Shortcuts\Practice* folder.

2. Configure Civil 3D to reduce the fading of XREF files. Type *Options* on the command line. In the Options window, go to the *Display* tab and use the slider in the lower left corner to change the *Fade control* from the default value of 50% to 6% for the *Xref display*, as shown in Figure 4–40. Click **OK**.

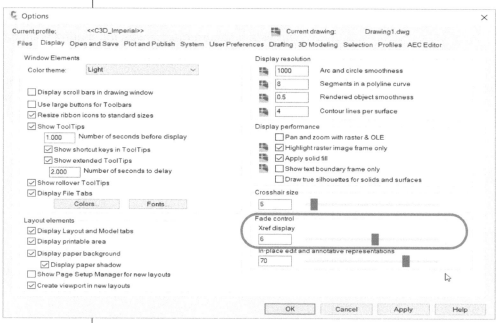

Figure 4–40

© 2021, ASCENT - Center for Technical Knowledge®

3. In the *Manage* tab>Data Shortcuts panel, click ⬜ (Set Working Folder), as shown in Figure 4–41.

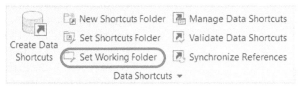

Figure 4–41

4. In the Set Working Folder dialog box, select the *C:\Civil 3D Projects\Data Shortcuts* folder, right-click to create a new folder, and name it **Lesson**.

5. Click **Select Folder**.

Task 2 - Create new Shortcuts folders.

In this task, you will create a new folder for storing a set of related project drawings and Data Shortcuts. A second project folder is created to help you understand how to change the project in which you are working.

1. Continue working with the drawing from the previous task.

2. In the *Manage* tab>Data Shortcuts panel, click 🖳 (New Shortcuts Folder), as shown in Figure 4–42.

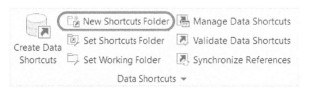

Figure 4–42

3. In the New Data Shortcut Folder dialog box, type **Ascent Phase 1** for the name and select the **Use project template** option. Templates are found in the default folder *C:\Civil 3D Templates*; however, you will be using customized project templates. Pick on the ellipses, as shown in Figure 4–43, and browse to *C:\Civil 3D Projects\Ascent-Config\Ascent Project Templates.* From the Project templates available, select *Base Project*. The Autodesk Civil 3D software will replicate this template folder structure and all included forms and documents in the *Ascent Phase 1* project folder. Click **OK**.

Figure 4–43

4. In the Toolspace, *Prospector* tab, a Data Shortcut folder is displayed in *C:\Civil 3D Projects\Data Shortcuts\ Lesson\Ascent Phase 1*. In Windows Explorer, verify that the *Civil 3D* folder structure is created for this project, as shown on the right in Figure 4–44.

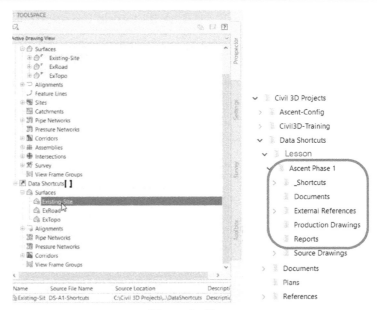

Figure 4–44

5. Create another new shortcuts folder. In the *Manage* tab>Data Shortcuts panel, click 🗀 (New Shortcuts Folder).

6. In the New Data Shortcut Folder dialog box, type **Ascent Phase 2** for the name and uncheck the **Use project template** option. Click **OK** to close the dialog box.

You now have two projects in the working folder: *Ascent Phase 1* and *Ascent Phase 2*, as shown in Figure 4–45. Notice the additional folders in *Ascent Phase 1*. These have been copied from the *Base Project* project template.

Figure 4–45

Task 3 - Set up the shortcuts folder.

Setting the shortcuts folder specifies the project path for Data Shortcuts. The path to the current *Data Shortcuts* folder (also known as the project folder) is specified in the Toolspace, *Prospector* tab, in the *Data Shortcuts* collection. The project folder typically contains both Data Shortcuts and source objects for data references.

1. In the *Manage* tab>Data Shortcuts panel, click 🔲 (Set Shortcuts Folder).

2. The current *Data Shortcut* folder is indicated by a green circle with a checkmark. Select **Ascent Phase 1** to make it current and click **OK**, as shown in Figure 4–46.

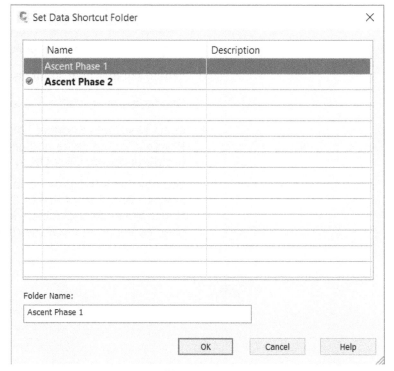

Figure 4–46

3. In the Toolspace, *Prospector* tab, right-click on Data Shortcuts and select **Associate Project to Current Drawing**, as shown in Figure 4–47.

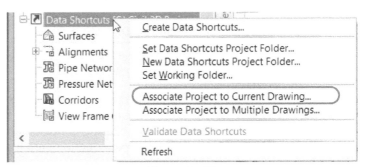

Figure 4–47

4. Verify that **Ascent Phase 1** is the selected project. Click **OK**.

5. Note that in the center of the title bar of Civil 3D (top of the Civil 3D window), the project name appears in parentheses after the drawing name: **DS-A1-Shortcuts.dwg (Ascent Phase 1)**.

6. Save the drawing.

Practice 4c

Manage File Sizes with Data Shortcuts

Practice Objective

- Create Data Shortcuts from objects in a drawing to share with other team members.

In this practice, you will walk through the steps of creating project-based *Data Shortcuts* folders. It simulates a situation in which the existing conditions and/or design work has been done and you now need to share elements of the design with team members.

Task 1 - Create Data Shortcuts.

1. In the Toolspace, *Prospector* tab, verify that the Data Shortcuts points to the correct folder, as shown in Figure 4–48. By hovering over the Data Shortcuts heading, the full path gets revealed in the tooltip. If it is not set to *Ascent Phase 1*, then repeat the steps from the previous exercise.

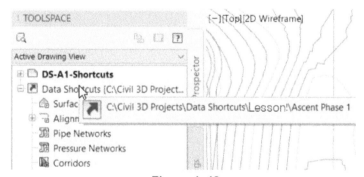

Figure 4–48

2. In the *Manage* tab>Data Shortcuts panel, click (Create Data Shortcuts).

3. If you receive a message that the drawing has not yet been saved, click **OK**. Save the drawing and start the **Create Data Shortcuts** command again.

4. In the Create Data Shortcuts dialog box, a list of all of the available objects for use in shortcuts displays. Select **Surfaces**, **Alignments**, and **Corridors** (as shown in Figure 4–49) and click **OK**.

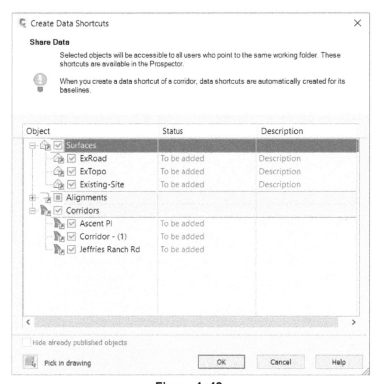

Figure 4–49

5. You have now created shortcuts for the surfaces, alignments, and corridors. This means that if the shortcuts and drawings are in a shared network folder, anyone on the network has access to these Autodesk Civil 3D objects.

   Note that in the Toolspace, *Prospector* tab, under the *Data Shortcuts* and *Surfaces* collections, you can now access all of the surfaces. In the list view, the source filename and source path display, as shown in Figure 4–50.

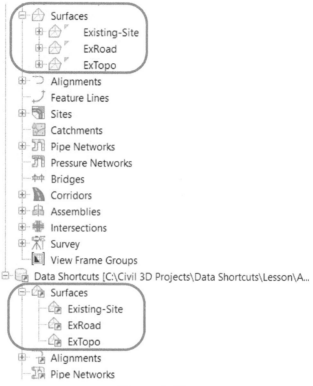

Figure 4–50

6. Save the drawing, but do not close it.

Task 2 - Data-reference Data Shortcuts.

---

1. Start a new drawing from the **ASC-C3D (CA83-VIF) NCS.dw**t file from the *C:\Civil 3D Projects\Ascent-Config* folder.

2. Save the file in *C:\Civil 3D Projects\Data Shortcuts\DWG* as **Reference File.dwg**.

3. In the Toolspace, *Prospector* tab, ensure that *Data Shortcuts* point to the *C:\Civil 3D Projects\Data Shortcuts\ Lesson\Ascent Phase 1* folder.

4. In the Toolspace, *Prospector* tab, right-click on **Data Shortcuts** and select **Associate Project to Current Drawing**, as shown in Figure 4–51.

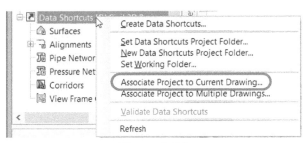

Figure 4–51

5. In the Toolspace, *Prospector* tab, under the *Data Shortcuts* collection, expand the *Surfaces* collection (if not already expanded) and expand the *Alignments>Centerline Alignments* collection, as shown in Figure 4–52.

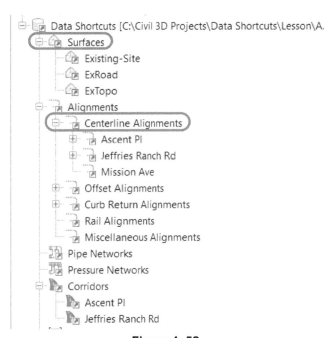

Figure 4–52

6. Under the *Surfaces* collection, select the surface **Existing-Site**, right-click, and select **Create Reference**, as shown in Figure 4–53.

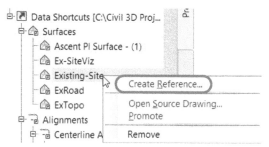

Figure 4–53

7. In the Create Surface Reference dialog box, do the following:

- Type **ExSurface** for the *Name*.
- Type **Data referenced surface** for the *Description*.
- Select **Contours 2' and 10' (Background)** for the *Style*, as shown in Figure 4–54.
- Click **OK** to close the dialog box.
- Type **ZE** and press <Enter> to display the surface reference.

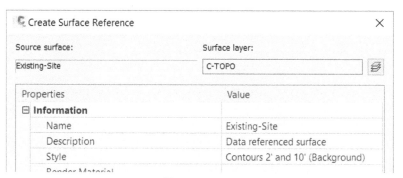

Figure 4–54

8. You will now create a data reference to the alignment. In the *Alignments* collection, right-click on **Ascent PI** and select **Create Reference**.

9. In the Create Alignment Reference dialog box, accept the default for the *Name*. Type **Data referenced alignment** for the *Description*. Set the *Alignment style* to **ASC-Layout** and set the *Alignment label set* to **ASC-Major and Minor only**. Click **OK** when done, as shown in Figure 4–55.

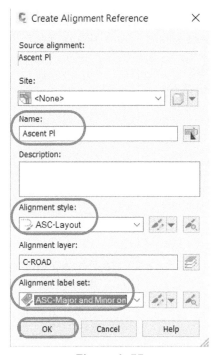

Figure 4–55

10. Zoom in to the end of the Ascent PI alignment, as shown in Figure 4–56.

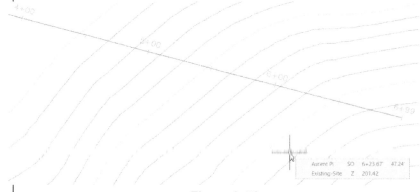

Figure 4–56

11. Create a data reference to the corridor: in the *Corridors* collection, right-click on **Ascent PI** and select **Create Reference**. Accept all of the defaults and then click **OK**.

12. In Model Space, select the **Ascent PI** referenced alignment.

Note that there are no grips and you cannot graphically redefine this alignment. However, you can add labels using the contextual tab.

13. In the contextual tab>Labels & Tables panel, expand Add Labels and select **Station/Offset - Fixed Point**, as shown in Figure 4–57.

Figure 4–57

14. When prompted to select a point, select the end point of Ascent PI, as shown on the left in Figure 4–58. Select the label and move its location so that it is easier to read, as shown on the right in Figure 4–58. Note that the station is **6+98.72**.

Figure 4–58

15. In the Toolspace, *Prospector* tab, expand the *Surfaces* and *ExSurface* collections, as shown on the left in Figure 4–59. Note that it does not contain the definition elements that might otherwise be displayed in a surface that is not data-referenced, as shown on the right in Figure 4–59. Therefore, you cannot edit or make design changes to a referenced surface.

Figure 4–59

16. Save the drawing but do not close it.

Task 3 - Revise original referenced object.

---

1. In the Toolspace, *Prospector* tab, ensure that *Data Shortcuts* point to the *C:\Civil 3D Projects\Data Shortcuts\Lesson\ Ascent Phase 1* folder.

2. Ensure that the **Master View** is enabled in Toolspace so that all of the drawings that are loaded display. Select **DS-A1-Shortcuts**, right-click and select **Switch to**, as shown in Figure 4–60. **DS-A1-Shortcuts.dwg** is now the current drawing. However, if you had closed the drawing, you need to open **DS-A1-Shortcuts.dwg**.

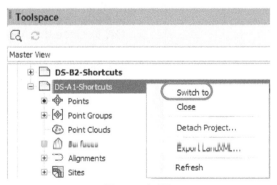

Figure 4–60

3. Zoom into the end of Ascent Pl to get a better view of the cul-de-sac.

---

4. You will now change the length of this alignment. In Model Space, select the alignment, select the grip that signifies the end of the alignment, and move it to the intersection where it crosses the cul-de-sac bulb, as shown in Figure 4–61.

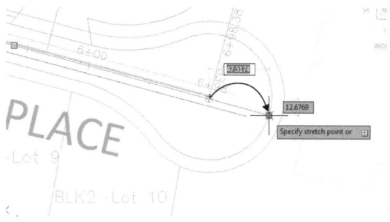

Figure 4–61

5. In the contextual tab>Modify panel, select **Alignment Properties**, as shown in Figure 4–62.

Figure 4–62

6. In the *Station Control* tab in the Alignment Properties - Ascent PI dialog box, set the reference point Station to **100**, as shown in Figure 4–63. A warning displays prompting you that changing the station will affect objects and data that have already been created. Click **OK** to dismiss the warning. Click **OK** to close the Alignment Properties dialog box.

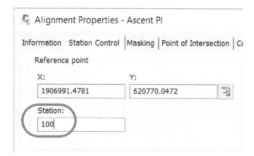

Figure 4–63

7. Save the drawing. This updates the Data Shortcut.

*If you closed the drawing in Step 8, open the drawing **Reference File.dwg**.*

8. If you are continuing with the drawing from the previous task, ensure that the Master view is enabled in the Toolspace so that you can see all of the drawings that are loaded. Select **Reference File**, right-click, and select **Switch to**. **Reference File.dwg** is now the current drawing.

9. In the Status Bar, you should see ⚿ (Data Shortcut Reference), as shown on the left in Figure 4–64. To synchronize your current drawing, right-click on see ⚿ (Data Shortcut Reference) and select **Synchronize**, as shown on the right in Figure 4–64.

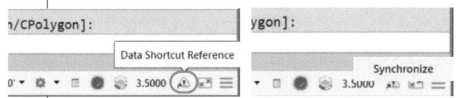

Figure 4–64

10. Alternatively, in the Toolspace, *Prospector* tab, select the alignment **Ascent PI** in the *Alignments* collection. Right-click and select **Synchronize**, as shown in Figure 4–65.

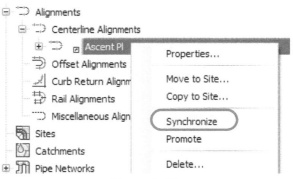

Figure 4–65

11. Note that the alignment has updated geographic information, as shown in Figure 4–66. The end of the alignment has been extended to intersect the cul-de-sac bulb, and the station label is updated to reflect the change to the original alignment design.

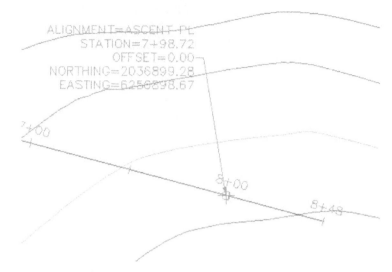

Figure 4–66

12. Save the drawing.

Chapter Review Questions

1. In the Autodesk Civil 3D workflow, what are the two main methods of project collaboration (or the sharing of intelligent Autodesk Civil 3D design data)?

   a. Windows Explorer and XREFs

   b. Data Shortcuts and Vault references

   c. XREFs and Data Shortcuts

   d. Vault references and XREFs

2. Why would you want to use Vault references over Data Shortcuts?

   a. Added security and version control.

   b. Permit more people to have access.

   c. It works more like regular AutoCAD.

   d. It works better with multiple offices.

3. When sharing data in a project collaboration environment, what is the recommended number of levels into which the data should be broken?

   a. 1 level

   b. 2 levels

   c. 3 levels

   d. 4 levels

4. How can you edit an object referenced through Data Shortcuts?

   a. Open the source drawing.

   b. With grips.

   c. Using the Panorama view.

   d. You cannot.

5. What is the file format that Data Shortcuts use to share design data between drawing files?

   a. .SHP

   b. .DWT

   c. .DWG

   d. .XML

6. How do you force the styles in a design file to update every time the CAD Manager makes a change to the styles in the company CAD Standards template file?

    a. In the *Manage* tab>Styles panel, click (Reference).

    b. In the *Manage* tab>Styles panel, click (Purge).

    c. In the *Manage* tab>Styles panel, click (Import).

    d. You have to create a new style manually because there is no way to force an update to styles in an existing drawing.

Command Summary

Button	Command	Location
	Create Data Shortcuts	**Ribbon:** *Manage* tab>Data Shortcuts panel
		Command Prompt: CreateDataShortcuts
	Manager Reference Styles	• **Ribbon:** *Manage* tab>Styles panel
		• **Command Prompt:** AttachReferenceTemplate
	Import Styles	• **Ribbon:** *Manage* tab>Styles panel
		• **Command Prompt:** importstylesandsettings
	New Shortcuts Folder	**Ribbon:** *Manage* tab>Data Shortcuts panel
		Command Prompt: NewShortcutsFolder
	Style Purge	• **Ribbon:** *Manage* tab>Styles panel
		• **Command Prompt:** purgestyles
	Set Shortcuts Folder	**Ribbon:** *Manage* tab>Data Shortcuts panel
		Command Prompt: SetShortcutsFolder
	Set Working Folder	**Ribbon:** *Manage* tab>Data Shortcuts panel
		Command Prompt: SetWorkingFolder

Alignments

#10

Alignments can represent the center line of a road, a curb return, the edge of a travel way, paths and walkways, dams, breakwaters, and much more. In this chapter, you will learn how to create an alignment, move an alignment to another site, and adjust an alignment. Then, you will create an alignment table and labels to communicate the design information to contractors and other stakeholders.

Learning Objectives in This Chapter

- List the various types of projects that are going to use alignments and profiles in their designs.
- Create a site for alignments, parcels, grading objects, etc. to be located.
- Create an alignment from existing design data.
- Create an alignment from scratch using specific design criteria and the Alignment Layout Tools.
- Control the station numbering and design speeds along the alignment using alignment properties.
- Communicate design information by adding alignment labels and tables.

5.1 Roadway Design Overview

Alignments and Profiles are used in nearly every civil engineering project to help lay out roads, railways, runways, and walking and bike trails (any kind of linear design feature). In these types of applications, alignments are used to represent center lines, lane boundaries, shoulders, right-of-ways, construction baselines, and similar features. In addition, many other kinds of projects can benefit from alignments, such as swales, waterways, utilities, and some types of earthwork (such as levee, dam, and landfill designs).

Roads are typically designed through multiple 2D views: plan (top view), profile (side view), and cross-section (left to right view). The result of this approach is a set of documents showing the alignment as a plan, a profile as part of a profile view, and a series of cross-sections. The Autodesk® Civil 3D® software uses these views, resulting in a 3D roadway model called a corridor. An example is shown in Figure 5–1.

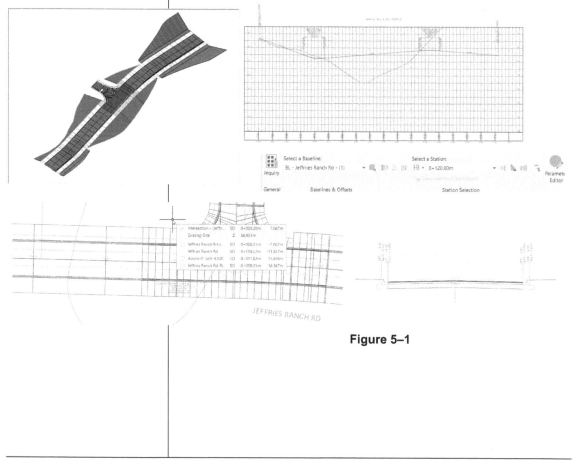

Figure 5–1

5.2 Autodesk Civil 3D Sites

Alignments, profiles, cross-sections, feature lines, grading groups, and parcels can be organized into containers referred to as *sites* in the Autodesk Civil 3D software. A site serves as a logical grouping of design data, such as:

- A specific phase of a project.

- A named geographic area in a larger project.

- A design alternative.

Sites are managed using a collection in the Toolspace, *Prospector* tab (as shown in Figure 5–2). A drawing can have any number of sites, or none at all.

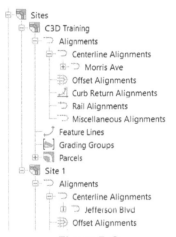

Figure 5–2

Profiles and cross-section data display in the Toolspace, *Prospector* tab below the alignment tree on which they are based. Corridors are stored in their own collection in the Toolspace, *Prospector* tab, separate from the site's collection.

Parcel lines only interact with other parcels and alignments in the same site. This enables multiple parcel and road alternatives to be present in the same drawing at the same time.

Alignments and their profiles and cross-sections might exist in a drawing without being part of a specific site. Those that are not, are located in the separate *Alignment* collection below the *Surfaces* collection in the Toolspace, *Prospector* tab. This enables alignments to exist in the drawing and not interact with any parcels, or to create a parcel if the alignment closes on itself (e.g., the bulb of a cul-de-sac).

5.3 Introduction to Alignments

An Autodesk Civil 3D alignment is an AEC object that resembles an AutoCAD® polyline. Alignments have rule-based constraints that make them very powerful design tools. Alignments can contain tangents (line segments), circular curves, and spirals.

The appearance and annotation of alignments are controlled by object and label styles. These styles are flexible, have an extensive list of label properties, and control layer assignments for objects and their labels.

Autodesk Civil 3D alignments can be created in the following ways:

- If previously defined, alignments can be imported from Autodesk LandXML® or from InfraWorks planning roads.

- A polyline can be converted directly to an alignment. Converted polylines follow the direction of the original polyline object.

- An alignment can be created interactively using the Alignment Layout toolbar.

- Individual AutoCAD lines and arcs can be converted to alignments using the Layout toolbar as well.

When creating new alignments, remember that you can use transparent commands to draw line segments by:

- **Angle Distance**
- **Bearing Distance**
- **Azimuth Distance**
- **Deflection Distance**

These commands are available in the *Transparent Commands* ribbon tab, as shown in Figure 5–3. They are extremely helpful when you need to stay within a specific right-of-way and you have the legal description of that right-of-way.

Figure 5–3

These transparent commands are also available in the
Transparent Commands toolbar (by default, docked vertically on
the right side of the Civil 3D window), as shown in Figure 5–4.

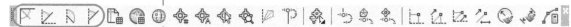

Figure 5–4

They are also available through the right-click menu when
AutoCAD or Civil 3D is searching for a point, as shown in
Figure 5–5.

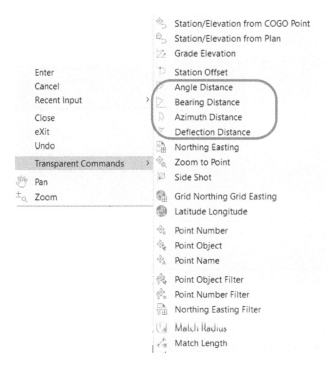

Figure 5–5

Criteria-Based Design

Default or custom standards can be used in the Autodesk Civil 3D software to evaluate alignment and profile designs. The Design Criteria Editor enables you to view, edit, or create criteria files (such as AASHTO tables). When you create a new alignment, the Create Alignment dialog box opens, as shown in Figure 5–6. You can tell the software what type of alignment you are creating to make intersection design easier later. The dialog box includes a *Design Criteria* tab that enables you to type the starting design speed, use criteria-based design, use a design criteria file, or use a design check set.

Figure 5–6

When an entity does not meet the criteria in the file it displays with a warning marker. Hover over the marker and note which criteria the entity violates, as shown in Figure 5–7.

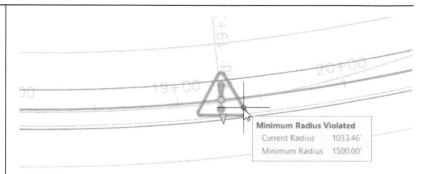

Figure 5–7

A warning marker also displays in the sub-entity and grid view editors when a violation occurs. This marker disappears when the value meets the required criteria.

Alignment Types

There are 5 different types of alignments that can be used in a design.

1. A **Centerline alignment** is the most commonly used type of alignment. You can use it when you know the location and design parameters of the centerline of the road, trail, or other linear feature being designed.

2. An **Offset alignment** is used to create transitions in a corridor design. You can use it when you want to target a transition line, such as a curb return, bus turnout lane, or other deviation from the original widths.

3. A **Curb Return alignment** is used when you want to base the design of the road from the curb location or when you need to connect the edges of two intersecting roadways.

4. A **Rail alignment** is the newest type of alignment. You can use it when you need to calculate curves along chords rather than arcs. It also enables you to set the track width and calculate cants.

5. A **Miscellaneous alignment** is available when the type of alignment you are creating does not fall into any of the other categories.

Alignment Segment Types

Each alignment tangent, circular curve, and spiral falls into one of three categories.

1. A **fixed segment** is one that is defined by specific criteria that only have a limited ability to be dynamically updated. Fixed curves hold their initial constraints (such as length and radius) and do not remain tangent at either end if a neighboring line segment is adjusted. You should avoid fixed curves in alignments that you might want to dynamically update (such as proposed alignments).

   Alignments imported from the Autodesk LandXML software contain all fixed segments. Alignment segments created from individual lines and arcs are also created as fixed segments. These fixed curves can be deleted and replaced with other types as required.

2. A **floating element** is one that depends entirely on the object before it in the alignment. If a preceding object is moved, stretched, or adjusted, a floating element (and everything following it) translates accordingly while holding all of the initial constraints (length, radius, pass-through-points, etc.).

   For example, the alignment shown in Figure 5–8 begins with a fixed line followed by a series of floating curves and a floating line that together define a cul-de-sac. Changing the end point of the fixed line causes all of the floating elements to translate while maintaining the original length of the floating line, and the original length, radius, and direction of the following curves. Floating elements only stay tangent at one end to neighboring segments if they are adjusted.

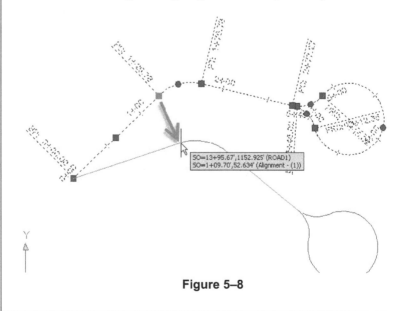

Figure 5–8

3. A **free segment** is one that is adjusted if the geometry of either neighboring segment is changed. Free segments always adjust to remain tangent to adjacent segments at both ends. For example, the free line shown in Figure 5–9 was drawn connected to two fixed arcs. If either of the arcs were assigned a different property (such as a new radius), the line would be completely redrawn to remain tangent to both.

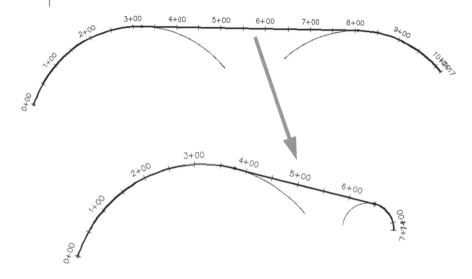

Figure 5–9

•   Alignments created by layout and polyline are made of fixed lines and free curves and spirals. These tend to be the most flexible types of alignments.

•   Because of their flexibility and ability to remain tangent through changes, free and floating elements are more useful in alignments that are subject to change, such as those for proposed roadway center lines.

Practice 5a

Creating Alignments from Objects

Practice Objective

- Create alignments from objects in the drawing or in an external reference file attached to the drawing.

In this practice, you will create horizontal alignments using two methods. First, you will create an alignment from an existing polyline that defines a road center line alignment. Second, you will create an alignment from a XREF file that defines a proposed center line alignment.

In this drawing, the **Existing Surface** has already been referenced in from the *Ascent-Development* Data Shortcut project and the surface style has been set to **_No Display**. The drawing has also been associated to the *Ascent-Development*. project.

Task 1 - Create an alignment from a polyline.

---

1. Open **ALN1-A.dwg** from the *C:\Civil 3D Projects\Working\ Alignments* folder.

See the Chapter 4: Project Management for how to work with Data Shortcuts.

2. Hover the cursor over the Data Shortcuts and review the tooltip that displays, as shown in Figure 5–10. Ensure that your Data Shortcuts are set so the **Working Folder** is set to *C:\Civil 3D Projects\Data Shortcuts\Fundamentals* and the **Data Shortcuts Project Folder** to *Ascent-Development*. If required, right-click on Data Shortcuts to set the **Working Folder** and **Data Shortcuts Project Folder**.

Figure 5–10

3. In the drawing, note that the red polyline running east-west represents the existing center line alignment of Mission Avenue, as shown in Figure 5–11.

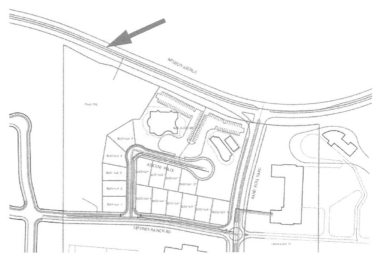

Figure 5–11

4. In the *Home* tab>Create Design panel, expand Alignment, and select (Create Alignment from Objects), as shown in Figure 5–12. Select the west end of the polyline representing **Mission Ave polyline** (as shown above in Figure 5–11) and press <Enter>.

Selecting the west end of the polyline identifies the start direction of the alignment.

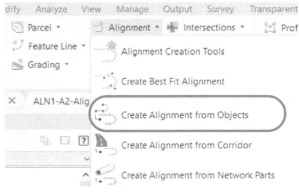

Figure 5–12

If you want to reverse the direction of the alignment, you need to select Reverse.

5. Verify that the alignment direction arrow is pointing East and press <Enter> to accept the alignment direction. If the direction arrow is pointing West, then press **R** to reverse the alignment direction.

6. In the Create Alignment from Objects dialog box, assign the values shown in Figure 5–13 to define the properties of this alignment:

- *Name:* **Mission Ave**
- *Type:* **Centerline**
- *Description:* Type a description, if required
- *Starting station:* **0** (Even though this is an existing roadway and the starting station should be an existing value, you will leave it set to 0 for simplicity's sake).
- *Site* (*General tab*): **None**
- *Alignment style:* **ASC-Proposed**
- *Alignment label set:* **ASC-All Labels**
- Clear the **Add curves between tangents** option.
- Accept the remaining default values, but **do not** click **OK**, for you need to check the design criteria in the next step.

Figure 5–13

*The Autodesk Civil 3D software will reference the design criteria file **Autodesk Civil 3D Imperial (2011) Roadway Design Standards.xml**.*

An Autodesk Civil 3D alignment is created, complete with labeling.

7. Select the *Design Criteria* tab shown in Figure 5–14. Ensure that the following are set, then click **OK**:

   - Design speed is set to **60 mi/h**.
   - Both the **Use criteria-based design** and **Use design criteria file** options should be selected.

Figure 5–14

8. Select the preset view **Aln-Warning**. Hover the cursor over the exclamation mark at approximately the station 19+26 on the alignment and note which design criteria was violated, as shown in Figure 5–15. In this case, the radius is 1033.46', but the minimum radius for a 60 mi/h road based on the AASHTO table must be greater than 1500'.

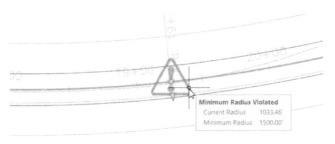

Figure 5–15

9. Save the drawing.

Task 2 - Create alignments from objects (XREFs).

1. Select the preset view **Aln-xref**.

2. In the *Home* tab>Create Design panel, expand **Alignment**, and select  (Create Alignment from Objects). When prompted to select an object, type **Xref** or **X** and press <Enter>. You will then be prompted to select a XREF object.

3. Select the west end of the polyline representing **Jeffries Ranch Rd** center line (the dashed gray line), as shown in Figure 5–16, and press <Enter>.

Selecting the west end of the XREF line identifies the start direction of the alignment.

Figure 5–16

4. Verify that the alignment direction arrow is pointing East and press <Enter> to accept the alignment direction.

5. In the Create Alignment from Objects dialog box, type **Jeffries Ranch Rd** for the alignment name, uncheck the **Add curves between tangents** checkbox, and accept all of the default values. Again you leave the starting station at Zero, although it is an existing roadway.

For this alignment, you will not be using design criteria.

6. In the *Design Criteria* tab, ensure that the **Use criteria-based design** option is cleared, as shown in Figure 5–17.

General   Design Criteria

Starting design speed:

60 mi/h

☐ Use criteria-based design

Use design criteria file

C:\ProgramData\Autodesk\C3D Stowe\enu

Figure 5–17

7. Click **OK** to close the dialog box and create the alignment.

8. Select the preset view **Aln-Create-Rand**.

9. Select 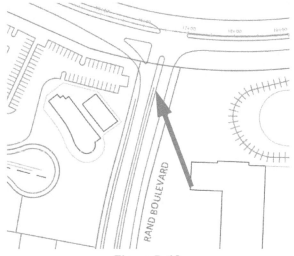 (Create Alignment from Objects) again. When prompted to select an object, type **Xref** or **X** and press <Enter>.

10. Select the north end of the polyline representing **Rand Boulevard** center line (the gray line in the boulevard island), as shown in Figure 5–18, and press <Enter>.

Figure 5–18

11. Verify that the alignment direction arrow is pointing south and press <Enter> to accept the alignment direction.

12. In the Create Alignment from Objects dialog box, type **Rand Boulevard** for the alignment name, uncheck the **Add curves between tangents** checkbox in the *Conversion options* section (as shown in Figure 5–19), and accept all of the default values.

Figure 5–19

For this alignment, you will be using design criteria.

13. In the *Design Criteria* tab, ensure that the following are set then click **OK**.

- Design speed is set to **40 mi/h**.
- Select both the **Use criteria-based design** and **Use design criteria file** options.

14. Save the drawing.

5.4 Alignments Layout Tools

Alignments are created and edited using the Alignment Layout toolbar, which can be opened from the *Home* tab>Create Design panel. Expand Alignment and select ![icon](Alignment Creation Tools), as shown at the top of Figure 5–20. The Alignment Layout Tools toolbar displays, as shown at the bottom of Figure 5–20.

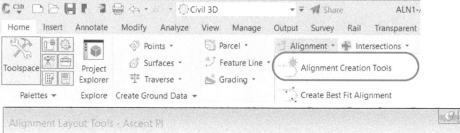

Figure 5–20

To create or add to an alignment interactively by locating new Points of Intersection (PIs), select one of the first two options in the Draw Tangents drop-down list, as shown in Figure 5–21.

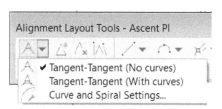

Figure 5–21

These two methods (with or without curves) are similar to drawing an AutoCAD polyline. If the **With Curves** option is selected, default curve information can be assigned in the Curve and Spiral Settings dialog box, as shown in Figure 5–22.

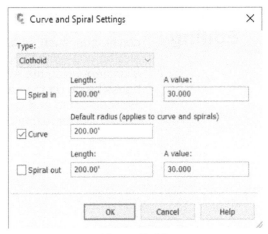

Figure 5–22

The Alignment Layout Tools toolbar also includes tools that enable you to:

	Create new Points of Intersection (PIs).
	Delete PIs (and associated curves).
	Break apart PIs.
	Convert AutoCAD lines and arcs to alignment segments.
	Delete a line, circular curve, or spiral segment.
	Reverse sub-entity's direction.
	Edit best-fit data for all entities.
	Select an individual segment for editing in the Sub-Entity Editor.
	Edit sub-entity components.
	Review and adjust alignment properties (length, radius, etc.) in the Alignment Entities vista.
	Undo a recent alignment edit.
	Redo a recent alignment edit.

Most of the other tools in the Alignment Layout Tools toolbar are intended for creating segments with various constraints.

Alignment Editing

In addition to the Edit tools available in the Alignment Layout toolbar, alignments can be edited using the AutoCAD **Modify** commands, such as **Move** and **Stretch**. Alignment entities can also be grip-edited into new positions. You can delete an alignment using the AutoCAD **Erase** command, or by right-clicking on the name of the alignment in the Toolspace, *Prospector* tab and selecting **Delete**. To open the Alignment Layout toolbar, expand Alignments and select **Edit Alignment Geometry**.

Practice 5b

Creating and Modifying Alignments

Practice Objective

- Create an alignment from scratch using the Alignment Layout tools.

In this practice, you will create a free form alignment, based on some design parameters. You will create an alignment for Ascent Place based on existing design data, as shown in Figure 5–23. According to this data, the street right-of-way extends north at a bearing of N1d18'04.79"E and then east at a bearing of S75d18'31.56"E. The north center line leg is 353.17' to the point of intersection and the east leg is -381.93' from the point of intersection. In addition, the center line of Ascent Place intersects Jeffries Ranch road at sta 5+79.13'.

Figure 5–23

Task 1 - Create an alignment by layout.

1. Continue working with the drawing from the previous practice or open **ALN1-B.dwg**.

2. Select the preset view **Aln-Create**.

3. In the *Home* tab>Create Design panel, expand **Alignment** and select 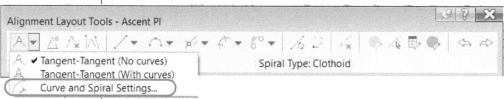 (Alignment Creation Tools).

4. In the Create Alignment Layout dialog box, type **Ascent PI** for the alignment name and accept all of the default values.

For this alignment, you will not be using design criteria.

5. In the *Design Criteria* tab, ensure that the **Use criteria-based design** option is not selected. Click **OK** to close the dialog box and create the alignment.

6. Expand the **Tangent** tool icon and select (Curve and Spiral Settings), as shown in Figure 5–24.

Figure 5–24

7. For the curve settings, ensure that the **curve** option is selected. Set the curve radius to **30.00'**, and click **OK** to close the Curve and Spiral Settings dialog box.

8. Expand the Tangent tool icon and select the ⬟ (Tangent-Tangent (With curves)) to start creating the horizontal alignment.

You want to start the alignment at a reference station to Jeffries Ranch Rd.

9. When prompted for the start of the alignment, click (Station Offset) on the *Transparent Commands* tab (or on the Transparent Tools toolbar).

10. Toggle on selection cycling by clicking  (Selection Cycling) in the Status Bar, as shown in Figure 5–25. (The alignment object and XREF center line occupy the same location in space and the selection cycling enables you to select the alignment.)

Figure 5–25

11. When prompted for an alignment, select **Jeffries Ranch Rd**. In the Selection Cycling dialog box, click **Alignment**.

12. When prompted for a station, type **579.13'** and press <Enter>.

13. When prompted for the offset, type **0** and press <Enter>. Press <Esc> to exit the transparent command.

14. You will specify the next point using the transparent command to enter a bearing and a distance. Click (Bearing Distance) on the *Transparent Commands* tab and enter the following:

- Type **1** and press <Enter> for the NE quadrant.
- Type **1.180479** and press <Enter> for the bearing (the transparent command will translate this to 1 deg, 18 min, and 04.79 sec).
- Type a distance of **353.17'** and press <Enter>.
- Press <Esc> once to exit the transparent command.

15. You will specify the next point using the transparent command to enter a turned angle and a distance. Click

 (Angle Distance) on the *Transparent Commands* tab and do the following:

- Type **C** and press <Enter>, since you will be entering a counter-clockwise include angle.
- Type the include angle of **76.6101** and press <Enter>
- Type **381.93** and press <Enter> for the distance.

16. Press <Esc> once to exit the transparent command and press <Enter> to complete the horizontal alignment.

The Autodesk Civil 3D software has now established the starting location of the alignment by converting the station/offset to a X,Y value.

17. Close the **Alignment** layout tool by clicking **X** in the top right of the dialog box.

18. Save the drawing.

Task 2 - Edit alignments.

In this task, we will study three methods of correcting the curve that was automatically inserted:

- Adjusting the radius with grips.
- Adjusting the radius in the Layout Parameter table.
- Deleting and re-creating the curve.

1. Set **Aln-Curv Radius** as the active view.

2. Select the alignment **Ascent PI**. Select the cyan triangular grip at the midpoint of the curve and drag it so it lies perpendicular to the gray curve segment of the XREF, as shown in Figure 5–26. Use the Perpendicular Osnap.

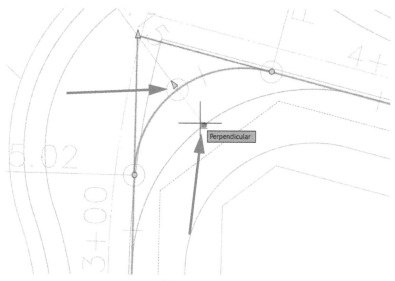

Figure 5–26

3. Undo the action by clicking ⟲ (Undo) in the Quick Access Toolbar. This restores the original curve radius so you can use another method.

4. Select the alignment **Ascent PI** again. In the *Alignment* contextual tab>Modify panel, click ⤳ (Geometry Editor).

5. In the Alignment Layout Tools toolbar, click [icon] (Pick Sub-entity), as shown in Figure 5–27.

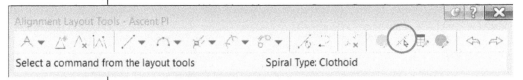

Figure 5–27

6. When prompted to select the sub-entity, select the curve. Change the radius to **50'** and press <Enter>, as shown in Figure 5–28.

Note that the radius dynamically changes in the graphics view.

Figure 5–28

7. Now you will use the third method by deleting and re-creating the curve. Select [icon] (Delete Sub-entity) in the Alignment Layout Tools toolbar, as shown in Figure 5–29. Select the curve and press <Enter> to exit the command.

Figure 5–29

8. In the Alignment Layout Tools toolbar, expand the curve

   drop-down list and select 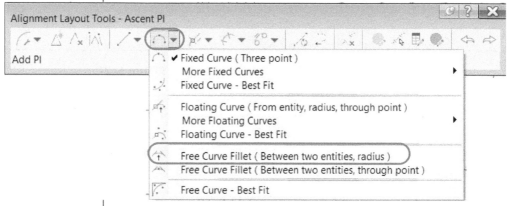 (Free Curve Fillet (between two entities, radius)), as shown in Figure 5–30.

Figure 5–30

9. Select the incoming tangent (running north-south) and the outgoing tangent (running eastward) and press <Enter> to accept that the angle is **less than 180 deg**. For the radius, type **50'**, press <Enter>, and press <Enter> again to complete the command. The results are shown in Figure 5–31.

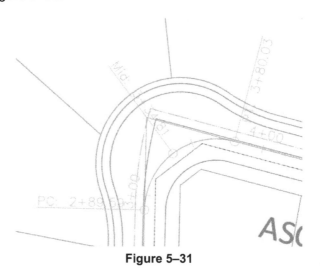

Figure 5–31

10. Close the Alignment Layout Tools toolbar and save the drawing.

11. Save the drawing.

5.5 Alignment Properties

The Alignment Properties dialog box (found by right-clicking on the alignment name in the Toolspace, *Prospector* tab and selecting Properties) controls stationing, station equations, references to the alignment by profiles and profile views, design speeds, superelevation settings, and related controls.

Station Control Tab

The *Station Control* tab sets the beginning station of the alignment. All labeling referencing the alignment dynamically updates its values when any change occurs to the alignment.

The *Station Equation* area of the panel adds and deletes equations from the alignment. A station equation is a point along the alignment where the stationing changes. The equation can represent the meeting of two stationing systems, a realignment of the alignment, or the change in authority over the center line.

When adding an equation, the Autodesk Civil 3D software displays a station jig reporting its station at the cursor. You set the station by selecting a point along the center line or entering a specific station value. After identifying the station equation point, set the station ahead value and whether the stationing increases or decreases.

Design Criteria Tab

Each roadway can have multiple design speeds that reflect the conditions, design, and type of roadway surface. Design speeds affect the amount of superelevation and other safety concerns (stopping sight distance, passing sight distance, etc.) surrounding the roadway design.

When working with superelevations and vertical curves, the design speed of the roadway is critical for computing the correct parameters for the road design. When setting design speeds, the Autodesk Civil 3D software displays a station selection jig and prompts for a station at the Command Line. After setting the station for the speed, you set the speed and enter any comments. You set the station in the drawing and refine its value in the *Design Speeds* tab in the Alignment Properties dialog box.

The option to **Use criteria-based design** is also found here, as shown in Figure 5–32. Select this option, and then decide whether you plan to use a design criteria file or design checks that you have created yourself.

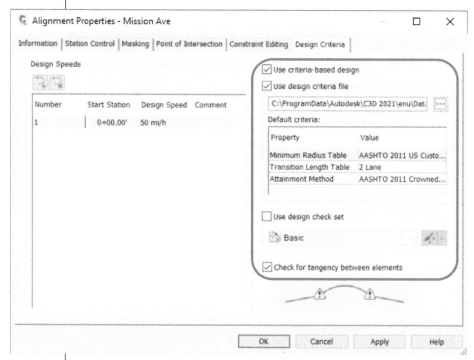

Figure 5–32

5.6 Labels and Tables

Alignment labels fall into two general categories: those controlled as a group using the **Edit Alignment Labels** command (referred to here as *Alignment Point Labels*), and those managed individually (referred to here as *Independent Alignment Labels*). Alignment labels of both types can be selected, repositioned, and erased separate from the alignment object itself.

Alignment Point Labels

Alignment point labels are organized into five categories, each of which is controlled by specific label styles:

*   Major and Minor Stations

*   (Horizontal) Geometry Points, such as Points of Curvature (PCs)

*   Station Equations

*   Design Speeds

*   Profile Geometry Points, such as Points of Vertical Curvature (PVCs)

*   Superelevation Critical Points

The Autodesk Civil 3D software enables you to organize various alignment point labels into **Alignment Label Sets**, as shown in Figure 5–33, to simplify adding a group of them at the same time.

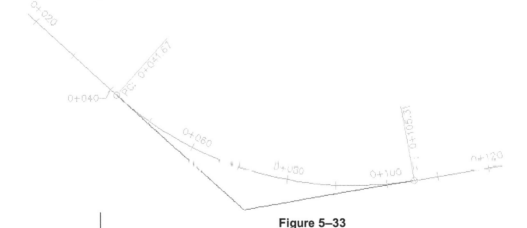

Figure 5–33

Alignment point labels can be added when the alignment is defined and can later be managed by right-clicking on an alignment and selecting **Edit Alignment Labels**. You can also edit existing labels by clicking on an alignment label element and selecting **Edit Label Group** from the contextual ribbon, as shown in Figure 5–34.

Figure 5–34

When an alignment has no labels, the easiest way to assign label sets is through the right-click menu by selecting **Edit Alignment Labels**.

Label sets are managed in the Alignment Labels dialog box, as shown in Figure 5–35.

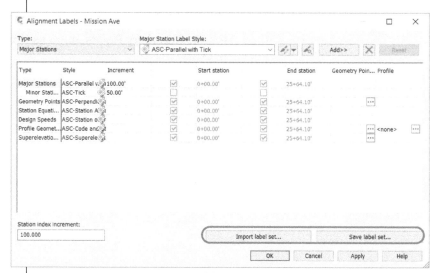

Figure 5–35

In the Alignment Labels dialog box, you can do the following:

- Add or delete components to the label set.
- Set the style of the components.
- Set the station spacing for the components.
- Determine the start and ending station location for the components.

- Determine which geometry points are labeled by clicking on the ellipses to launch the Geometry Points dialog box (shown in Figure 5–36).

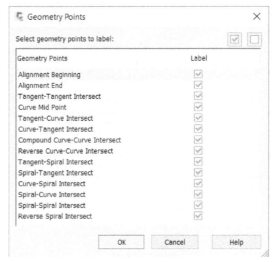

Figure 5–36

- Determine which profile points are labeled by clicking on the ellipses to launch the Profile Points dialog box (shown in Figure 5–37).

Figure 5–37

Once a label set is established, it can be saved for easy reuse in other alignments by clicking on the **Save Label Set** and **Import Label Set** buttons, respectively, as shown previously in Figure 5–35. Importing a label set will **replace** the existing label set; it will not add on to the existing labels.

Alignment point labels are organized into *label groups*, so that when one is selected, all similar labels on the alignment are also selected, as shown in Figure 5–38. This enables you to change their properties (e.g., using the AutoCAD Properties dialog box), or erase them all at once.

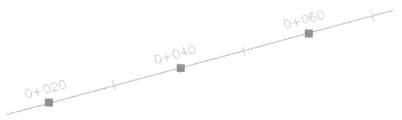

Figure 5–38

If you only want to select one of these labels (e.g., to erase one of them), hold <Ctrl> when selecting.

If you select an alignment and a large number of regularly spaced grips highlight, you have probably selected an alignment station label group, as shown in Figure 5–39. If you want to select the alignment itself (rather than the labels), press <Esc>, zoom in, and try again.

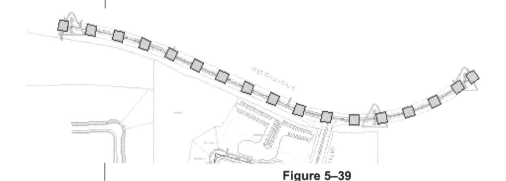

Figure 5–39

Independent Alignment Labels

Independent Alignment Labels can be used to add labels to alignment segments, and station and offset labels. They can be added using the Add Labels dialog box, which can be opened from the *Annotate* tab>Add Labels panel. Expand Alignment and select **Add Alignment Labels...**, as shown in Figure 5–40.

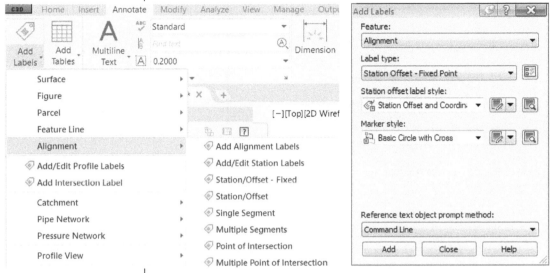

Figure 5–40

These labels include:

- **Station and offset label type:** Moves with the alignment if it changes to maintain the same station and offset, as shown in Figure 5–41.

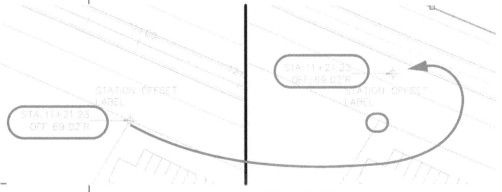

Figure 5–41

- **Station and offset – fixed point label type:** Does not move if the alignment changes, and its station and offset values update to reflect the alignment edit, as shown in Figure 5–42.

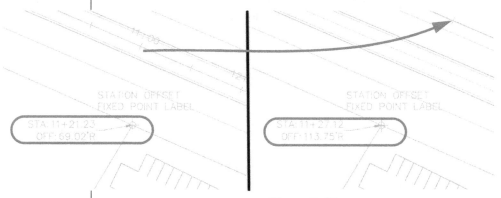

Figure 5–42

- **Single segment label type:** Adds a single line, curve, or spiral label to one alignment segment.

- **Multiple segment label type:** Adds a single line, curve, or spiral label to each alignment segment at the same time, as shown in Figure 5–43.

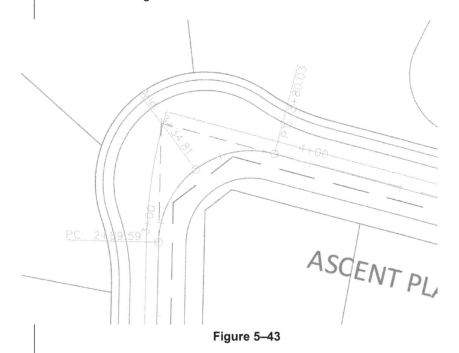

Figure 5–43

- **Point of intersection label type:** Adds a curve (or spiral-curve-spiral group) label at the tangent intersection, and labels the intersection of two tangents (sometimes called an *angle point*).

- **Multiple point of intersection label type:** Adds a curve (or spiral-curve-spiral group) to all of the intersections in the alignment.

Alignment Table Styles

If required, alignment segments can be given *tag* labels (such as **C1** shown in Figure 5–44) and the segment data can be tabulated. This is very similar to the procedures covered in the Parcels chapter for adding tags and tables.

Mission Ave				
Number	Radius	Length	Line/Chord Direction	A Value
L1		98.15	S81° 52' 26.21"E	
C1	2132.54	558.44	S74° 22' 19.17"E	
L2		743.18	S66° 52' 12.12"E	
C2	1033.46	1054.09	N83° 54' 37.46"E	
L3		110.26	N54° 41' 27.03"E	

Figure 5–44

Hint: Project Explorer

The new Project Explorer offers alternatives to creating tables and reports, providing additional flexibility and improvements. For more information, see *Appendix B: Project Explorer*.

Practice 5c | Alignment Properties and Labels

Practice Objective

- Communicate design information by adding alignment labels and tables.

Task 1 - Edit alignment properties.

1. Continue working with the drawing from the previous practice or open **ALN1-C.dwg**.

2. Set **Aln-Warning** as the active view.

   When you created this alignment, you typed 60 mi/h as the speed. Note that, based on the design criteria, the radius is below the minimum. The warning displays both in Model Space and in the Panorama view, as shown in Figure 5–45.

   - If the yellow triangular warning symbol is too small, zoom out and regenerate the drawing (**Regen** command). The symbol resizes itself proportionally to the screen size.

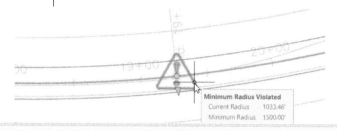

Figure 5–45

You need to fix the properties of this alignment to reflect the correct speed.

3. Select the alignment **Mission Ave**. In the *Alignment* contextual tab>Modify panel, select 🔧 (Alignment Properties).

In practice, you would add design speed zones to decrease the design speed for the intersection and restore the design speed after.

4. In the *Design Criteria* tab, change the *Design Speed* to **50 mi/h** and clear **Use design check set**, as shown in Figure 5–46, and click **OK** to exit.

   • Now that you have the correct design speed, the radius is within the minimum requirements.

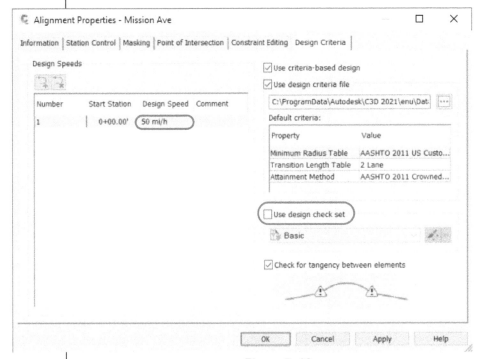

Figure 5–46

5. Press <Esc> to clear the selection and save the drawing.

Task 2 - Add and change alignment labels.

---

1. Select the **Rand Boulevard** alignment.

2. Note that in the alignment contextual ribbon, there is no option to add a label set to the alignment. This is available through the right-click menu.

3. In the right-click menu, select **Edit Alignment Labels**, as shown in Figure 5–47.

4. In the Alignment Labels dialog box, select **Import label set....**

5. In the Select Label Set dialog box, use the drop-down list to select **ASC-All Labels**, as shown in Figure 5–47. Click **OK** to close the dialog box.

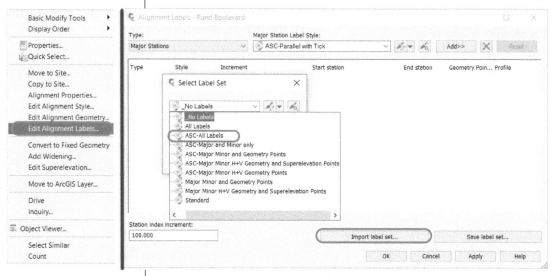

Figure 5–47

6. Click **OK** to close the Alignment Labels dialog box.

7. Note the warning about a tangency being violated, as shown in Figure 5–48. This is due to the polyline on the base place that you picked to create the alignment. For now, you will simply not check for tangencies on this alignment.

Figure 5–48

8. With the **Rand Boulevard** alignment still selected, in the *Alignment* contextual tab>Modify panel, select

 (Alignment Properties).

9. In the Alignment Properties dialog box, in the *Design Criteria* tab, clear **Check for tangency between elements**. Click **OK** to close the dialog box.

10. Currently, the station label intervals for Mission Ave. are every **100'**. The labels run parallel to the alignment. Select the alignment **Mission Ave**, right-click, and select **Edit Alignment Labels**.

11. In the Alignment Labels dialog box, leave the *Increment* for the Major labels to **100'** but change the Minor labels to **25'**, and in the *Style* drop-down list for *Major Station Label*, select **ASC-Perpendicular with Tick**, as shown in Figure 5–49. Click **OK** to close the Pick Label Style dialog box, then click **OK** to apply the changes and close the Alignment Labels dialog box.

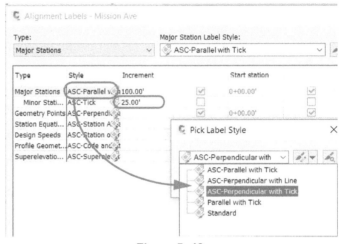

Figure 5–49

12. With the **Mission Ave** alignment still selected, in the Labels & Tables panel, expand **Add Labels** and select **Multiple Segment**, as shown in Figure 5–50.

Figure 5–50

13. When prompted to select the alignment, select the **Mission Ave** alignment again (as shown in Figure 5–51), and press <Enter> to complete and exit the command.

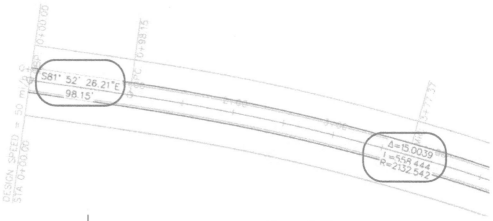

Figure 5–51

14. Select **Aln-Labels** as the active view.

15. To create a table listing the segments, select the alignment again, and in the Labels & Tables panel, expand **Add Tables** and select **Add Segments**, as shown in Figure 5–52.

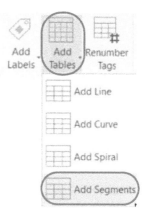

Figure 5–52

16. In the Alignment table creation dialog box, select **Mission Ave** in the Select alignment drop-down list. Set the options as shown in Figure 5–53 and click **OK** when done.

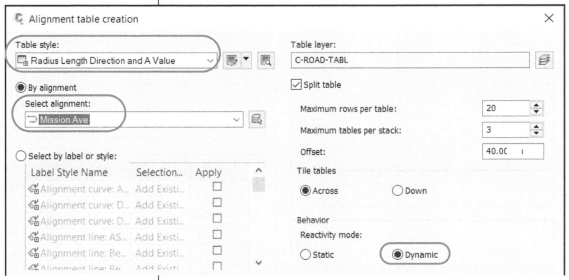

Figure 5–53

17. The Autodesk Civil 3D software will convert the labels to tags. Select a point in Model Space to set the location of the table, as shown in Figure 5–54.

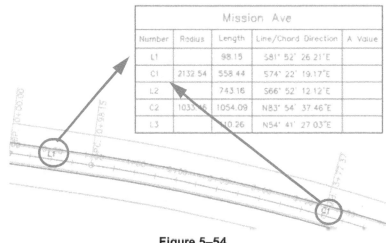

Mission Ave				
Number	Radius	Length	Line/Chord Direction	A Value
L1		98.15	S81° 52' 26.21"E	
C1	2132.54	558.44	S74° 22' 19.17"E	
L2		743.16	S66° 52' 12.12"E	
C2	1033.16	1054.09	N83° 54' 37.46"E	
L3		10.26	N54° 41' 27.03"E	

Figure 5–54

18. Select **Aln-Sta Label** as the active view.

19. Select the **Jeffries Ranch Rd** alignment and in the contextual tab>Labels & Tables panel, expand **Add Labels** and select **Station/Offset - Fixed Point**, as shown in Figure 5–55.

Figure 5–55

20. Select the end point where the Ascent PI alignment intersects with Jeffries Ranch Rd, as shown in Figure 5–56. Because of all of the Autodesk Civil 3D labels around the intersection, it might be advisable to use the Endpoint Osnap.

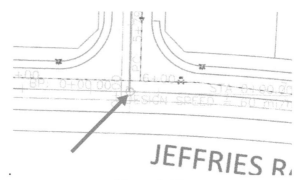

Figure 5–56

21. Press <Enter> to end the command and press <Esc> to clear the selection.

22. Select the label and using the Move grip, move the label to a location to avoid clutter, as shown in Figure 5–57.

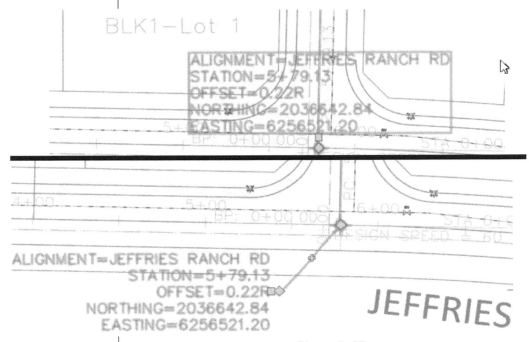

Figure 5–57

23. Save the drawing.

24. (Optional) Save the drawing as **<Your Initials>-Alignment-Complete.dwg** in the *C:\Civil 3D Projects\References\DWG\ Proposed* folder.

25. Update the relative paths of the referenced drawings in the alert box.

See the Chapter 4: Project Management for how to work with Data Shortcuts.

26. Add the four alignments to the project as Centerline Alignment Data Shortcuts, as you have done previously.

Chapter Review Questions

1. When can an alignment subdivide parcels?

   a. When it is a design style.

   b. When the parcels are ROW parcels.

   c. When they are in the same drawing file.

   d. When they are in the same site.

2. How do you open the Alignment Layout toolbar for an existing alignment?

   a. Select the Geometry Editor from the alignment's contextual ribbon.

   b. Right-click on **Alignments** in the Toolspace, *Prospector* tab.

   c. In the *Home* tab>Create Design panel, select **Edit Alignments**.

   d. Select **Alignments** in the Toolspace, *Prospector* tab.

3. How do you select an individual alignment Station label for deletion?

   a. Click on it.

   b. Right-click on it.

   c. Hold <Ctrl> as you select it.

   d. Hold <Shift> as you select it.

4. To change minor stations in the alignment from 50 feet to 25 feet...

   a. Change the settings in the alignment.

   b. Change the minor increment in the label set to 25 feet.

   c. Change the station style.

   d. Change the alignment label style.

5. The Alignment Style controls the color of the major and minor ticks.

   a. True

   b. False

Command Summary

Button	Command	Location
	Alignment Creation Tools	• **Ribbon:** *Home* tab>Create Design panel • **Command Prompt:** CreateAlignmentLayout
	Alignment Properties	• **Contextual Ribbon:** *Alignment* tab> Modify panel • **Command Prompt:** editalignmentproperties
	Create Alignment from Objects	• **Ribbon:** *Home* tab>Create Design panel • **Command Prompt:** CreateAlignmentEntities
	Curve & Spiral Settings	• **Toolbar:** Alignment Layout Tools
	Delete Sub-entity	• **Toolbar:** Alignment Layout Tools
	Free Curve Fillet	• **Toolbar:** Alignment Layout Tools
	Geometry Editor	• **Contextual Ribbon:** *Alignment* tab> Modify panel • **Command Prompt:** editalignment
	Pick Sub-entity	• **Toolbar:** Alignment Layout Tools
	Sub-entity Editor	• **Toolbar:** Alignment Layout Tools
	Tangent-Tangent (with Curves)	• **Toolbar:** Alignment Layout Tools

Profiles

Profiles are lengthwise vertical representations of an alignment. In this chapter, you will learn how to show what the existing ground is doing vertically along an alignment. Then, you will create a design profile to control the vertical slope and vertical curves for the final design.

Learning Objectives in This Chapter

- List the various items that form a profile view.
- Set the grid spacing and required labels for displaying a profile in a profile view.
- Create a surface profile to indicate what the ground is doing vertically along an alignment.
- Create a profile view to display an alignment vertically with a grid and preset labels included.
- List the various types of vertical curves and why they are used in profiles.
- Create a profile that previews the finished ground by following specific design parameters.

6.1 Profiles Overview

A profile is the second plane of a roadway design. It is a view of the alignment from one side of the center line with elevations along the alignment. An Autodesk® Civil 3D® profile is a combination of a *profile view* and any number of *profiles* displayed in the view, as shown in Figure 6–1.

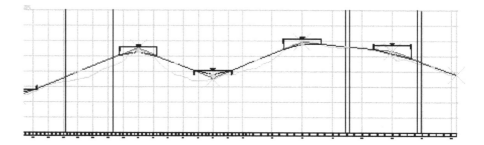

Figure 6–1

- A *profile view* consists of a profile grid and its annotation. The view's vertical lines represent alignment stationing and the horizontal lines represent elevations.

- A *profile* represents a surface or roadway vertical design. A typical road design profile view contains two profiles: the existing ground and a proposed vertical design. The existing ground profile represents elevations along the path of the alignment, usually from a sampled surface. The proposed vertical design defines elevations along the path of the proposed top surface of the roadway. You can have any number of existing and proposed vertical alignments displayed in the same profile view.

Autodesk Civil 3D Profiles are managed by:

- **Profile View Properties:** Control settings specific to individual profiles, such as datum elevation and maximum height.

- **Profile View Styles:** Affect how the grid and its annotations display.

- **Profile Styles:** Control how the profile linework displays.

- **Bands:** Control optional, additional annotation that can be displayed across the top or bottom of a profile view. Bands are grouped into Band Sets to make it easier to apply multiple, related bands at the same time. An example of a profile band is the elevation and station data shown in Figure 6–2.

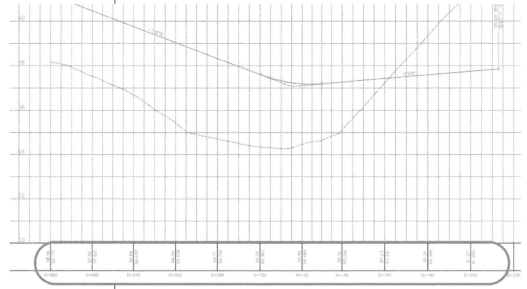

Figure 6–2

Repositioning and Deleting Profile Views

Autodesk Civil 3D profile views are safe to reposition as required with the AutoCAD® **Move** command, and copy with the AutoCAD **Copy** command. They can also be erased with the AutoCAD **Erase** command. Erasing a profile view also erases the design profile grade line that is attached. However, if the profile grade line exists in another profile view, the profile grade line data is saved.

6.2 Create a Profile View Style

Profile view styles control the format of the grid, titles, axis annotations, and other elements used for displaying profiles. To set up a new profile view style, select the Toolspace, *Settings* tab. Expand the *Profile View* collection, right-click on *Profile View Styles*, and select **New**. Typically, this is already set up for you by the BIM Manager in the drawing template, although some changes in the settings may be required based on specific project needs.

Information Tab

The *Information* tab enables you to enter basic information about the style, such as the name, a description, who it was created by and when, and who it was last modified by and when, as shown in Figure 6–3.

Figure 6–3

Graph Tab

The *Graph* tab enables you to set the vertical exaggeration for greater visibility in the profile view and the profile direction. The vertical scale can be set in two ways:

1. By dividing the current horizontal scale of the drawing by the vertical scale value, which gives you the vertical exaggeration value. This is usually set at a one to ten ratio. Therefore, if the horizontal scale is 1"=60', the *Vertical exaggeration* is set to **10** and the *Vertical Scale* is set to **1"=6'**.
2. You can select the vertical scale from a list, as shown in Figure 6–4.

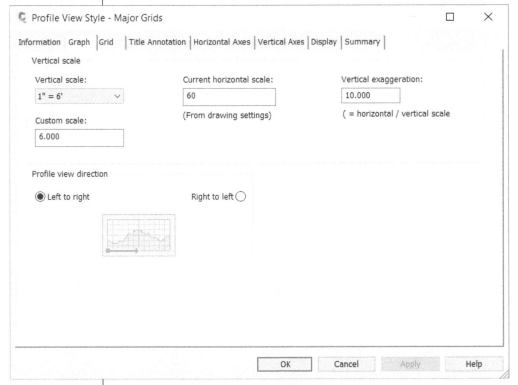

Figure 6–4

3. If required, you can change the view direction from left to right (the default is right to left).

Grid Tab

The *Grid* tab is used to specify the clipping, padding, and axes offset in the profile view grid.

- The **Clip vertical grid** option enables you to trim the vertical grid lines at either the existing ground or finished ground profiles, the highest profile, or select which profile will clip the grid (when the profile view is created).

- The **Clip horizontal grid** option does the same for the horizontal grid lines, as shown in Figure 6–5.

- The **Grid padding** enables you to add extra grid boxes at the beginning and end of the profile, and to the top and bottom.

- The **Axis offset** specifies the distance to offset the axis beyond the profile extents.

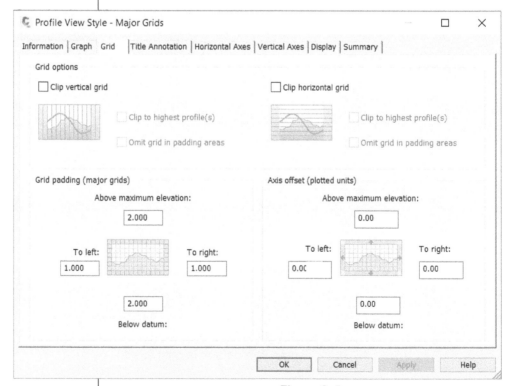

Figure 6–5

Title Annotation Tab

The *Title Annotation* tab enables you to specify the text style, contents, justification, and location of the profile view and axis titles, as shown in Figure 6–6.

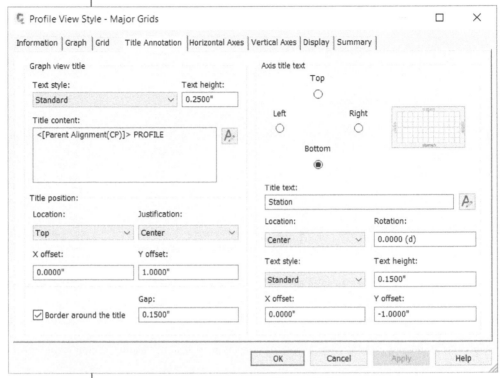

Figure 6–6

Horizontal Axes Tab

Note: *You can have different values for top and bottom.*

The *Horizontal Axes* tab enables you to specify the annotation for the top and bottom axes of the profile view. From here you can set the major and minor intervals for station labels and/or ticks, and the horizontal geometry tick details, as shown in Figure 6–7.

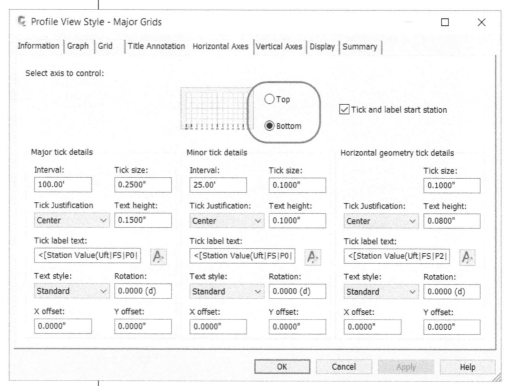

Figure 6–7

Vertical Axes Tab

Note: You can have different values for left and right.

The *Vertical Axes* tab enables you to specify the elevation label details, such as vertical interval, justification, content, text styles, and tick sizes, as shown in Figure 6–8.

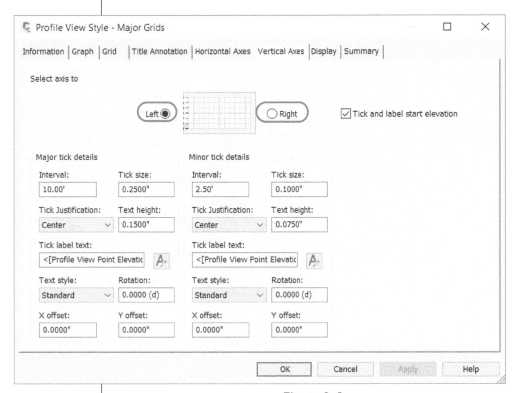

Figure 6–8

Display Tab

The *Display* tab enables you to set which components display and which layer, color, linetype, and other properties they use, as shown in Figure 6–9.

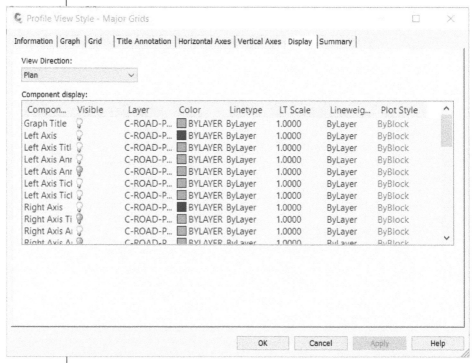

Figure 6–9

Summary Tab

The *Summary* tab enables you to review all of the settings that were selected on the other tabs for a quick reference, as shown in Figure 6–10.

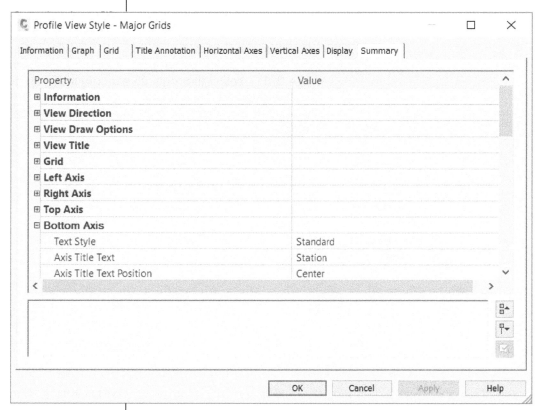

Figure 6–10

6.3 Create Profiles from Surface

Most profile views display at least one profile based on a surface, such as from an existing ground terrain model. To create a profile from a surface, use the following steps:

1. In the *Home* tab>Create Design panel, click 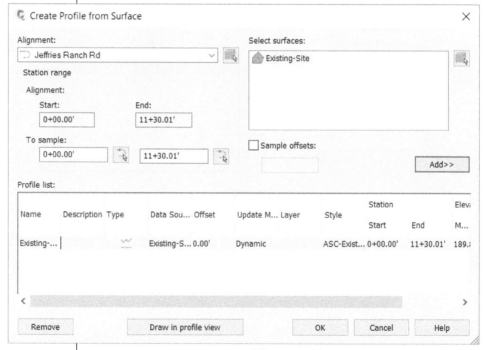 (Profile> Create Surface Profile).
2. In the Create Profile from Surface dialog box (shown in Figure 6–11), select the required alignment and surface(s).
3. Enter the required station range.
4. Click **Add>>** to sample each surface based on these settings.

Figure 6–11

This creates a profile along the alignment itself with a zero offset. If you want to sample at an offset from the alignment, select the **Sample Offsets** option. Enter a positive (+) value to sample the right side and a negative (-) value to sample the left side of the alignment, and then click **Add>>**. You can sample multiple offsets by entering values one at a time and clicking **Add>>** after each or putting a comma between offset values to add them all at the same time.

There are two ways to exit this dialog box (other than clicking **Cancel**):

- If you do not have a profile view of this alignment in the drawing, click **Draw in profile view**. This opens the Create Profile View dialog box.

- If you already have a profile view of this alignment, click **OK** and any new profiles are added to the existing view. If you clicked **OK** accidentally without having a view in which to display the profile, go to the *Home* tab> Profile and Section Views panel, and click (Profile View>Create Profile View).

6.4 Create Profile View Wizard

You can create a profile view at any time using  (Profile View>Create Profile View). All of the settings selected in the wizard can be reassigned later using Profile View Properties (except for the alignment on which they are based).

*Clicking **Draw in profile view** in the Create Profile from Surface dialog box opens the same wizard.*

The *General* page in the Create Profile View wizard enables you to select the alignment that you want to work with and to assign the profile view a name, description, view style, and layer. The **Show offset profiles by vertically stacking profile views** option (shown in Figure 6–12), enables you to display offset profiles in a different view from the center line profile without overlapping.

Figure 6–12

The *Station Range* page (shown in Figure 6–13), enables you to select the station range with which you want to work. The **Automatic** option includes the entire alignment's length.

Figure 6–13

The *Profile View Height* page (shown in Figure 6–14), enables you to select the required height of the profile grid.

Figure 6–14

- The **Automatic** option creates a profile view that is sized to avoid having to be split.

- The **User Specified** option enables you to assign specific minimum and maximum heights to the profile view. If a profile in one of these views has an elevation below or above the specified values, the profile view is split to accommodate it. If a profile needs to be split you can assign different styles to control the different portions of the split profile.

Figure 6–15 shows a profile view that has been split.

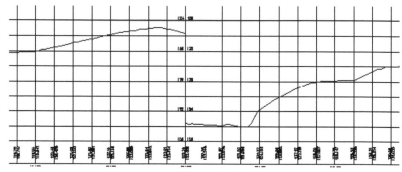

Figure 6–15

The *Stacked Profile* page (shown in Figure 6–16) enables you to set the number of stacked views, the gap between those views, and the styles for each one.

- This page is only available if you selected the **Show offset profiles by vertically stacking profile views** on the General page.

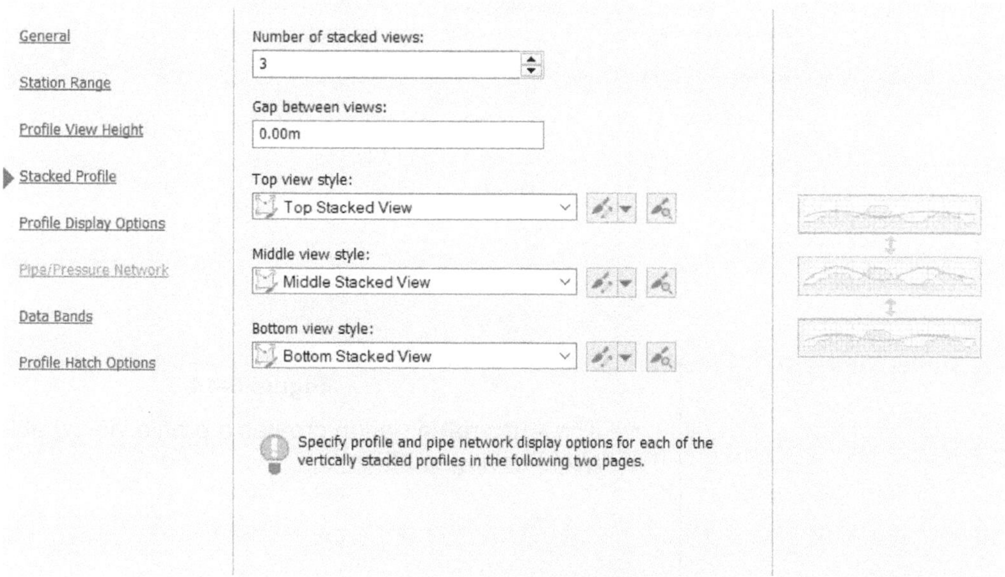

General

Station Range

Profile View Height

▶ Stacked Profile

Profile Display Options

Pipe/Pressure Network

Data Bands

Profile Hatch Options

Number of stacked views:

3

Gap between views:

0.00m

Top view style:

Top Stacked View

Middle view style:

Middle Stacked View

Bottom view style:

Bottom Stacked View

Specify profile and pipe network display options for each of the vertically stacked profiles in the following two pages.

Figure 6–16

The *Profile Display Options* page (shown in Figure 6–17) enables you to apply specific controls to profiles that display in the views.

Some of the most important options include:

- **Draw:** Disabling this option prevents the profile from being displayed in the view.

- **Style:** Sets the profile style to display in the profile.

- **Labels:** Sets the profile label set to display in the profile.

Figure 6–17

The *Data Bands* page (shown in Figure 6–18) enables you to select the bands that you want to include. Bands are additional profile information that can be included along the top or bottom of a profile. Bands are applied in this dialog box by selecting a Band Set.

Figure 6–18

You can only create the **Profile Hatch** *when there are at least two profiles in the profile view.*

The **Profile Hatch** option is shown in Figure 6–19. You can hatch the profile according to the *Cut Area*, *Fill Area*, *Multiple boundaries*, or *From criteria* that you import. If you select one of these options, the software enables you to specify the upper and lower boundaries for the hatch area.

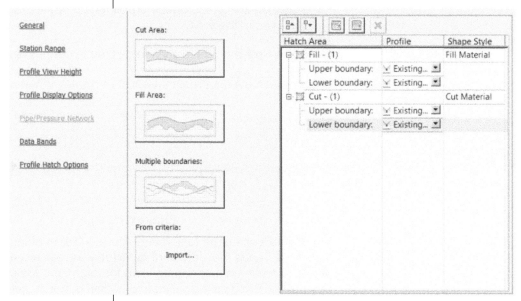

Figure 6–19

When satisfied, click **Create Profile View** to create the profile view. After the profile view is created these settings can be reviewed and adjusted using **Profile View Properties**. To open this dialog box, select the profile view, right-click and select **Profile View Properties**.

Practice 6a

Working with Profiles Part I

Practice Objective

*   Create profile views and the profile line of the existing ground.

In the following practices, you will create profile views and a profile vertical design. In a production collaboration environment, you can use data references to share data between team members, i.e., surfaces and horizontal alignments.

Based on specific design workflow, the horizontal alignment and design profiles often reside in the same drawing. This is the workflow that you will use. However, you can assume that the horizontal alignments are fixed and that you only need to reference them into the profile drawing. In that case, you can practice using data shortcuts or Vault shortcuts.

The *Existing-Site* surface is part of the Data-Shortcut Project *Ascent-Development* and has been referenced into this drawing. Its style has been set to *ASC-Border Only*.

Task 1 - Create surface profiles.

1. Open **PRF1-A1.dwg** from the *C:\Civil 3D Projects\ Working\Profiles* folder.

See the Project Management for how to work with Data Shortcuts.

2. Hover the cursor over the Data Shortcuts and review the tooltip which displays, shown in Figure 6–20. Ensure that your Data Shortcuts are set so the **Working Folder** is set to *C:\Clvll 3D Projects\Data Shortcuts\Fundamentals* and the **Data Shortcuts Project Folder** to *Ascent-Development*. If required, right-click on Data Shortcuts to set the **Working Folder** and **Data Shortcuts Project Folder**.

Figure 6–20

3. In the *Home* tab>Create Design panel, click 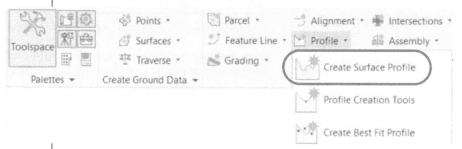 (Profile> Create Surface Profile), as shown in Figure 6–21.

Figure 6–21

4. In the Create Profile from Surface dialog box:

- Select the **Jeffries Ranch Rd** alignment.
- Highlight the **Existing-Site** surface and click **Add>>**.
- Click **Draw in profile view**, as shown in Figure 6–22.

This samples an existing ground profile along the center line, the entire length of Jeffries Ranch Rd.

Figure 6–22

*If you clicked **OK** instead, expand Profile View and select **Create Profile View** in the Home tab>Profile & Section Views panel.*

5. In the Create Profile View wizard, set the following options, as shown in Figure 6–23:

- In the *General* page, confirm **Jeffries Ranch Rd** as the alignment.
- Set the *Profile view style* to **Profile View**.
- Click **Next>**.

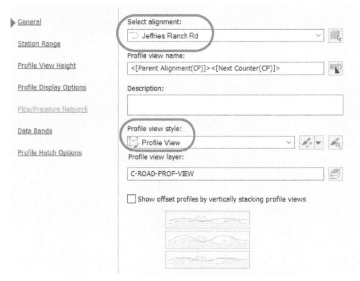

Figure 6–23

6. Accept the defaults in the *Station Range* page and click **Next>**.

7. Accept the defaults in the *Profile View Height* page and click **Next>**.

8. Accept the defaults in the *Profile Display Options* page and click **Next>**.

Note: You will set which profiles to use for profiles 1 and 2 in the data bands after a finish ground profile has been created.

9. In the *Data Bands* page, accept **EG-FG Elevations and Stations** for the band set, and click **Next>**.

10. In the *Profile Hatch Options* page, accept the default of no hatching and click **Create Profile View**.

11. If the event viewer displays, close it by clicking the checkmark in the top right corner. When prompted for a location for the profile, click a point to the right of the plan view to define the lower left corner of the profile view, as shown in Figure 6–24.

   • **Note:** The surface profile displays although the surface contours are not displayed in the plan view. This is because the surface exists in the drawing but is set to a **No Display** style.

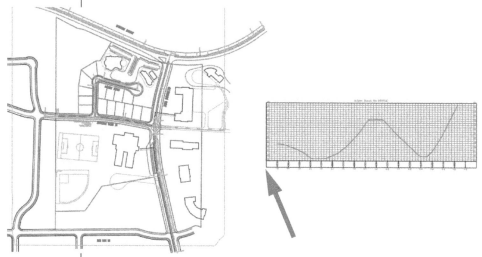

Figure 6–24

*If you are accepting all the defaults, you can simply click **Create Profile View** rather than stepping through all the pages of the Create Profile View wizard.*

12. Repeat Steps 3 to 11 for the alignment **Ascent Pl** and **Rand Boulevard**. Place the profile views underneath the previous one.

13. If you need to move a profile view, simply use the AutoCAD **Move** command or move it using the grip when you select the profile view.

14. Save the drawing.

Task 2 - Create named viewports.

---

1. In the top left corner of the drawing window, select - (dash or minus symbol) for Viewport Control. Expand **Viewport Configuration List** and select **Two: Horizontal**, as shown on the left in Figure 6–25.

   • Alternatively, in the *View* tab>Model Viewports panel, expand **Viewport Configuration** and select **Two: Horizontal**, as shown on the right in Figure 6–25.

Figure 6–25

2. Decide which viewport you want to use for the profile. In this case, it will be the upper viewport. Make the upper viewport active by clicking in it, then zoom and pan so that the Jeffries Ranch Rd profile view is centered.

3. Since Jeffries Ranch Rd runs west to east, you can enlarge the upper (profile view) viewport. Hover over the dividing line between the viewports until a double arrow appears, then click and drag to resize both viewports.

4. Adjust the zoom and pan levels for both viewports so the alignment in plan and profile view fit properly, as shown in Figure 6–26.

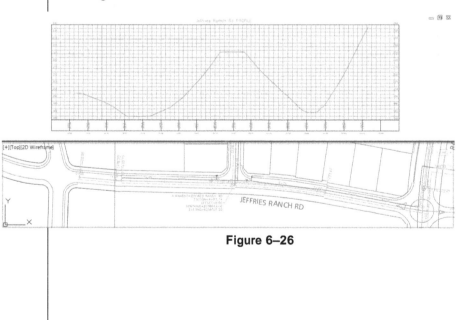

Figure 6–26

5. In the *View* tab>Model Viewports panel, select 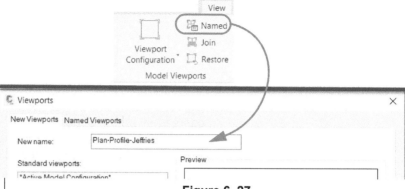 (Named). In the Viewports dialog box, select the *New Viewports* tab and type **Plan-Profile-Jeffries** for the name of this viewport configuration, as shown in Figure 6–27.

Figure 6–27

6. Click **OK** to close the Viewports dialog box.

7. In the top left corner of the drawing window, select **+** (plus symbol) for Viewport Control, expand **Viewport Configuration List**, and select **Single**.

8. To restore the Viewport Configuration, in the top left corner of the drawing window, select **-** (dash or minus symbol) for Viewport Control, expand **Viewport Configuration List> Custom Viewport Configuration**, and select **Plan-Profile-Jeffries**.

9. Time permitting, establish named viewport configurations for Ascent Place and Rand Boulevard. If you do not complete this step, you can open the next drawing for the next task.

10. Save the drawing.

Task 3 - Adjust the profile view.

You might sometimes be required to modify some of the selections that you made in the Create Profile View Wizard, specifically the datum elevation or grid height. In this task, you will adjust the profile view.

1. Continue with the previous drawing or open **PRF1-A2.dwg** if you did not complete Task 2.

2. Make the **Plan-Profile-Ascent** viewport configuration current.

3. Select the **Ascent PI** profile view, right-click, and select **Profile View Properties**, as shown in Figure 6–28.

*You can also select the Toolspace, Prospector tab and expand Alignments> Centerline Alignments> Ascent PI>Profile Views. Right-click on Ascent PI and select **Properties**.*

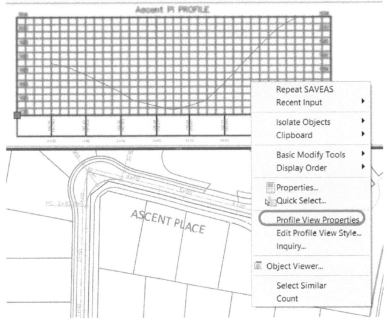

Figure 6–28

4. In the *Elevations* tab, select the **User specified height** option. Type a *Minimum* of **165** and a *Maximum* of **210**, as shown in Figure 6–29. Click **OK**.

Figure 6–29

5. The profile view will be adjusted as shown in Figure 6–30.

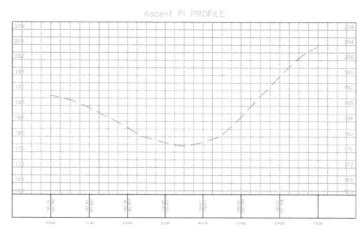

Figure 6–30

6. Save the drawing.

6.5 Finished Ground Profiles

Finished ground profiles (also referred to as proposed profiles or proposed vertical alignments) are often created interactively using the Profile Layout Tools toolbar, as shown in Figure 6–31. This is similar to how alignments are created by layout. The toolbar can be opened by going to the *Home* tab>Create Design panel and expanding Profile and selecting **Profile Creation Tools**.

Figure 6–31

- Using these tools, you can add tangents and vertical curves.

- Vertical curves transition a vehicle from one tangent grade to another and occur in two situations: Crest (top of a hill) and Sag (valley).

- There are multiple types of vertical curves to transition between changing the tangent grades of a crest or sag: **Circular**, **Parabolic**, **Asymmetric Parabolic**, and **Best Fit**. Roadways almost always use parabolic (equal length) curves. Asymmetric parabolic curves are usually only used if layout constraints do not permit an equal-length curve. True circular curves are used in some parts of the world for low-speed rail design. Generally, they should *never* be used for roadways (which could lead to vehicle vaulting or bottoming out). Best fit curves follow the most likely path through a series of points.

- In the Toolspace, *Settings* tab, in the Profile heading, the Edit Features Settings set the default curve type, styles, and command settings.

Most vertical designs have regulations affecting the minimum and maximum values for tangent slopes, distances along tangents between vertical curves, and safety design parameters for passing sight and stopping sight distances. Refer to local design manuals for more information on these design constraints.

The Surface Profile is linked to the alignment and the surface elevations at the alignment. Thus, if either the alignment or the surface (or both) change, the Surface Profile will update automatically.

However, the design profile(s) is not linked to the surface profile or the alignment and will not update to reflect changes to the surface and/or alignment. However, a circular yellow alert marker will be displayed on the affected profile where changes have occurred, as shown on the right in Figure 6–32. You can dismiss these notifications through the profile contextual ribbon, as shown on the left in Figure 6–32.

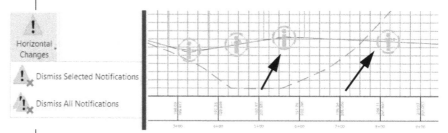

Figure 6–32

The points connecting tangents in a finished ground profile are referred to as a *Point of Vertical Intersection* (PVI).

Profiles are listed in the Prospector in the **Alignments** branch, as shown in Figure 6–33.

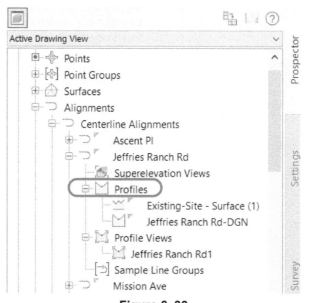

Figure 6–33

6.6 Create and Edit Profiles

Similar to the Alignments Layout toolbar, the Profile Layout Tools toolbar contains an overall vista (Profile Grid View) and Profile Layout Parameters (segment data viewer). These vistas enable you to review and edit the vertical design. The settings used when creating a finished ground profile can be selected in the Draw Tangents flyout in the toolbar, as shown in Figure 6–34. This toolbar is used to edit any kind of profile, including profiles created from surfaces.

Figure 6–34

Other toolbar commands, enable you to **Add**, **Delete**, or **Move** individual tangents, PVIs, or vertical curve segments.

- When editing a profile in the layout parameters or grid view, editable parameters display in black.

- You can graphically edit a design profile using grips. As soon as you select the profile, a contextual tab (shown in Figure 6–35) displays in the ribbon that is specific to that profile.

Figure 6–35

- When graphically editing a vertical alignment, the tangents, PVIs, and vertical curves display grips that represent specific editing functions, as shown in Figure 6–36.

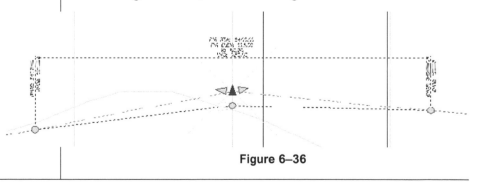

Figure 6–36

- The center triangular grip moves the PVI to a new station and/or elevation.

- The triangles left and right of the center extend the selected tangent, hold its grade, and modify the grade of the opposite tangent to relocate the PVI.

- The middle or end circular grips lengthen or shorten the vertical curve without affecting the location of the PVI.

- When you move the cursor to the original location of the grip, the cursor snaps to that location.

Superimposing Profiles

When there are multiple design profiles in a project, it may become necessary to see the different profiles together to understand how they relate and at which elevations they may intersect.

You select a profile in the originating profile view, and then select the profile view you want the profile superimposed on. The Superimpose Profile Options dialog box opens. It contains two tabs: *Limits* and *Accuracy*. The *Limits* tab prompts for the limits of the profile, meaning the extents the superimposed profile is displayed. If you do not want the entire length of the profile to be superimposed, enable the **Select start** and/or **Select end** checkboxes in order to type in the station values. You can also select the stations in Model Space by clicking 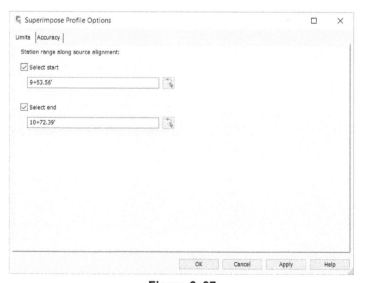 (Pick station), as shown in Figure 6–37.

Figure 6–37

The *Accuracy* tab is for setting the horizontal and vertical accuracy. You can set the mid-ordinate distances based on the source profile, as shown in Figure 6–38.

Figure 6–38

Transparent Commands

The Autodesk Civil 3D software has several transparent commands that can be extremely helpful when creating or editing a finished ground profile. They are listed below, in the order in which they display in the *Transparent* tab and in the toolbar on the right hand side of the drawing window, as shown in Figure 6–39.

Transparent tab

Toolbar

Figure 6–39

The Transparent commands are also available through the right-click menu when AutoCAD or Civil 3D is searching for a point, as shown in Figure 6–40.

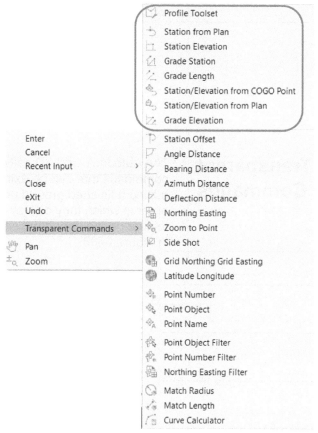

Figure 6–40

- **(Profile Station from Plan):** When creating or adjusting a PVI, this command enables you to pick a point in plan view next to the base alignment. The Autodesk Civil 3D software then calculates the station value automatically and prompts you for the elevation to use at that station.

- **(Profile Station and (surface) Elevation from Plan):** This command is similar, except that it enables you to determine an elevation from a surface.

- **(Profile Station and Elevation from COGO Point):** This command enables you to determine station and elevation values for a PVI based on the location of a point object.

- 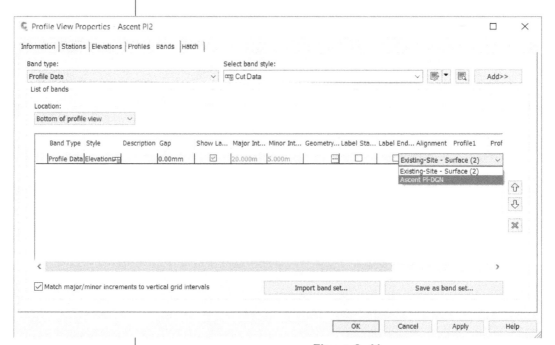 **(Profile Station Elevation):** By default, when adding a PVI you are prompted for a drawing's X,Y location. If you would rather enter a station value and elevation, use this command.

- **(Profile Grade Station):** This command enables you to locate a PVI based on a grade and an ending station value.

- **(Profile Grade Elevation):** This command enables you to locate a PVI based on a grade and an ending elevation value.

- **(Profile Grade Length):** This command enables you to locate a PVI based on a grade and tangent length.

Assigning Profile Band Elevations

Profile band elevations are assigned using Profile View Properties, in the *Bands* tab. When you create a profile view, you should review the band settings and verify that each profile band is assigned the correct profile in the *Profile1* and *Profile2* fields, as shown in Figure 6–41. The Autodesk Civil 3D software does not make any assumptions about which profile to use in either field.

Figure 6–41

Using the styles supplied with the Autodesk Civil 3D templates, the existing ground surface would be assigned the *Profile1* field, and the finished ground profile would be assigned the *Profile2* field. This can be swapped depending on your organization's standards.

Profile Segment Types

Profile segments created by layout (tangent lines, parabolas, and circular curves) can be created as fixed, floating, or free.

Profile Labels

Profiles have dynamic labels that are organized into two categories:

- **Profile labels:** Include labels for Major and Minor Stations, Horizontal Geometry Points, Profile Grade Breaks, Lines, and Crest and Sag curves. These can be selected when the profile is created and managed later by right-clicking on a profile and selecting **Edit Labels**, or by selecting <img> (Edit Profile Labels) from the contextual Profile ribbon.

- **Profile View labels:** Include a Station & Elevation label type and a Depth label type. These are created by going to the *Annotate* tab>Labels & Tables panel, expanding Add Labels, expanding Profile View, and selecting **Add Profile View Labels**, as shown in Figure 6–42. They can be removed using the AutoCAD **Erase** command.

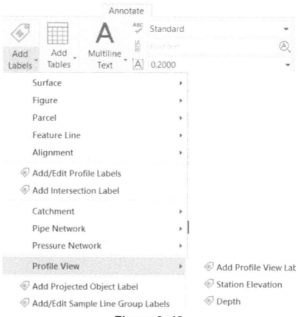

Figure 6–42

Label sets are managed in the Profile Labels dialog box, as shown in Figure 6–43.

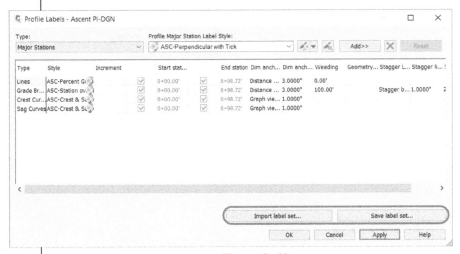

Figure 6–43

In the Profile Label dialog box, you can do the following:

- Add or delete components to the label set.
- Set the style of the components.
- Set the station spacing for the components.
- Determine the start and ending station location for the components.
- Determine which geometry points are labeled by clicking on the ellipses to launch the Geometry Points dialog box, (shown in Figure 6–44).

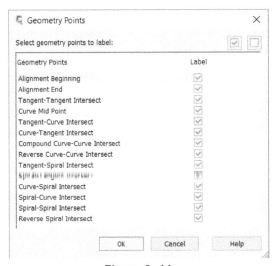

Figure 6–44

- Set the location and the length of the dimension line anchors for certain labels.
- Set the options for staggering labels, as follows:
1. No staggering
2. Stagger both sides
3. Stagger to right
4. Stagger to left
5. Stagger line heights

Once a label set is established, it can be saved for easy reuse in other profile views by clicking on the **Save Label Set** and **Import Label Set** buttons, respectively, as shown previously in Figure 6–43.

Practice 6b

Working with Profiles Part II

Practice Objective

- Create finished ground profiles using specific design parameters.

Before starting any type of design, you need to obtain all of the constraints. The tie in elevation for Jeffries Ranch Rd at the east end is 200.02', for this is an existing road to be lengthened. You also know that based on survey data that the tie in elevations at the west end at station 0+06.17' is 207.78', with an existing grade of approximately 3.80%. The cul-de-sac will be based on the grade of Jeffries Ranch Rd and an adjacent grade at Ascent Blvd. The low point overflow drainage in the knuckle will be addressed by an overland gutter to the pond.

For Rand Boulevard, you will use the values Civil 3D provides as the basis of your rough design. Figure 6–45 roughly shows the type of street drainage that you want to establish.

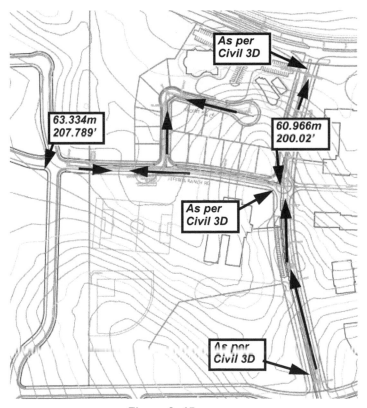

Figure 6–45

Task 1 - Create the Finished Ground Profile.

1. Continue with the previous drawing or open **PRF1-B1.dwg**.

2. In the top left corner of the drawing window, select **+** (plus symbol) for Viewport Control, expand **Viewport Configuration List**, and select **Plan-Profile-Jeffries**.

Alternatively, select the **Jeffries Ranch Rd** *profile view, and in the contextual tab>Launch Pad panel, select* **Profile Creation Tools**.

3. In the *Home* tab> Create Design panel, expand **Profile** and select **Profile Creation Tools**. When prompted to select a profile view, select the **Jeffries Ranch Rd** profile view.

4. In the Create Profile dialog box that opens, for the *Name*, click 🔲 (Edit name template) to the right.

5. In the Name Template dialog box, set the following, as shown in Figure 6–46:

   - In the *Property fields* field, select **Alignment Name** and then click **Insert**.
   - In the *Name* field, after **<[Alignment Name]>**, type -**DGN**.
   - Click **OK** to close the dialog box.

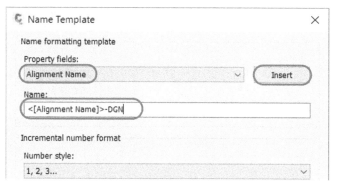

Figure 6–46

6. Set the *Profile style* to **ASC-Design Profile** and the *Profile label set* to **ASC-Complete Label Set** as shown in Figure 6–47. Click **OK**.

Figure 6–47

7. Note in the title of the Profile Layout Tools toolbar, the profile name is listed (*Jeffries Ranch Rd-DGN*), as shown in Figure 6–48. It is prudent to always check this when creating or editing profiles to ensure you are working on the right one.

8. Expand the drop-down list in the Profile Layout Tools toolbar and select **Draw Tangents**, as shown in Figure 6–48. The Autodesk Civil 3D software prompts you for a start point, which indicates the location of the road's first PVI.

Figure 6–48

9. In the *Transparent* tab (or the toolbar or right-click menu),

   click ⊟ (Profile Station Elevation), and then proceed as follows:

   • Select any part of the Jeffries Ranch Rd profile view.
   • Type a starting station of **6.17'** and press <Enter>.
   • Type a starting elevation of **207.78'**, and press <Enter>.
   • Press <Esc> to exit this transparent command.

*You want to set the next point based on a grade to a given station, so you will use the **Profile Grade Station** transparent command.*

10. Click 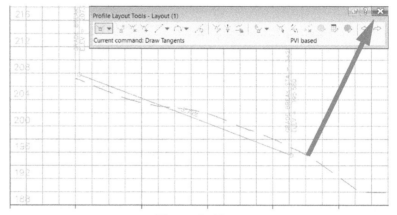 (Profile Grade Station) in the *Transparent Commands* tab to enter a grade followed by a station, as follows:

- For the grade, type **-3.79** and press <Enter>. (This indicates -3.79%. Note the minus sign to indicate going downhill).
- For the station, type **328.08'** and press <Enter>.
- Press <Esc> to end the transparent command.
- Press <Esc> again to end the layout command.

The profile is shown in Figure 6–49. Close the Profile Layout Tools, as shown on the top right of Figure 6–49.

Figure 6–49

11. At any time, you can continue to edit a profile by selecting it, right-clicking, and selecting **Edit Profile Geometry**. In the Jeffries Ranch Rd profile view, select the **Jeffries Ranch Rd-DGN** grade line drawn in Step 8. In the contextual

tab>Modify Profile panel, click (Geometry Editor) to edit it.

12. To continue adding PVIs, return to the Profile Layout Tools

toolbar and expand and select **Draw Tangents**. When prompted for the start point, snap to the end point of the last segment that you drew (i.e., **sta=328.08', elev=195.58')**.

13. In the *Transparent* tab, click (Profile Grade Length), and then proceed as follows:

- Select the **Jeffries Ranch Rd** profile view.
- For the grade, type **0.8** and press <Enter>.
- For the length, type **482.283'** and press <Enter>.
- Press <Esc> to exit the transparent command.

14. To tie back to the next design point, click ⌐ (Profile Station Elevation) in the *Transparent* tab, and then proceed as follows:

- Type an end alignment station of **1130.01'** and press <Enter>.
- Type a tie in elevation of **200.02'** and press <Enter>.
- Press <Esc> to exit the transparent command.
- Press <Enter> to exit the **Draw Tangent** command.

15. In the Profile Layout Tools toolbar, click **X** to close it. You will finish the design profile later in the chapter.

Task 2 - Adjust the FG Profile.

---

1. Select the **Jefferies Ranch Rd-DGN** profile that you drew in the previous task and note the grips that display.

2. In the contextual tab>Modify Profile panel, click

   ⌐ (Geometry Editor).

   The PVIs do not have any vertical curves. You will add them to the design using the **Free Vertical Curve (Parabola)** option, as shown in Figure 6–50. You could have also done this at the initial stage of the design using the **Draw Tangent with Curves** tool rather than the **Draw Tangent** tool.

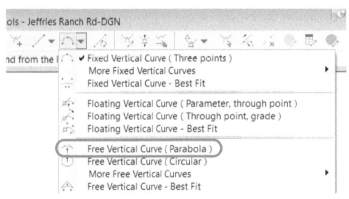

Figure 6–50

3. In the Curve drop-down list, select ⚆ (Free Vertical Curve (Parabola)), and when prompted to select the first entity, select the incoming grade (**A**) and then select the outgoing grade (**B**), as shown in Figure 6–51. Type **100'** for the length of vertical curve.

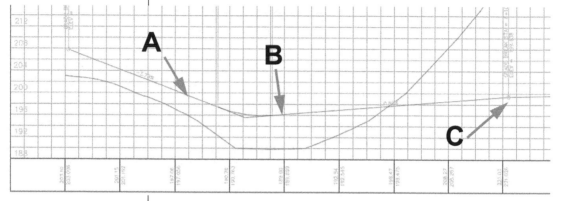

Figure 6–51

4. Note that the labels have not been updated to include the new curve and that you are prompted for another incoming entity. Press <Enter> to exit the command, and note that now the labels update to include the vertical curve information.

5. You could do the same for the second vertical curve; however, you will use another method. From the Curves drop-down list, expand **More Vertical Free Curves** and select **Free Vertical Parabola (PVI based)**, as shown in Figure 6–52. This option allows you to pick the PVI rather than the incoming and outgoing entities.

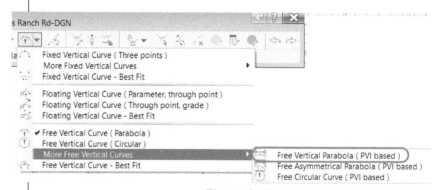

Figure 6–52

6. Select the PVI marked (**C**), as shown previously in Figure 6–51, and type **100'** for the length of the vertical curve. Press <Enter> to exit the command. Once again, the labels update with the new curve information.

7. In the Profile Layout Tools toolbar, click 🌸 (Profile Grid View).

The Profile Entities vista should display in the Panorama.

8. The *Grade In* elevation at the station **11+30.01'** is **0.18%**. This is less than minimum, so you need to change it to **-0.8%** while maintaining both PVI stations. However, the elevation at station **8+10.37'** will be revised. Select the *Grade In* elevation and change *0.18* to **-0.8**, as shown in Figure 6–53.

Figure 6–53

9. You will change the *Grade In* elevation at station **8+10.37'** to also be **0.80%**. Select the *Grade In* elevation and change it to **0.8**, as shown in Figure 6–54. This affects the elevation at station **3+28.08'**.

Figure 6–54

10. Close the Panorama.

Task 3 - Continue creating the profile.

1. Expand the drop-down list in the Profile Layout Tools toolbar and select 🐂 (Curve Settings), as shown in Figure 6–55.

Figure 6–55

---

2. In the Vertical Curve Settings dialog box, for both the Crest and Sag curves:

   • Set the curve type to **Parabolic**.
   • Select the **Length** option and type **200'** as the length.
   • Click **OK** to close dialog box.

3. Click 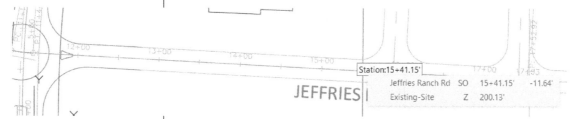 (Draw Tangent with Curves).

4. The Autodesk Civil 3D software prompts you for a start point, which indicates the location of the road's first PVI. Use the Endpoint Osnap to continue from the last segment.

5. Click (Profile Station from Plan) in the *Transparent Commands* tab. If prompted, select the Jeffries Ranch Rd-DGN profile view.

6. Select the lower viewport containing the plan and click on a point near the second eastern intersection, as shown in Figure 6–56. It should be around 15+50, although the exact station is not necessary (that is why these transparent commands are so useful!).

Figure 6–56

7. You are now prompted for an elevation. Type **210.0** for the elevation and press <Enter>. Press <Esc> once to exit the transparent command but to remain in the Tangent-Curve command.

8. To finish the final design profile, click (Profile Station Elevation) in the *Transparent* tab, then proceed as follows:

   • Type an end alignment station of **1631.0'** and press <Enter>.
   • Type a tie in elevation of **216.0'** and press <Enter>.
   • Press <Esc> to exit the transparent command.
   • Press <Enter> to exit the **Draw Tangent** command.

9. In the Profile Layout Tools toolbar, click **X** to close it.

10. The last grade needs adjusting. You could use the Panorama as done previously, but this time you will use the grips. In the **Jeffries Ranch Rd-DGN** profile view, select the design profile and the grips appear. Select the last square grip. The tooltip appears, specifying the station. Press <Tab> to toggle to the elevation, as shown in Figure 6–57.

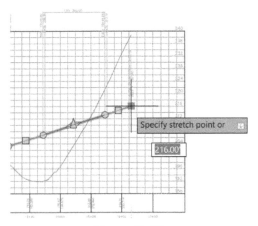

Figure 6–57

11. Type **225.0** for the final elevation and press <Enter>.

12. Save the drawing.

Task 4 - Update profile bands.

The profile views display existing ground elevations in both the existing and proposed slots of the profile bands, as shown in Figure 6–58. In this task, you will change the right label to a finished ground profile label.

Figure 6–58

1. To update, select the Jeffries Ranch Rd profile view, right-click, and select **Profile View Properties**. In the *Bands* tab, assign *Profile2* to reference **Jeffries Ranch Rd-DGN**, as shown in Figure 6–59. Click **OK**.

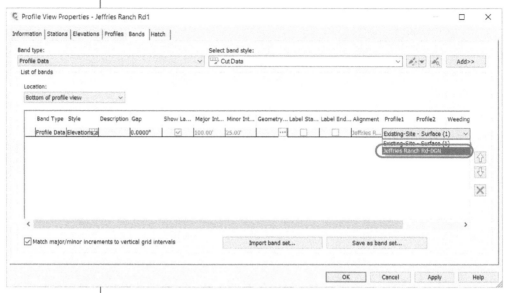

Figure 6–59

The profile band displays existing ground elevations on the left and design elevations on the right, as shown in Figure 6–60.

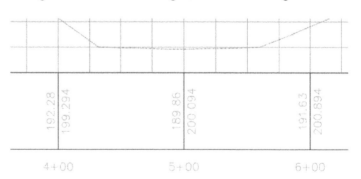

Figure 6–60

2. Save the drawing.

Practice 6c

Working with Profiles Additional Practice

Practice Objective

- Create finished ground profiles using specific design parameters.

Task 1 - Create the Ascent Place FG Profile.

In this task, you will create a design grade for Ascent Place. To do this, you will use the tie in elevation at Jeffries Ranch Rd of **200.72'**. Design requirements include PVI at station **3+77.461'** elev **187.237'** and a slope of **0.8%** to the end station of **6+89.72'**.

If you are not able to complete this task on your own, use the following steps.

1. Continue with the drawing from the previous practice or open **PRF1-B2.dwg**.

2. In the top left corner of the drawing window, select **+** (plus symbol) for Viewport Control, expand **Viewport Configuration List**, and select **Plan-Profile-Ascent**.

3. In the top left corner of the drawing window, select **+** (plus symbol) for Viewport Control and click **Maximize Viewport**, as shown in Figure 6–61.

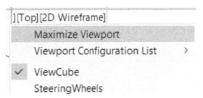

Figure 6–61

4. In the *Home* tab> Create Design panel, expand **Profile**, and click 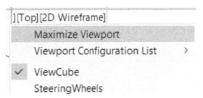 (Profile Creation Tools). When prompted to select a profile view, select the **Ascent PI** profile view.

5. The Create Profile dialog box opens. Do the following, as shown in Figure 6–62:

- Set the name as you did in the previous practice, or type **Ascent PI-DGN** for the *Name*.
- Set the *Profile style* to **ASC-Design Profile**.
- Set the *Profile label set* to **ASC-Complete Label Set**.
- Click **OK**.

Figure 6–62

6. Expand the drop-down list in the Profile Layout Tools toolbar and select (Curve Settings), as shown in Figure 6–63.

Figure 6–63

7. In the Vertical Curve Settings dialog box, for both the Crest and Sag curves:

- Set the curve type to **Parabolic**.
- Select the **Length** option and type **100'** as the length.
- Click **OK** to close dialog box.

8. Click ☒ ▾ (Draw Tangent with Curves).

9. The Autodesk Civil 3D software prompts you for a start point, which indicates the location of the road's first PVI. Proceed as follows:

   • In the *Transparent Commands* Ribbon tab or toolbar, click

     🔲 (Profile Station Elevation).
   • When prompted for a profile view, select the **Ascent PI** profile view.
   • Type a starting station of **0** and press <Enter>.
   • Type **200.72'** and press <Enter> for the starting elevation.
   • For the next station, type **377.46'**and press <Enter>.
   • Type **187.24'** and press <Enter> for the elevation.
   • Press <Esc> to exit this transparent command.

10. In the *Transparent Commands* tab, click 🔲 (Profile Grade Station).

    • For the grade, type **0.80** and press <Enter>.
    • For the station, type **698.72'** and press <Enter>
    • Press <Esc> to exit the transparent command.
    • Press <Enter> to exit the **Profile Draw** command.
    • Click the **X** to close the Profile Layout Tools toolbar.

11. Update the Databands, similar to the steps used in the previous practice.

12. In the top left corner of the drawing window, select **+** (plus symbol) for Viewport Control and click **Restore Viewport**, as shown in Figure 6–64.

Figure 6 64

13. Save the drawing.

Task 2 - Create the Rand Boulevard FG Profile.

In this task, you will create a rough design grade for **Rand Boulevard**. To do this, rather than relying on predetermined values, you will use Civil 3D for determining the stations and elevations. Thus, you will first draw a simple tangent from the start to the end of the surface profile in the profile view. Then, you will superimpose a small segment of the Jeffries Ranch Road FG profile into the profile view in order to see where they intersect. Finally, you will insert a PVI at the intersection point and place a vertical curve.

1. Continue with the drawing from the previous practice or open **PRF1-B3.dwg**.

2. In the top left corner of the drawing window, select **+** (plus symbol) for Viewport Control, expand **Viewport Configuration List**, and select **Plan-Profile-Rand**.

3. In the *Home* tab>Create Design panel, expand **Profile** and click ⌇ (Profile Creation Tools). When prompted to select a profile view, select the **Rand Boulevard** profile view.

4. The Create Profile dialog box opens. Do the following:

    - Set the name as you did in the previous practice, or type **Rand Boulevard-DGN** for the *Name*.
    - Set the *Profile style* to **ASC-Design Profile**.
    - Set the *Profile label set* to **ASC-Complete Label Set**.
    - Click **OK**.

Remember, if these are to be your organization's standard procedures, your BIM manager can preset these in the command settings.

5. In the Profile Layout Tools toolbar, select ⟋ (Draw fixed tangent by two points).

6. Use the Endpoint Osnap to snap to the beginning and the end of the red **Existing Site** surface profile.

7. Press <Enter> to exit the command, and note that now the labels update.

8. Leave the Profile Layout Tools toolbar open for later use.

The Create Superimposed Profile command is also available in the Profile View contextual tab.

9. In the *Home* tab>Create Design panel, expand **Profile** and click ⌄ (Create Superimposed Profile).

10. For the **source profile**, pan up to the **Jeffries Ranch Rd** profile view and select the cyan **Jeffries Ranch Rd-DGN** profile.

11. For the **destination profile view,** select the **Rand Boulevard** profile view.

12. In the Superimpose Profile Options dialog box, click 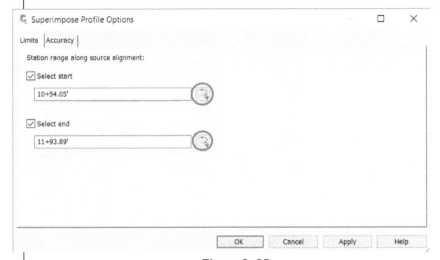 (Pick station) for both the **Select start** and **Select end** values, as shown in Figure 6–65.

Figure 6–65

13. Select near the incoming and outgoing islands of the sketched roundabout for start and end stations, respectively, as shown in Figure 6–66.

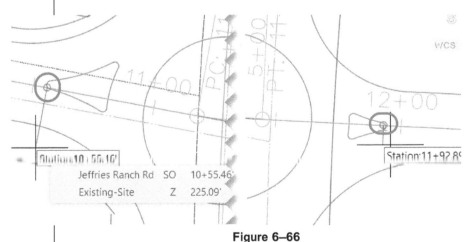

Figure 6–66

14. Click **OK** to close the Superimpose Profile Options dialog box.

15. Near Station 5+33 and Elevation 200', you will note a small cyan line segment, which is the superimposed profile, as shown in Figure 6–67.

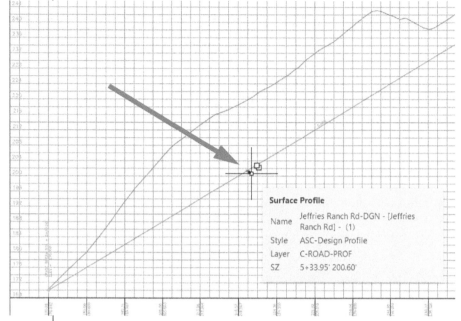

Surface Profile

Name	Jeffries Ranch Rd-DGN - [Jeffries Ranch Rd] - (1)
Style	ASC-Design Profile
Layer	C-ROAD-PROF
SZ	5+33.95' 200.60'

Figure 6–67

16. In the Profile Layout Tools toolbar, select (Insert PVI).

17. For the point for new PVI, select near the middle of the superimposed profile. Press <Enter> to finish the Insert PVI command.

18. From the Curves drop-down list, expand **More Vertical Free Curves** and select **Free Vertical Parabola (PVI based)**.

19. Select near the new PVI you just created to add the curve. Make the curve length **200.00'** and press <Enter> to finish the command.

20. Select the curve label and drag it into the profile view by its grip, as shown in Figure 6–68.

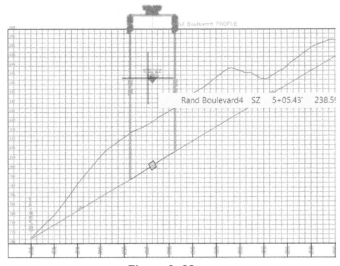

Rand Boulevard4   SZ   5+05.43'   238.5⁹

Figure 6–68

21. Also adjust the curve labels in the other two profile views so they do not interfere with other labeling.

22. Save the drawing.

23. (Optional) Save the drawing as **<Your Initials>-Profile-Complete.dwg** in the *C:\Civil 3D Projects\References\DWG\Proposed* folder.

24. Update the relative paths of the referenced drawings in the alert box.

Chapter Review Questions

1. You can safely relocate profile views in the Autodesk Civil 3D software using the AutoCAD **Move** command.

   a. True

   b. False

2. Which of the following is not a vertical curve option in the Autodesk Civil 3D software?

   a. Circular

   b. Parabolic

   c. Spiral

   d. Asymmetric Parabolic

3. Which grip do you use to move the PVI to a new station and elevation at the same time?

   a. ⌖ Circular

   b. ⌂ Center Triangle

   c. ◁ Sideways Triangle

   d. ▢ Square

4. What do Profiles 1 and 2 annotate in profile bands?

   a. Profile elevations of two different profiles from the same alignment.

   b. Alignment stations.

   c. Tangent Slopes.

   d. Vertical curve lengths.

5. Which of the following **Transparent** command tools helps you to design a finished ground profile?

   a. ⊿

   b. ⏏

   c. ⊿

   d. ⊔

Command Summary

Button	Command	Location
	Create Profile from Surface	• **Ribbon:** *Home* tab>Create Design panel • **Command Prompt:** CreateProfileFromSurface
	Create Profile View	• **Ribbon:** *Home* tab>Create Design panel • **Command Prompt:** CreateProfileView
	Curve Settings	• **Toolbar:** Profile Layout Tools
	Draw Tangents	• **Toolbar:** Profile Layout Tools
	Draw Tangents with Curves	• **Toolbar:** Profile Layout Tools
	Free Vertical Curve (Parameter)	• **Toolbar:** Profile Layout Tools
	Geometry Editor	• **Contextual Ribbon:** *Profile* tab>Modify panel • **Command Prompt:** editprofilelayout
	Profile Creation Tools	• **Ribbon:** *Home* tab>Create Design panel • **Command Prompt:** CreateProfileLayout
	Profile Properties	• **Contextual Ribbon:** *Profile* tab>Modify panel • **Command Prompt:** editprofileproperties
	Draw fixed tangent by two points	• **Toolbar:** Profile Layout Tools
	Superimpose Profile	• **Contextual Ribbon:** *Profile View* tab>Launch Pad panel • **Command Prompt:** superimposeprofile

Assemblies

Corridors are 3D representations of a road design. In this chapter, you will create a typical cross-section of a road (called an assembly) to study how the road is laid out perpendicular to its center line. Next, you will reference assemblies that have already been created.

Learning Objectives in This Chapter

- List the various types of assemblies available and their uses.
- Design the typical cross-section of a road by creating an assembly and adding subassemblies to it.
- Create a corridor model using previously created alignments, profiles, and assemblies.

7.1 Assembly Overview

Assemblies

An *assembly* defines the attachment point of a roadway cross-section to the horizontal and vertical alignments. This attachment point occurs at the midpoint of the assembly marker (or assembly baseline), as shown in Figure 7–1. The 3D progression of the attachment point along the corridor is also sometimes referred to as the *profile grade line*.

Figure 7–1

Assemblies can be placed anywhere in a drawing (centerline of roads, curb returns, sidewalks, off ramps, railways, etc). Assembly styles only affect the display of the marker itself (i.e., color, layer, etc.).

Assembly Types

The type of road or railway that an assembly represents is important, especially if it is used in a corridor that requires superelevation axis of rotation or cant. When a superelevation or cant is calculated for an alignment, it is also important to select an assembly type that matches design needs. There are six types of assemblies:

- **Undivided Crowned Road:** Enables you to specify the axis about which the corridor is superelevated.

- **Undivided Planar Road:** Enables you to specify the axis about which the corridor is superelevated and the default highside location for planar roads.

- **Divided Crowned Road:** Enables you to specify the axis about which the corridor is superelevated and whether the median maintains its shape or becomes distorted as the corridor superelevates.

- **Divided Planar Road:** Enables you to specify the axis about which the corridor is superelevated and whether the median maintains its shape or becomes distorted as the corridor superelevates.

Railways are not covered in this course.

- **Railway:** Enables you to specify the cant about which the corridor is going to bank.

- **Other:** Used for all other types of corridors that are not listed above.

Subassemblies

Assemblies are assigned *subassemblies*, which represent individual components of the proposed cross-section (such as lane or curb subassemblies). Subassemblies attach to the left or right side of an assembly's attachment point. When building an assembly, you build from the middle out to the left or right edges.

- The library of stock subassemblies supplied with the Autodesk Civil 3D® software uses a wide array of dynamic parameters (e.g., dimensions of lane width and slope). These stock subassemblies routinely expand and evolve as Civil 3D matures from release to release.

- When parameter values change, the corridor model gets updated.

- You can create static subassemblies (without dynamic parameters) from polylines.

- Each point (vertex) of a subassembly can be assigned a name or *point code* for reference later. A point is a potential location for offset and elevation annotation. It is also a connection point for an adjacent subassembly. When such a point is stretched onto the next assembly, it generates a line (known as a *feature line*). For example, points are commonly assigned at edge-of-travelways, back-of-curbs, gutters, etc. Marker styles define the properties for points and their labels.

- Corridors generate *feature lines* at every location that is assigned a point code. These linear 3D objects can be used as input for surfaces and grading solutions.

- Lines in subassemblies are referred to as *links*. A link can be automatically given a slope or grade label in the cross-sections as required. When such a link is stretched onto the next assembly, it generates a plane, which can be used to create Civil 3D surfaces. Link styles define the properties of a link and its labels.

- A subassembly *shape* is an area enclosed by links. When such a shape is stretched onto the next assembly, it generates a solid, which can be assigned material types and can be used to calculate quantities. Shape styles define the display properties of a shape.

- Marker styles, feature line styles, and link and shape styles are all assigned based on a Code Set Style. The Code Set Style assigns the styles to be applied based on the codes assigned to these objects. Code Sets and each of these styles are all configured under the *Multipurpose Styles* collection in the Toolspace, *Settings* tab.

The example in Figure 7–2 shows an assembly containing lane, curb, and daylight subassemblies. This assembly has been assigned to display an offset and elevation marker (point) label at the edge of the lane, a pavement slope (link) label, and shape labels displaying the area of the sub-base.

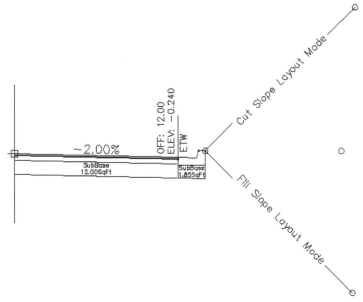

Figure 7–2

- Each subassembly attaches to the assembly connection point or to a point on an adjacent subassembly. You should assign each assembly a logical, unique name during creation. This is helpful later in the corridor creation process when you are working with very complex corridors that include intersections, transitions, and other components.

- Autodesk Civil 3D Help contains extensive documentation for each subassembly.

The Toolspace, *Prospector* tab lists each assembly with a further breakdown of each subassembly associated with it, in a tree structure, as shown in Figure 7–3.

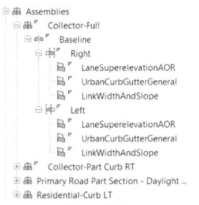

Figure 7–3

To review their interconnections and parameters, select the assembly, right-click, and select **Assembly Properties**. The Assembly Properties dialog box opens as shown in Figure 7–4.

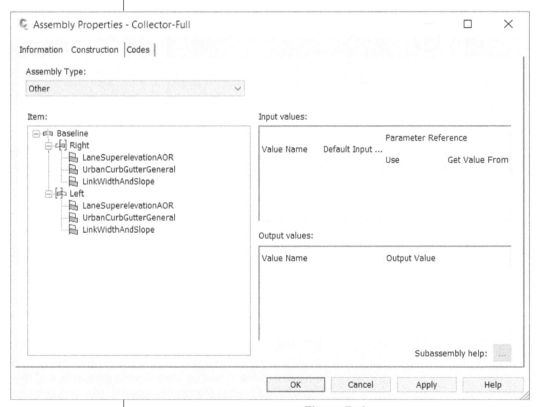

Figure 7–4

Subassembly Composer

As mentioned previously, Civil 3D comes with stock subassemblies covering a wide variety of situations. In most cases, these will suffice for any situation land development or road projects encounter.

However, these stock subassemblies are not dynamic. Dynamic subassemblies can be created using the dot net (.net) programming language, using the Subassembly Composer, which is an additional program that is included with Autodesk Civil 3D.

The Subassembly Composer is rather complex and is not covered in extensive detail in this course; however, an overview is provided for you to understand its capabilities and potential use.

The Subassembly Composer interface is broken down into four major areas plus a toolbox side panel, as shown in Figure 7–5

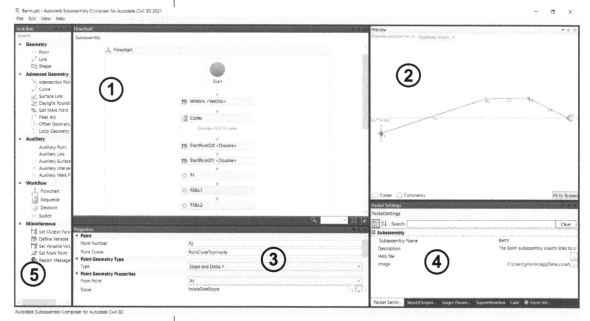

Figure 7–5

1. **Flowchart** - This area provides a logical, graphical overview of the subassembly. Place and rearrange the various elements that make up the subassembly. Parts can be moved by clicking and dragging them to their new position.
2. **Preview** - This area provides a preview of the selected element of the subassembly. As the properties of the element are altered (in the Properties panel), the preview updates to provide a graphical view of the element.

3. **Properties** - This area is where the details of the selected element are manipulated. Many of the entries are controlled through populated lists and defaults to ensure the proper variables are entered to prevent mistakes and typos. Ordinary values can also be entered.

4. **Multi-use panel** - This area contains the following tabs:

   - **Packet Settings** - General information of the packet.
   - **Input/Output Parameters** - Tabular view of the various input and output parameters along with their default values.
   - **Target Parameters** - Tabular view of the various target parameters along with their values used for the preview panel.
   - **Superelevation** - Settings for the superelvations, their values used for the preview panel, and a toggle if they are enabled for the preview.
   - **Cant** - Settings for the cants (superelvations for rail) and their values used for the preview panel.
   - **Event Viewer** - A record of all the events (errors and triggers) that have occurred.

5. **Toolbox** - This is a collection of various generic, auxiliary, and advanced geometry elements, flowchart components, and miscellaneous tools.

7.2 Modifying Assemblies

Attaching Subassemblies

The easiest way to add an Autodesk Civil 3D subassembly to an assembly is using the Tool Palettes. You can open the Tool Palettes by clicking 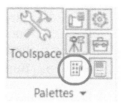 in the *Home* tab>Palettes panel, as shown in Figure 7–6, or in the *View* tab>Palettes panel. You can also use <Ctrl>+<3>.

Figure 7–6

The Autodesk Civil 3D software provides a number of stock subassembly tool palettes, as shown in Figure 7–7. In addition, it is continually updating and adding new subassemblies with every release.

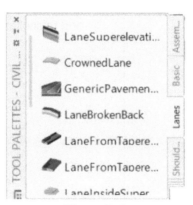

Figure 7–7

There are separate Tool Palettes for metric and imperial units. Ensure that you are using the correct palette. To select the correct palette, right-click on the Tool Palette band and select the required palette, as shown in Figure 7–8.

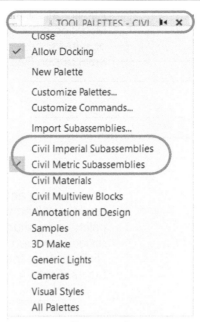

Figure 7–8

The Help file is an invaluable resource for an updated list, and information about the specific attributes and properties of each subassembly, as shown in Figure 7–9.

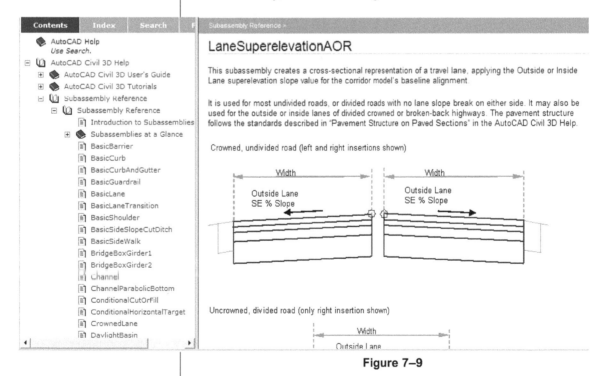

Figure 7–9

Additional subassemblies can be accessed using the Corridor Modeling catalogs. Open the catalog by selecting an assembly or subassembly from the drawing. In the *Assembly/Subassembly* tab>Launch Pad panel, click **Catalog**, as shown in Figure 7–10.

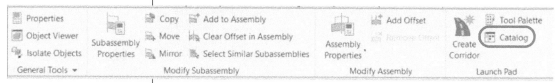

Figure 7–10

You can drag and drop the catalog onto a Tool Palette, if required. When working with the Tool Palettes and Properties palette, you might find it helpful to toggle off the **Allow Docking** option to prevent them from docking on the sides of the screen. Right-click on the palette's title bar to set the option, as shown in Figure 7–11.

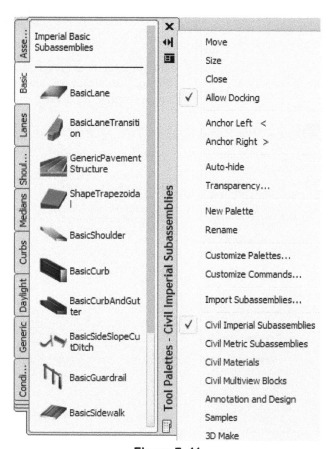

Figure 7–11

Detaching Subassemblies

Individual subassemblies can be deleted directly from an assembly with the AutoCAD® **Erase** command or using Assembly Properties. Assemblies can also be deleted with the **Erase** command.

Copying Assemblies

Assemblies can be copied with the AutoCAD **Copy** command. Copying an assembly creates an independent assembly without a relationship to the original. Select the assembly by selecting the **Assembly Baseline**.

Modifying Subassemblies

In the Autodesk Civil 3D software, subassemblies can be mirrored, copied, and moved across the assembly to which it is attached by selecting the subassemblies, right-clicking, and

selecting **Mirror**, **Copy to**, or **Move to** or by clicking (Mirror),

(Copy), or (Move), in the *Assembly* tab>Modify Subassembly panel. This enables you to create one side of the roadway and to create a mirrored image for the other side in one step.

Hint: AutoCAD Mirror, Move, or Copy Commands

The basic AutoCAD **Mirror**, **Move**, or **Copy** commands do not work for subassemblies. You need to use the special commands from the shortcut menu or in the Modify Subassembly panel.

Select Similar Subassemblies

It is often necessary to create multiple assemblies with the same subassemblies for various purposes. For example, a corridor that includes an intersection might need a full assembly that includes both sides of the road, an assembly that includes just the right side of the road, and another that includes just the left side of the road. It might also include two other assemblies that require the assembly marker to be placed at the edge of pavement rather than the crown, as shown in Figure 7–12.

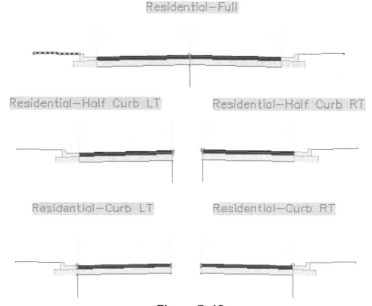

Figure 7–12

However, making changes to all of the assemblies when a design parameter changes can be time consuming. To ensure that all similar subassemblies are modified at the same time when a design change occurs you can select one subassembly, click (Select Similar Subassemblies) in the *Assembly* tab> Modify Subassembly panel, and change the parameter in the AutoCAD properties palette.

Getting More Information on Subassemblies

Many subassemblies have a large number of parameters. If you want to read the documentation on a subassembly, right-click on its tool icon in a Tool Palette and select **Help**. You can also find out more from Subassembly Properties and Assembly Properties using the **Subassembly help** icon, as shown in Figure 7–13.

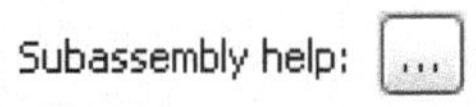

Subassembly help: [...]

Figure 7–13

Practice 7a | Creating Assemblies

Practice Objective

- Create and modify assemblies for use in a corridor model.

In this practice, you will create two assemblies: one for Jeffries Ranch Rd and the second for the Ascent Place. Create the Collector Road assembly.

Task 1 - Create the Collector Road assembly.

A typical cross-section of Jeffries Ranch Rd is shown in Figure 7–14. (See *A.4 Design Data* for the design criteria.)

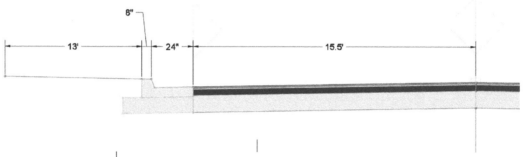

Figure 7–14

1. Open **ASM1-A.dwg** from the *C:\Civil 3D Projects\ Working\Assemblies* folder.

2. In the *Home* tab>Create Design panel, click ▦ (Create Assembly).

3. In the Create Assembly dialog box, name the new assembly **Collector-Full**. Set the *Assembly Type* to **Undivided Crown Road,** and leave the other settings at their defaults, as shown in Figure 7–15. Click **OK** to close the dialog box.

Figure 7–15

4. When prompted, locate the assembly baseline to the left of the profile view Jeffries Ranch Rd in the current drawing, as shown in Figure 7–16.

Once selected, the Autodesk Civil 3D software will change the view to zoom into the assembly baseline location.

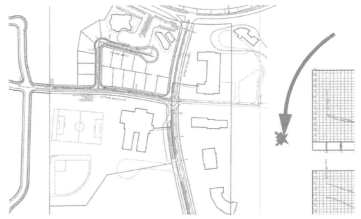

Figure 7–16

5. Open the Tool Palettes by clicking (Tool Palettes) in the *Home* tab>Palettes panel.

6. In the Lanes Tool Palette, select the **LaneSuperelevationAOR** subassembly to add it to your assembly. In the Properties palette, set the following, as shown in Figure 7–17:

- *Side:* **Right**
- *Width:* **15.5'**
- *Slope:* **-2%**
- Select the assembly baseline to attach the subassembly to the assembly.

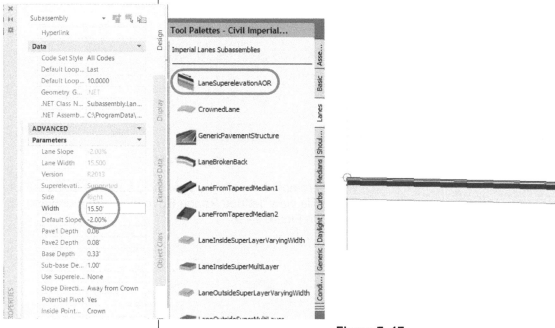

Figure 7–17

7. In the Subassemblies Tool Palette, select the *Curbs* tab and select the **UrbanCurbGutterGeneral** subassembly. In the Advanced Properties, set the following:

- *Side:* **Right**
- *Dimension B:* **24"**
- Insert the subassembly by selecting the upper most circle at the end of the **LaneSuperelevationAOR** subassembly, as shown in Figure 7–18. Do not Osnap to the endpoint, for this may not connect the two subassemblies properly. Press <Esc> to exit the subassembly command.

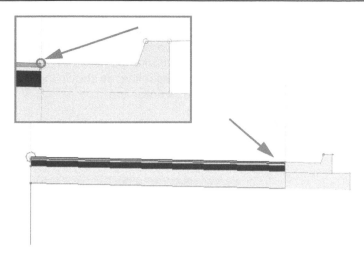

Figure 7–18

8. You will now create a subassembly that links the back of curb to property line. In the Subassemblies Tool Palette, select the *Generic* tab, and select the **LinkWidthAndSlope** subassembly. In the Advanced Properties, set the following:

- *Side parameter:* **Right**
- *Width*: **13'**
- Insert the subassembly by selecting the circle at the end of the **UrbanCurbGutterGeneral** subassembly, as shown in Figure 7–19.
- Press <Esc> to exit the subassembly command.

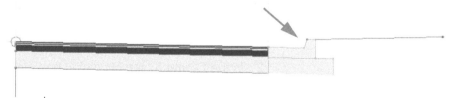

Figure 7–19

9. Select the three sub-assemblies that you just created, but do not select the on the right side, assembly baseline (the red vertical line), and right-click, and select **Mirror**. At the *select marker point within assembly:* prompt, select the assembly baseline, as shown in Figure 7–20, which represents the road center line.

Figure 7–20

10. Save the drawing.

Task 2 - Create the Residential Road assembly.

A typical cross-section of Ascent Pl is shown in Figure 7–21. (See *A.4 Design Data* for design criteria.)

Note that this task is similar to Task 1. You can use this Task as a test of your knowledge in creating a residential road assembly or you can skip this task and open the backup drawing in Task 3.

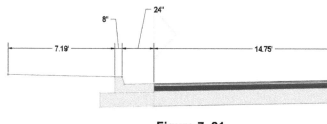

Figure 7–21

1. In the *Home* tab>Create Design panel, click 🗔 (Create Assembly).

2. In the Create Assembly dialog box, name the new assembly **Residential-Full**. Set the *Assembly Type* to **Undivided Crown Road,** and leave the other settings at their defaults and click **OK**. Click in the drawing to place the new assembly.

3. Follow the same steps in Task 1 to create the residential assembly. For this assembly:

- Set the pavement LaneSuperelevationAOR *width* to **14.75'**.
- **UrbanCurbGutterGeneral** subassembly *Dimension B* is set to **24"**.
- LinkWidthAndSlope *width* to **7.193'**.

Task 3 - Copy and modify an assembly.

Copying an assembly can be helpful if you need another, similar assembly for other design purposes. In the following task, you will create assemblies that are required by the Intersection wizard for the intersection area of Jeffries Ranch Rd and Ascent Place. It would be helpful to understand the names and the configuration of the different assemblies.

You only need to select the red baseline, since all subassemblies are properly attached, they all will get copied with the baseline.

1. Start the AutoCAD **Copy** command. Copy the **Collector-Full** assembly to a location just below the original, as shown in Figure 7–22.

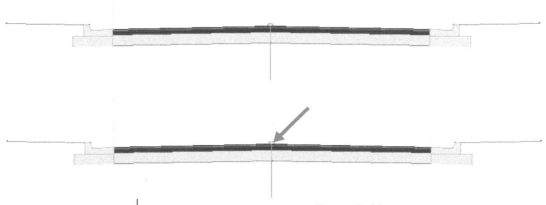

Figure 7–22

2. Select the bottom assembly baseline, right-click, and select **Assembly Properties**.

3. In the *Information* tab, change the *Name* to **Collector-Part Curb RT** and click **OK**.

4. Start the AutoCAD **Erase** command and erase the left **UrbanCurbGutterGeneral** and the left **LinkWidthAndSlope**, as shown in Figure 7–23.

Figure 7–23

5. Save the drawing.

Practice 7b

(Optional) Creating Assemblies Additional Practice

Practice Objective

- Create and modify assemblies for use in an intersection model.

In the previous practice, you created all of the Jeffries Ranch Rd assemblies that were required for the intersection. In this practice, you will create all of the required Ascent Place assemblies.

Task 1 - Create the assemblies required for the intersection.

1. Continue working with the drawing from the previous practice if you completed creating all of the subassemblies or open **ASM1-B.dwg** from the *C:\Civil 3D Projects\ Working\Assemblies* folder.

2. Start the AutoCAD **Copy** command. Copy the **Residential -Full** assembly to two locations below the original, as shown in Figure 7–24.

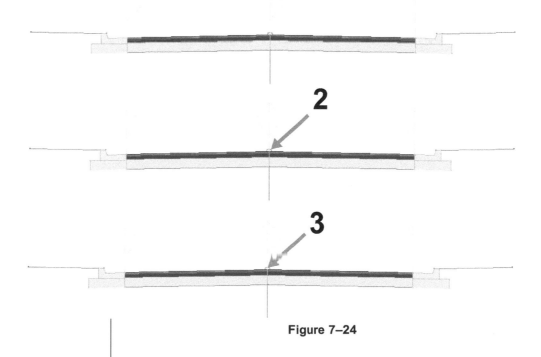

Figure 7–24

3. Select the second assembly baseline, right-click, and select **Assembly Properties**. In the *Information* tab, change the *Name* to **Residential-Half Curb LT** and click **OK**.

4. Start the AutoCAD **Erase** command and erase the right **LaneSuperelevationAOR**, the right **UrbanCurbGutterGeneral**, and the right **LinkWidthAndSlope**.

5. Select the third assembly baseline, right-click, and select **Assembly Properties**. In the *Information* tab, change the *Name* to **Residential-Half Curb RT** and click **OK**.

6. Start the AutoCAD **Erase** command and erase the left **LaneSuperelevationAOR**, the left **UrbanCurbGutterGeneral**, and the left **LinkWidthAndSlope**, as shown in Figure 7–25.

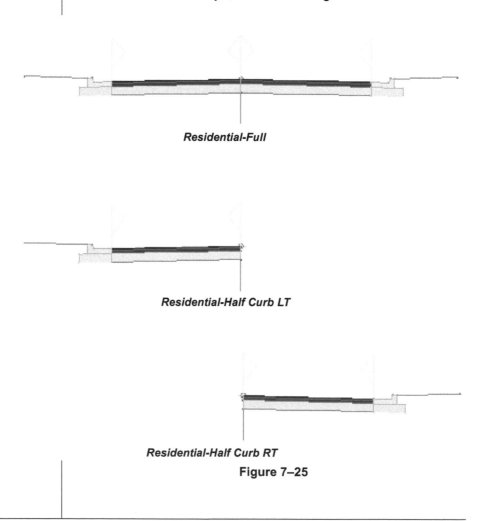

Residential-Full

Residential-Half Curb LT

Residential-Half Curb RT

Figure 7–25

Task 2 - Create a Curb Return assembly.

To include the intersection in the corridor model, you need another assembly to go around the curb returns. This assembly will have the assembly baseline at the edge of pavement or flange of the curb and gutter. It is important to create the assembly with the lane inserted first for the **Intersection** tool to be able to set the correct transitions at the centerline.

Open the Tool Palettes

by clicking 🔲 *in the View tab>Palettes panel, if it is not already open.*

1. In the *Home* tab>Create Design panel, expand **Assembly** and select **Create Assembly**.

2. In the Create Assembly dialog box, name the new assembly **Residential-Curb Return**. Leave the other settings at their defaults, and click **OK**. Click in the drawing to place the new assembly.

3. In the Lanes Tool Palette, select the **LaneSuperelevationAOR** subassembly to add it to your assembly. In the AutoCAD Properties Palette, confirm that the following are set:

   - *Side:* **Left**
   - *Width:* **14.75'**
   - *Slope:* **+2%**.

4. To add the Left lane subassembly, select the assembly baseline object.

5. In the Curbs tool palette, select the **UrbanCurbGutterGeneral** subassembly to add it to your assembly.

6. In the AutoCAD Properties Palette, confirm that the following are set:

   - *Side*: **Right**
   - *Dimensions B*: **24"**

7. Select the assembly baseline to add the curb and gutter, as shown in Figure 7–26.

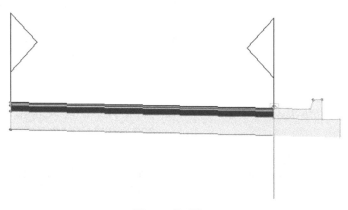

Figure 7–26

You will now create a subassembly that links the back of curb to the property line.

8. In the Subassemblies Tool Palette, select the *Generic* tab, and select the **LinkWidthAndSlope** subassembly.In the AutoCAD Properties Palette, in the Advanced Properties, set the following:

   - *Side*: **Right**
   - *Width*: **7.193'**

9. Insert the subassembly at the end of the **UrbanCurbGutterGeneral** subassembly, as shown in Figure 7–27.

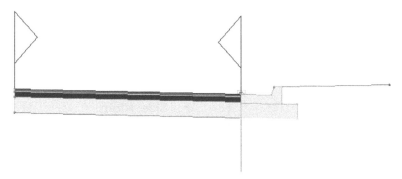

Figure 7–27

10. Press <Esc> to exit the subassembly command and save the drawing.

7.3 Managing Assemblies

Assemblies are small in size but very important components to a road design project. They are often standardized to meet requirements spelled out by the various governing agencies or project requirements; hence, the more they can be reused on a company-wide basis, the more efficient the overall design workflow becomes.

Identifying Assemblies

Assemblies are small and tend to get lost in the overall Model Space of the project. The following are some tips to make it easier to find, identify, and manage assemblies in a project:

- Name the assemblies with fields so the identification is easier.
- Establish AutoCAD Named Views where the assemblies are and name the views appropriately.
- Remove or insert assemblies from or to Model Space, as appropriate, using the right-click menu of the assembly in the Prospector, as shown in Figure 7–28.

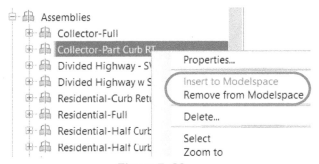

Figure 7–28

- Note that in the right-click menu of the assembly in the Prospector, there is also a **Zoom to** feature.

Sharing Assemblies

Assemblies can be shared with the Autodesk Civil 3D software in three ways:

- Assemblies can be dragged from the drawing area to a Tool Palette. The Tool Palette can then be shared, as shown in Figure 7–29

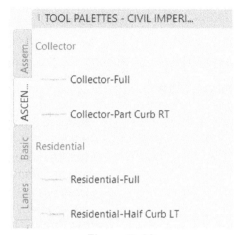

Figure 7–29

- The Content Browser can be used to add assemblies to a catalog.

- Assemblies can be placed in their own drawing files and shared by dragging the assembly drawing into the destination drawing file. If this method is used, the assembly drawing must only contain the assemblies that you want to share.

Practice 7c | Managing Assemblies

Practice Objectives

- Modify assemblies from another project.
- Create an Assembly library in the Tool Palettes.
- Create AutoCAD Named Views to find the assemblies.
- Insert fields for the assembly names.

In this practice, you will open a drawing containing other assemblies. You will modify one of them and then create a palette to share the assemblies. Finally, you will study ways of finding the assemblies within your current project.

Task 1 - Modify an assembly.

1. Open **ASM1-Reference.dwg** from the *C:\Civil 3D Projects\ Working\Assemblies* folder. If you currently have the previous drawing still open, leave it open.

2. Locate the assembly named **Divided Highway - SW - DL**, as shown in Figure 7–30.

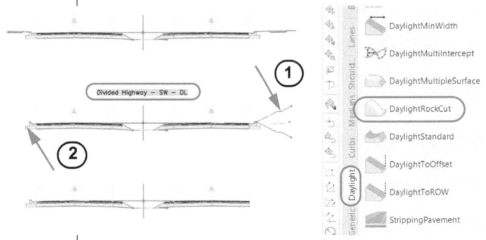

Figure 7–30

3. If needed, open the Tool Palettes by clicking 🗗 (Tool Palettes) in the *Home* tab>Palettes panel.

4. In the Daylight Tool Palette, select the **DaylightRockCut** subassembly.

5. When prompted for a marker point, select **Replace** (either from the command line or the right-click menu) instead. Then, select the existing daylight subassembly to be replaced, as marked **(1)** in Figure 7–30.

6. Press <Enter> to finish the command.

7. Select the newly inserted daylight subassembly, right-click, and select **Mirror**. At the *select marker point within assembly:* prompt, select the far left marker, as marked **(2)** in Figure 7–30.

8. Select the first daylight subassembly (on the right side) and erase it.

9. Save the drawing.

Task 2 - Create an assembly palette.

In order to share assemblies throughout an organization, the drawings containing the assemblies need to be centrally located so all users have access to them. Then, they can be used to create an Assembly palette to serve as a library.

1. Save the drawing as **<Your Initials>-Assemblies.dwg** in the *C:\Civil 3D Projects\Ascent-Config\Assembly Sets* folder.

2. In the Tool Palettes, right-click on the top tab (*Assemblies*) and select **New Palette** from the menu, as shown in Figure 7–31. Name the new palette **<Your Initials>-Assemblies**.

Figure 7–31

3. In the new palette, from the right-click menu, select **Add Text**, as shown in Figure 7–32. Type **Collector** for the text.

Figure 7–32

4. In the *Prospector* tab of the Toolspace, expand the Assemblies branch, right-click on **Collector-Full**, and select **Zoom to**, as shown in Figure 7–33.

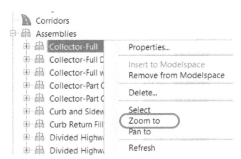

Figure 7–33

5. Select the assembly by picking the red vertical centerline, then click on the lower part of the red centerline and drag it into the Tool Palettes, as shown in Figure 7–34. Release it there. Do NOT select the grip when clicking and dragging.

Figure 7–34

6. Repeat this for **Collector-Part Curb RT**.

7. Create a **Residential** text and drag the following under it:

- **Residential-Full**
- **Residential-Half Curb LT**
- **Residential Half Curb RT**
- **Residential-Curb Return**

8. Create a **Boulevard** text and drag the following under it:

- **Divided Highway w SW**
- **Divided Highway -SW - DL**
- **Divided Highway Curb - NoCurb**

9. The final result should look like Figure 7–35.

Figure 7–35

10. Save and close the drawing.

Task 3 - Insert assemblies from the tool palette.

If you did not complete the previous task with the tool palettes, you can skip this task.

1. Continue working with the drawing from the earlier practice, or open **ASM1-C.dwg** from the *C:\Civil 3D Projects\ Working\Assemblies* folder.

2. Zoom and pan to the lower left corner of the **Rand Boulevard** profile view.

3. In your Assembly palette that you created in the previous task, select the **Divided Highway w SW** assembly. Release it (do not click and drag).

4. In Model Space, select a point left of the profile view to place the assembly.

5. Place the **Divided Highway -SW - DL** assembly by clicking the left mouse button.

6. Save the drawing.

Task 4 - Manage assemblies.

1. Continue working with the previous drawing if you completed Task 2, or open **ASM1-D.dwg** from the *C:\Civil 3D Projects\ Working\Assemblies* folder.

2. Zoom and pan to the lower left corner of the **Rand Boulevard** profile view, if not already there.

For more information on AutoCAD Named Views, consult the AutoCAD help section or the AutoCAD: Fundamentals guide (published by ASCENT).

3. In the *View* tab>Named Views panel, click (New View).

4. In the New View / Shot Properties dialog box, name the view **Assem-Collector**. If the dialog box is not expanded, click on the down arrow to expand it, as shown in Figure 7–36. Uncheck the **Save layer snapshot with view** checkbox.

Figure 7–36

For more information on AutoCAD Fields, consult the AutoCAD help section or the AutoCAD: Fundamentals guide (published by ASCENT).

5. Click **OK** to close the New View / Shot Properties dialog box.

6. Pan to the lower left corner of the **Ascent Place** profile view and repeat the process to create an **Assem-Residential** view.

7. Pan to the lower left corner of the **Jeffries Ranch Rd** profile view and repeat the process to create an **Assem-Collector** view.

8. In the *Insert* tab>Data panel, click ⬜ (Field).

9. In the *Field* dialog box, in the left column, select **Object** from the list. In the middle column, select **Name** from the list, then click (Select Object). In the drawing, select the assembly by picking the red vertical centerline, as shown in Figure 7–37.

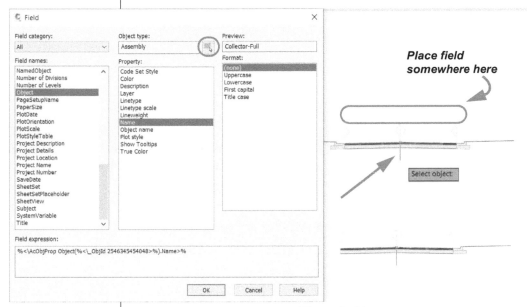

Figure 7–37

10. Click **OK** to close the Field dialog box. When prompted for the insertion point for the field, select **Height** (either from the command line or the right-click menu) and enter **1.2** for the height, then place the field above the assembly.

11. Time permitting, repeat this for the other assemblies.

12. In the *View* tab>Named Views panel, select the preset view **Assem-Collector** that you created earlier.

13. In the *Prospector* tab of the Toolspace, expand the **Assemblies** branch, right-click on **Collector-Full**, and select **Remove from Modelspace**, as shown in Figure 7–38.

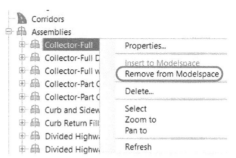

Figure 7–38

14. Right-click on **Collector-Full**, select **Insert to Modelspace**, and select a point to insert the assembly.

15. Save and close the drawing.

Chapter Review Questions

1. Where would you find subassemblies to attach to an assembly?

   a. Tool Palettes

   b. *Home* tab>Create Design panel

   c. *Modify* tab>Design panel

   d. *Insert* tab>Block panel

2. How do you change the width of a lane in the corridor model? (Select all that apply.)

   a. Advanced Properties

   b. Assembly Properties

   c. Subassembly Properties

   d. Corridor Properties

3. How do you Insert an assembly into the drawing? (Select all that apply.)

   a. Insert as a block

   b. Through a tool palette

   c. By right-clicking in the prospector

   d. Drag and drop from the Design Center

4. How do you Insert an assembly into a tool palette?

   a. Right-click in the tool palette

   b. Drag and drop from Model Space

   c. By right-clicking in the prospector

   d. You cannot place assemblies in a tool palette

Command Summary

Button	Command	Location
	Assembly Properties	• **Contextual Ribbon:** *Assembly* tab> Modify Assembly panel
		• **Command Prompt:** editassemblyproperties
	Copy Subassembly	• **Contextual Ribbon:** *Assembly* tab> Modify Subassembly panel
		• **Command Prompt:** copysubassemblyto
	Field	• **Ribbon:** *Insert* tab>Data panel, **Command Prompt:** Field
	Mirror Subassembly	• **Contextual Ribbon:** *Assembly* tab> Modify Subassembly panel
		• **Command Prompt:** mirrorsubassembly
	Move Subassembly	• **Contextual Ribbon:** *Assembly* tab> Modify Subassembly panel
		• **Command Prompt:** movesubassembly
	Subassembly Properties	• **Contextual Ribbon:** *Assembly* tab> Modify Subassembly panel
		• **Command Prompt:** editsubassemblyproperties
	Tool Palettes	• **Ribbon:** *Home* tab>Palettes panel
		• **Command Prompt:** <Ctrl>+<3>
	New View	• **Ribbon:** *View* tab>Named View panel
		• **Command Prompt:** View

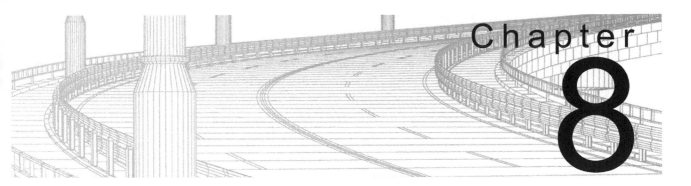

Corridors

Corridors are 3D representations of a road design, other travel ways, paths and walkways, dams, breakwaters, and much more. In some cases, corridors are used for strip-mining and grading.

In this chapter, you will explore creating corridors in road design. You will apply the assembly to an alignment and profile you have established previously. Then, you will create finished ground surfaces to continue on to the final design stage.

Learning Objectives in This Chapter

- Create a corridor model using previously created alignments, profiles, and assemblies.
- Modify a corridor by changing parameters and other properties.
- Create intersections.
- Create roundabouts.
- Create a corridor model representing the location where two roads intersect that accounts for lane widening and curb returns.
- Create a finished ground surface from the design corridor.
- Review and edit corridor sections to make changes to a selected station.
- Add sample lines for calculating quantities within the corridor.

8.1 Creating a Corridor

A corridor is a 3D model of a proposed design based on alignments or feature lines, profiles, and assemblies. Corridors can be used to create terrain models (such as a finished ground terrain model) and generate section data. Corridors display as complex drawing objects consisting of individual cross-sections, feature lines that connect marker points (locations where point codes are assigned), and other related data, as shown in Figure 8–1.

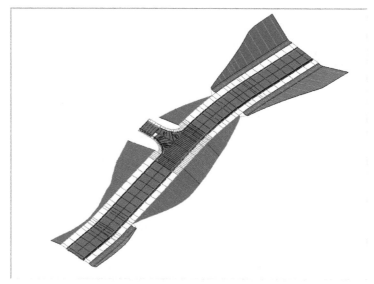

Figure 8–1

Corridors can be used to represent an individual alignment, profile, feature line and assembly (such as for a single road) or can contain multiples of each. When modeling intersections, it is often easiest to have all intersecting roads as part of the same corridor object. However, it might not be practical to include all of the proposed roads in a single corridor on large projects. You can have any number of corridors present in the same drawing file.

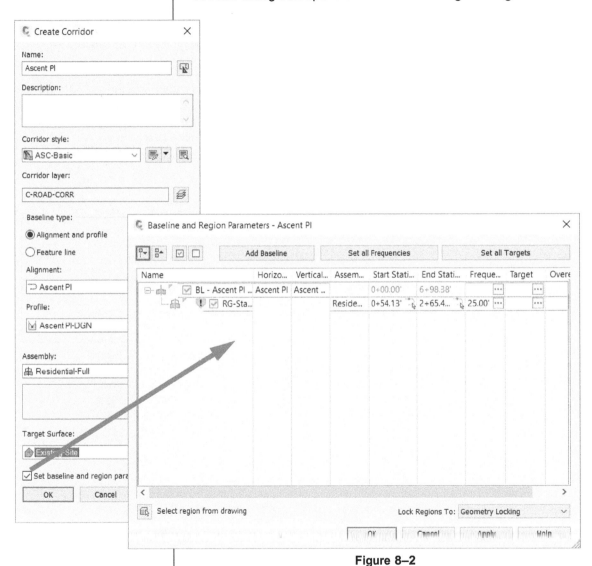

(Rehab Corridor) is also available in the Home tab>Create Design panel. However, this is not covered in this course.

To create a corridor, click (Corridor) in the *Home* tab>Create Design panel. A dialog box opens in which you can enter a description, corridor style, layer, alignment or feature line, profile, assembly, and target surface, as shown on the left in Figure 8–2. It also has an option that enables you to set the baseline and region parameters. By selecting this, when you click **OK** a second dialog box opens as shown on the right of Figure 8–2.

Figure 8–2

Target Mapping

Target Mapping is where you assign a surface to which daylight subassemblies are graded or alignments, feature lines, and polylines that cause lanes and other subassemblies to stretch.

Many stock subassemblies include transitional components, such as the lanes you added to the 2 Lane Road assembly. These lanes can have their outside edge-of-travelway (ETW) controlled by other alignments, feature lines, survey figures, and 3D polylines as required, which can be used to specify widening and contraction of the lanes. These lanes also include profile controls at the ETW points. These types of controls are all assigned using Target Mapping.

In the Target Mapping dialog box (shown in Figure 8–3), the subassembly name and assembly groups are listed. Giving these items logical names is important. Otherwise, it would be difficult to tell them apart in this dialog box.

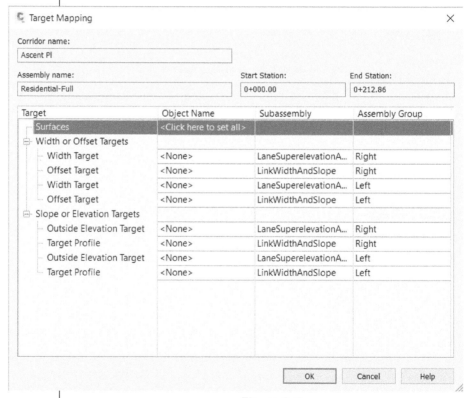

Figure 8–3

Corridor Frequency

The corridor frequency determines how often assemblies are applied to the corridor model, as shown in Figure 8–4. The frequency can be set for tangents separate from curves to provide more control over the model's size and accuracy. The more frequently the assembly is applied to the corridor model, the more accurate the model. A higher frequency also causes the model to require more computer resources, as it increases the size of the model. It is important to set the frequency at a level that balances the level of required accuracy with a reasonably sized corridor model.

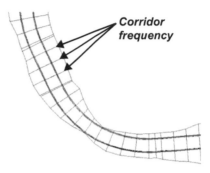

Corridor frequency

Figure 8–4

Frequency locations for curved baselines can be set **By curvature**, **At an increment**, or **Both**, as shown in Figure 8–5. If the **At an increment** option is selected, assemblies are applied at a specified number of units along the curve. If the **By curvature** option is selected, the radius of the curve determines how frequently the assemblies are applied to the corridor model. **Both** will use both options.

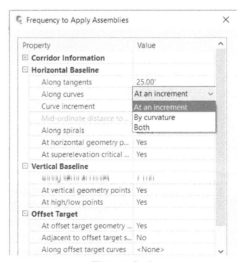

Figure 8–5

8.2 Corridor Properties

Once created, corridors are adjusted in the Corridor Properties dialog box.

Information Tab

The *Information* tab enables you to name the corridor (recommended), and add a description. The corridor style is not very pertinent since the **Code Set Styles** will control the appearance of the corridor.

Parameters Tab

The *Parameters* tab enables you to review and adjust corridor parameters, including which alignments, profiles, and assemblies are being used. Each unique road center line is listed as a *baseline*. In each baseline, there is at least one *region*. Each region is an area over which a specific assembly is applied. You can have multiple baselines and multiple regions in the same baseline as required. The *Parameters* tab is shown in Figure 8–6.

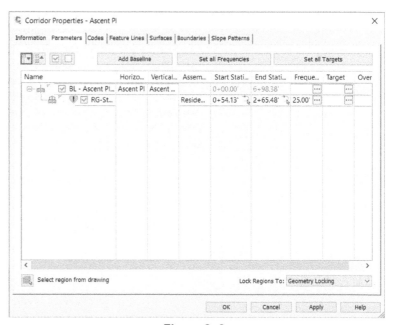

Figure 8–6

Each region has controls that enable you to review the Target Mapping, and the *Frequency* at which corridor sections should be created. If the corridor has had overrides applied using the Corridor Section Editor (select the corridor, *Corridor* tab> Modify panel), then those can be reviewed here as well.

At the top of the dialog box are two important icons: **Set all Frequencies** and **Set all Targets**. These can be used to assign frequencies and targets to all corridor regions. Otherwise, these properties can be adjusted for individual regions using ⬚ (Ellipsis), which is available in the *Frequency* and *Targets* columns.

Codes

The *Codes* tab lists all of the codes that are available in the corridor based on the subassemblies in the assembly, as shown in Figure 8–7. These codes are combined into Code set styles. They control the appearance of the corridor (as well as cross sections and assemblies) by applying styles to each of the subassemblies.

These codes can change the display of corridors, assemblies, and cross-sections from solid colors to hatch patterns to none, etc. Such codes are also used to set section labels and for quantity takeoff.

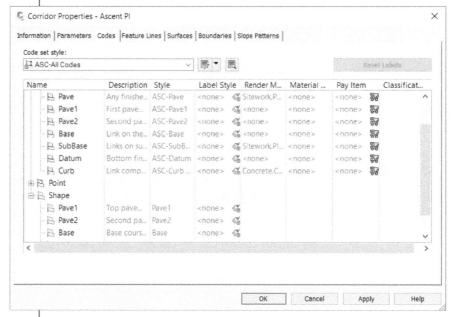

Figure 8–7

Feature Lines

Feature lines are named 3D linework that connect marker points (locations assigned point codes) in your assemblies, as shown in Figure 8–8. From any feature line listed in the *Feature Lines* tab, you can export a polyline or extract a linked or unlinked feature line (such as for grading purposes).These feature lines are generated from the subassembly Point codes.

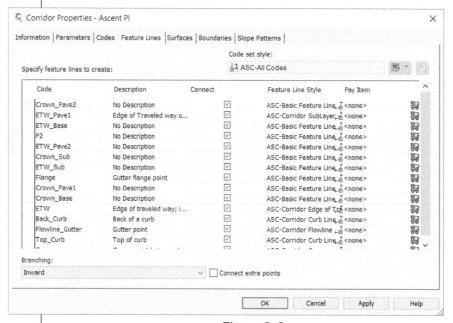

Figure 8–8

Slope Patterns

Slope patterns can be used to indicate whether an area of side slope is a cut or fill. The *Slope Patterns* tab is shown in Figure 8–9.

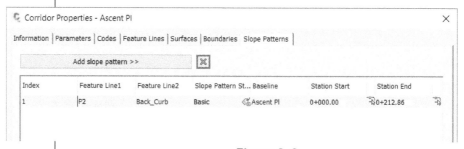

Figure 8–9

Corridor Contextual Ribbon

Most of the functions performed in the *Corridors Parameters* tab are also available in the ribbon in the *Corridor* contextual tab>Modify Region panel, as shown in Figure 8–10. For advanced users, this is the preferred option; they find it more intuitive because they can pick the regions of the corridor in the drawing and view the results.

Figure 8–10

The corridor contextual ribbon's Modify Corridor panel also has **Corridor Surfaces**, **Code Sets**, **Feature Lines** and **Slope Patterns**, as shown in Figure 8–11.

Figure 8–11

Exporting Corridors

Civil 3D corridors can be exported to:

- InfraWorks via the IMX format

- A file geodatabase (FGDB) that can be used in ArcGIS

- ArcGIS directly via the ArcGIS Connector

- To a LandXML exchange file

- To a regular AutoCAD drawing with the intelligent Civil 3D objects translated to regular AutoCAD objects

These export utilities are accessible though the *Output* and the *InfraWorks* tabs shown in Figure 8–12.

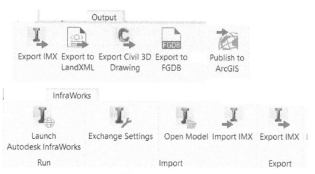

Figure 8–12

Practice 8a

Creating Corridors

Practice Objective

- Create a corridor model using previously created alignments, profiles, and assemblies.

In this practice, you will use the assemblies to create a corridor for both Jeffries Ranch Rd and Ascent Pl. You will also learn how to split a region.

Task 1 - Create a corridor with regions - Option #1.

1. Open **COR1-A.dwg** from the *C:\Civil 3D Projects\Working\ Corridors* folder.

See the Chapter 4: Project Management for how to work with Data Shortcuts.

2. Hover the cursor over the Data Shortcuts and review the tooltip that displays, shown in Figure 8–13. Ensure that your Data Shortcuts are set so the **Working Folder** is set to *C:\Civil 3D Projects\Data Shortcuts\Fundamentals* and the **Data Shortcuts Project Folder** to *Ascent-Development*. If required, right-click on Data Shortcuts to set the **Working Folder** and **Data Shortcuts Project Folder**.

Data Shortcuts [C:\Civil 3D Projects\Data Shortc...

C:\Civil 3D Projects\Data Shortcuts\Fundamentals\Ascent-Development

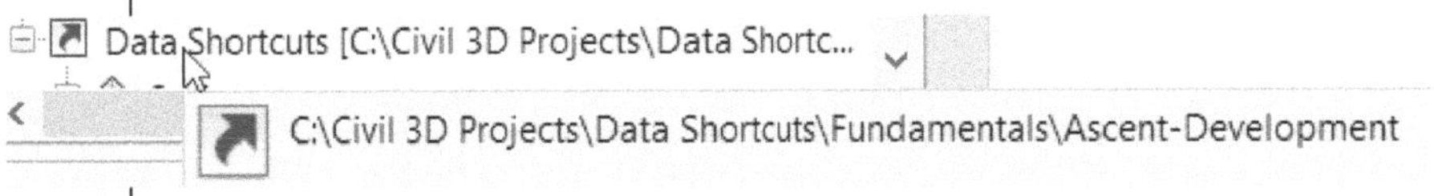

Figure 8–13

3. In the *Home* tab>Create Design panel, click  (Corridor). Enter the following (as shown in Figure 8–14):

- Name it **Jeffries Ranch Rd**.
- For the alignment, select **Jeffries Ranch Rd**.
- For the profile, select **Jeffries Ranch Rd-DGN**.
- For the assembly, select **Collector-Full**.
- Verify that the **Set baseline and region parameters** option is selected.

Figure 8–14

4. Click **OK**. The Baseline and Region Parameters dialog box opens.

You will be creating an intersection in the Jeffries Ranch Rd, so you will need to create two regions: one before the intersection and one after the intersection.

5. The Baseline and Region Parameters dialog box identifies the Baseline (BL) as *BL-Jeffries Ranch Rd - (1)*. This baseline currently has one Region (RG). In the Baseline and Region Parameters dialog box, set the following options, as shown in Figure 8–15:

- Change the region name to **RG-Before Intersection**.
- Adjust the start station to **117.03'**.
- Right-click on RG-Before Intersection and select **Split Region**.

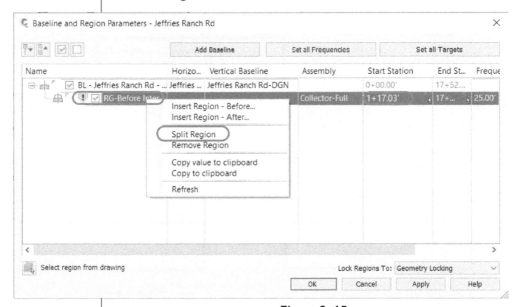

Figure 8–15

6. You now need to enter the start and end stations for the regions. In Model Space, you are prompted for the start station of the new region. Enter the following values, as shown in Figure 8–16:

- Type **1035.92'** and press <Enter>. This will create a region to the start of the roundabout.
- Type **630.74'** and press <Enter>. This will create a region between the end of the intersection with Ascent Pl and the start of the roundabout.
- Type **525.81** and press <Enter>. This will create a region at the end of the intersection of Ascent Pl (which you will erase later).
- Press <Esc> to stop creating regions and return to the Baseline and Region Parameters dialog box.

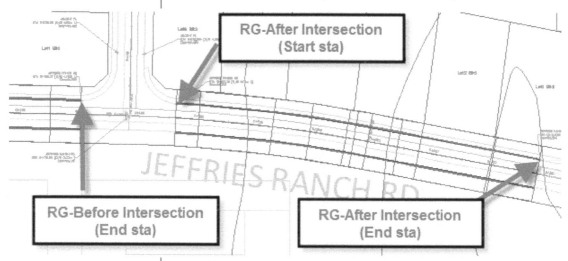

Figure 8–16

7. In the Baseline and Region Parameters dialog box, right-click on **RG - Collector-Full - (1)** and select **Remove Region**. This is the Ascent Pl Intersection region. Do the same for **RG - Collector-Full - (3)**, which is the region from the start of the roundabout to the end. You will re-create that region later.

8. Click on **RG - Collector-Full - (2)** and rename it **RG-After Intersection**, as shown in Figure 8–17.

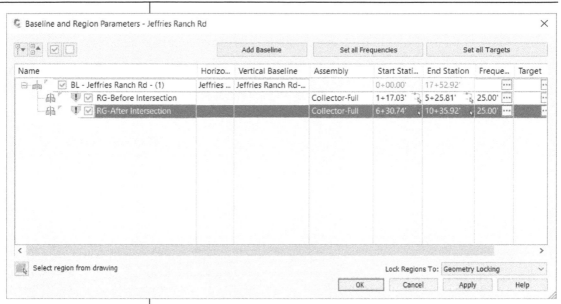

Figure 8–17

9. Click **OK** to apply the changes and close the dialog box. If prompted, rebuild the corridor.

10. Save the drawing.

Task 2 - Create a corridor with regions - Option #2.

In this task, you will create regions as in the previous task, but using the tools within the Corridor contextual ribbon and "eyeballing" the locations of the regions.

1. Do not continue from the previous drawing. Instead, open **COR1-B.dwg** from the *C:\Civil 3D Projects\Working\Corridors* folder.

2. As you did in Task 1, in the *Home* tab>Create Design panel,

   click ![icon] (Corridor). Enter the following:

   - Name it **Jeffries Ranch Rd**.
   - For the alignment, select **Jeffries Ranch Rd**.
   - For the profile, select **Jeffries Ranch Rd-DGN**.
   - For the assembly, select **Collector-Full**.

3. **Do not** select the **Set baseline and region parameters** option. You will be using the corresponding tools within the contextual ribbon instead.

4. Click OK to close the *Create Corridor* dialog box.

5. The corridor is built with the default settings.

6. Select the newly built corridor and in the *Corridor* contextual tab>Modify Region panel, select <img_1 /> (Split Region), as shown in Figure 8–18.

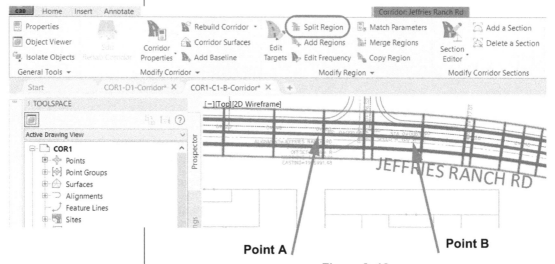

Point A   **Point B**

Figure 8–18

7. You are prompted to select the region to split. This is a newly created corridor, therefore it has only one region. Select anywhere within the corridor to select.

8. For the location to split the region, select somewhere near Point A. It does not need to be exact.

9. The **Split Region** command continues by asking for another region to split. Select the region to the east of the intersection.

10. For the location to split the region, select somewhere near Point B. It does not need to be exact.

11. Press <Enter> to finish the command.

12. There are now three regions, marked with triangular grips. Extend the Modify Region panel and select **Delete Regions**. Select the middle region, as shown in Figure 8–19. You will need to click twice to select the region.

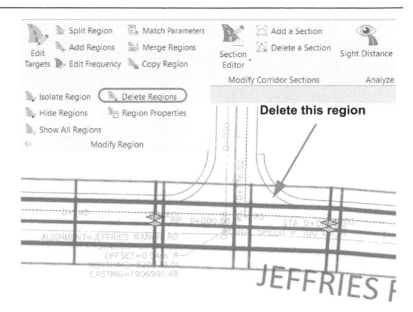

Figure 8–19

You did not really need to create three regions. You could have split the corridor into two regions and simply dragged their edges to the intersection limits.

13. Now you can adjust the edges of the two remaining regions with the triangular grips.

14. Pan over to the start of the corridor to the west.

15. If needed, reselect the corridor. To adjust the start station of the first region, click on the triangular grip at the start of the corridor and drag it to the right, then you can type in **117.03** for the start station, as shown Figure 8–20, and press <Enter>.

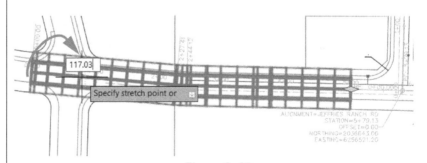

Figure 8–20

16. In the Prospector, note the yellow alert icon next to the Jeffries Ranch Rd corridor. Right-click on it and select **Rebuild**, as shown in Figure 8–21.

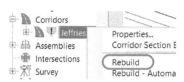

Figure 8–21

17. Save the drawing.

Task 3 - Create a residential corridor.

In this task, you will use the assemblies to create a corridor, applying the **Residential-Full** subassembly from station to station.

The steps to accomplish this are similar to those in Task 1. If you have time, you can complete this task; otherwise, skip this task and open the next drawing when instructed to do so in the next practice.

1. Continue working with either drawing from the previous tasks or open **COR1-C.dwg**.

2. In the *Home* tab>Create Design panel, click (Corridor).

3. Name it **Ascent PI**, then enter the following, as shown in Figure 8–22:

   • For the alignment, select **Ascent PI** from the list.
   • For the profile, select **Ascent PI-DGN** from the list.
   • For the assembly, select **Residential-Full**.
   • Verify that the **Set baseline and region parameters** option is selected.

Since you have no daylighting subassemblies in your assembly, the surface can be ignored.

Figure 8–22

4. Click **OK**. The Baseline and Region Parameters dialog box opens.

5. The dialog box identifies the Baseline (BL) as *BL-Ascent Pl*. This baseline currently has one Region, which is assigned the **Residential - Full Assembly**. Set the following options, as shown in Figure 8–23:

- Rename the region to **RG – Start**.
- Adjust the *Start Station* to **54.13'**
- Adjust the *End Station* to **265.48'**

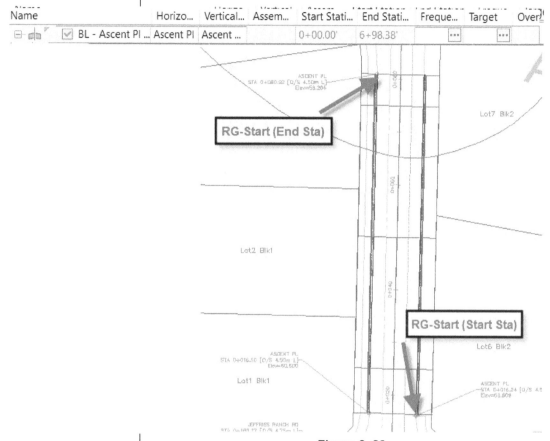

Figure 8–23

6. Click **OK** to create the corridor. If prompted, rebuild the corridor.

7. Save the drawing.

Task 4 - Build a Boulevard Corridor with Daylighting.

In this task, you will create another corridor that has daylighting on one side in a particular region. You will create the full corridor, split it at the intersection, and then apply another assembly to the newly created region.

1. In the *Home* tab>Create Design panel, click (Corridor). Do the following:

   - Name it **Rand Boulevard**.
   - For the alignment, select **Rand Boulevard**.
   - For the profile, select **Jeffries Ranch Rd-DGN**.
   - For the subassembly, select **Divided Highway - SW -DL**.
   - For the Target Surface, select **Existing Site**.

2. **Do not** select the **Set baseline and region parameters** option. You will be using the corresponding tools within the contextual ribbon instead.

3. Click **OK** to close the Create Corridor dialog box. The corridor is built with the default settings.

4. Select the newly built corridor.

5. Rather than splitting the region twice to make three regions, as you did earlier, you will split the region once and pull the two regions apart using the grips. In the *Corridor* contextual tab>Modify Region panel, select 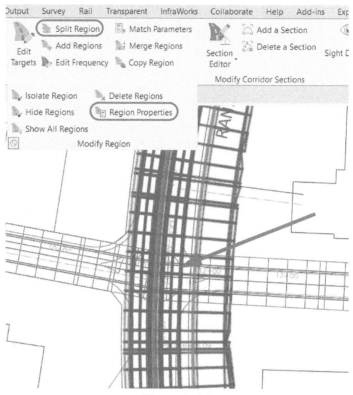 (Split Region), as shown in Figure 8–24.

Figure 8–24

6. The first click will select the region you want to split (even though there is only one region) and the second selects the station where the split occurs.

7. Press <Enter> to finish the command.

8. Zoom in more to see the grips better. Select the triangular grip pointed downward, as shown in Figure 8–25, and drag it so it is just barely beyond the boulevard island.

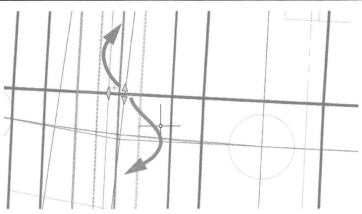

Figure 8–25

9. Repeat for the northern portion of the corridor.

10. Press <Esc> to deselect the corridor.

11. Select the **Jeffries Ranch Rd** corridor and repeat Steps 6 to 9 to split the corridor and drag it beyond the intersection. The result should be similar to Figure 8–26. The exact position of the regions is not important as they can be adjusted later.

Figure 8–26

12. Press <Esc> to deselect the corridor.

13. Select the **Rand Boulevard** corridor.

14. In the *Corridor* contextual tab>expanded Modify Region panel, select 📋 (Region Properties), as shown previously in Figure 8–24.

15. You are prompted for a region to edit. Select the northern region.

16. In the Corridor Region Properties dialog box, click in the *Value* column for the *Assembly*, and in the Edit Corridor Region dialog box, select the **Divided Highway w SW assembly**, as shown in Figure 8–27.

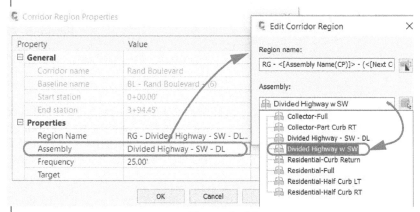

Figure 8–27

17. Click **OK** twice to get back to the drawing.

18. Press <Esc> to deselect the corridor

19. Save the drawing.

8.3 Designing Intersections

Intersection objects are complex corridor models that automatically create offset and curb return geometry where two intersecting alignments meet. As changes are made to the underlying information (alignments, profiles, assemblies, and surfaces) the intersection geometry is automatically updated. There are four types of Intersection objects, as shown in Figure 8–28. This training guide only covers the standard intersection.

Figure 8–28

To create an intersection, select the *Home* tab>Create Design panel and click (Create Intersection). You are prompted to pick the intersection of two roads. The Create Intersection Wizard then opens.

General Tab

The *General* tab enables you to name the intersection (recommended), add a description, and select intersection marker and label styles.

An important element on this tab is the intersection corridor type. You can keep the primary road crown maintained or have all road crowns maintained, as shown in Figure 8–29. If you only maintain the crown of the primary road, the secondary road's profile is adjusted automatically.

Note: The intersection corridor type cannot be changed once you click **Create Intersection** and exit the Create Intersection Wizard.

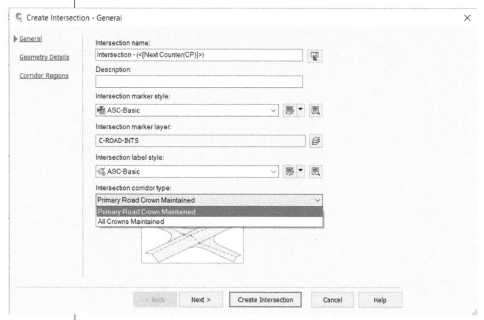

Figure 8–29

Geometry Details Tab

The *Geometry Details* tab enables you to set the road that is going to be the primary road, as shown in Figure 8–30. It is also where you set the **Offset** and **Curb Return** parameters, which include parameters for both alignments and profiles.

Figure 8–30

Corridor Regions Tab

The *Corridor Regions* tab enables you to create a new corridor or add the intersection corridor to an existing corridor.

This is also where you select the assemblies to use in each of the corridor regions. Some assembly sets ship with the Autodesk Civil 3D software and can be located by clicking **Browse**. By default, a Metric or Imperial assembly set displays various assemblies that are set in the window.

Note: Best practice would be for your organization to establish the assembly sets that you can use to create the required intersections. This would allow for consistent creation of intersections, according to your organization's design standards.

It is recommended that you add the resulting corridor (created within the intersection) to an existing corridor, selectable from the drop down list, as shown in Figure 8–31, rather than creating it as a new corridor (not recommended).

Click ⸬ for each Corridor Region Section Type and select the appropriate assembly, as required. As you select a region, the wizard highlights that region in the preview at the bottom of the window. If you select any assemblies that use daylight subassemblies, do not forget to set the target surface at the top right.

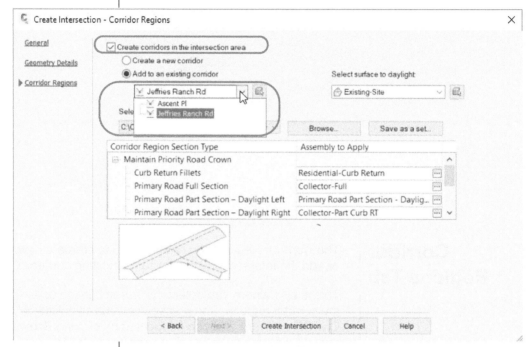

Figure 8–31

Once all of the parameters have been set, you can click **Create Intersection** to create the intersection object.

Practice 8b

Intersections

Practice Objective

- Create an intersection object to represent how two roads should meet.

Task 1 - Create an intersection.

In this task, you will create an intersection at Jeffries Ranch Rd and Ascent Pl. This intersection will fill in the gap you left in the Jeffries Ranch Rd corridor by setting regions.

1. Open **COR1-D.dwg** from the *C:\Civil 3D Projects\Working\Corridors* folder.

2. In the *View* tab>Named Views panel, select the preset view **Corr-inter**.

3. In order to make selecting the intersection of the two alignments easier, restore the **Intersection** layer state by selecting it from the Layer States drop-down list, as shown in Figure 8–32.

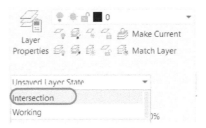

Figure 8–32

4. In the *Home* tab>Create Design panel, click 🞤 (Create Intersection).

5. The Autodesk Civil 3D software sets an **Intersection** object snap and prompts you to *Select Intersection Point*. Select the intersection of the Jeffries Ranch Rd and Ascent Pl alignments, as shown in Figure 8–33.

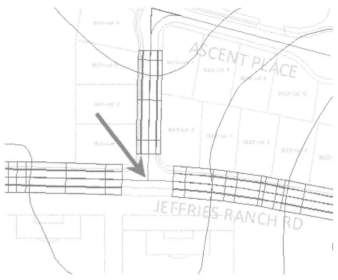

Figure 8–33

Note: If you are having problems selecting the intersection point, press <Esc> to exit the **Intersection** command. In Model Space, select the two alignments **Jeffries Ranch Rd** and **Ascent Pl**, right-click, expand *Display order* and select **Bring to front**. Then, create the intersection.

If this were a four-way intersection, you would be prompted to select the Primary road. In this case, the Autodesk Civil 3D software assumes that Jeffries Ranch Rd is the primary road.

6. Position the Create Intersection wizard so that the intersection is also displayed in the drawing.

7. In the *General* page, set the following options, as shown in Figure 8–34:

- *Intersection Name:* Type **Intersection–(Jeffries Ranch & Ascent Pl)**.
- Accept the default *Intersection Marker Style* and *Intersection Label Style* settings.
- *Intersection Corridor Type:* Select **Primary Road Crown Maintained**.

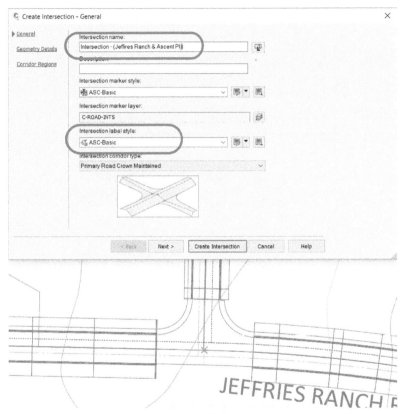

Figure 8–34

8. Click **Next>**.

9. In the *Geometry Details* page, the alignments, intersection stations, and profiles to be used are listed. The profile can be changed here, as required. In the *Offset and curb returns* area, select the **Create or specify offset alignments** option and click **Offset Parameters**, as shown in Figure 8–35.

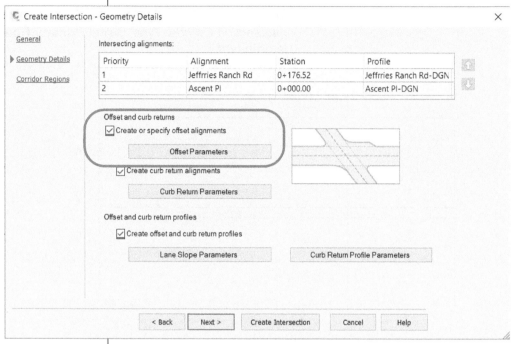

Figure 8–35

In the Intersection Offset Parameters dialog box, note that selecting the **Primary Road** or **Secondary Road** highlights the respective alignment in the drawing.

Because this is a simple intersection, you do not need to add additional offsets.

10. For this project, set the following options:

- Set the offset parameters for the Primary Road, Jeffries Ranch Rd to **15.5'** for the right and left sides.
- For the Secondary Road, Ascent Pl, set the offset parameters to **14.75'** for the right and left sides.
- Click **OK** to close the dialog box.

11. In the *Geometry Details* page, select the **Create curb return alignments** option and click **Curb Return Parameters**.

12. In the Intersection Curb Return Parameters dialog box, note the preview for the **NE-Quadrant** in the drawing. Set the *Curb Return Radius* to **38.55'**, as shown in Figure 8–36, and accept the remaining default values. Note the preview as you make the edits.

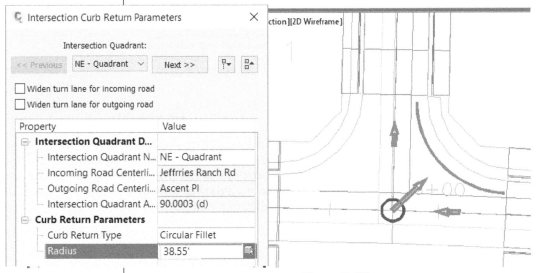

Figure 8–36

13. Click **Next>>** at the top of the dialog box to switch to the **NW-Quadrant**. Note the change in the drawing. Set the *Curb Return Radius* to **38.55'**, as shown in Figure 8–37, and accept the remaining default values. Click **OK** to return to the *Geometry Details* page.

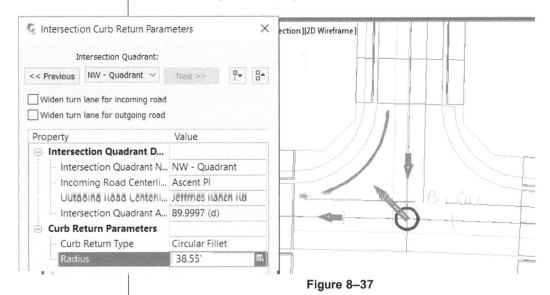

Figure 8–37

14. To automatically create curb return profiles, in the *Offset and curb return profiles* area, select the **Create offset and curb return profiles** option as shown in Figure 8–38. Accept the defaults for the **Lane Slope** and **Curb Return Profile** parameters and click **Next>**.

Figure 8–38

15. In the *Corridor Regions* page, you can create a new corridor or add this intersection to an existing corridor. Select the **Create corridors in the intersection area** option and select the **Add to an existing corridor** option, and select **Jeffries Ranch Rd** from the drop-down list, as shown in Figure 8–39.

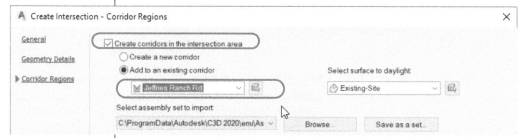

Figure 8–39

16. For the Curb Return Fillets, click on the [...] and select the **Residential – Curb Return** assembly, as shown in Figure 8–40. Click **OK**.

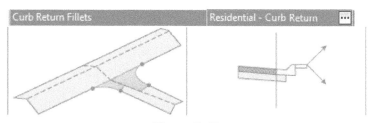

Figure 8–40

17. For the Primary Road Full Section, select the **Collector-Full** assembly, as shown in Figure 8–41.

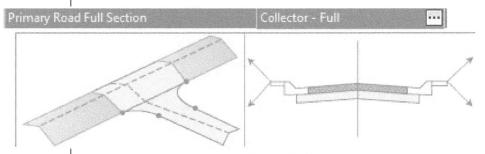

Figure 8–41

18. For the Primary Road Part Section – Daylight Left, accept the default value as shown in Figure 8–42, as this is not applicable to your intersection.

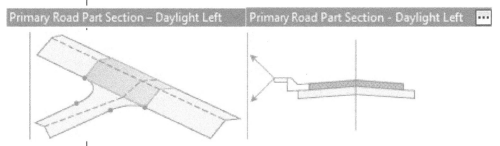

Figure 8–42

19. For the Primary Road Part Section – Daylight Right, select the **Collector-Part Curb RT** assembly, as shown in Figure 8–43.

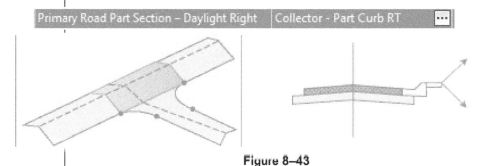

Figure 8–43

20. For the Secondary Road Full Section, select the
Residential-Full assembly, as shown in Figure 8–44.

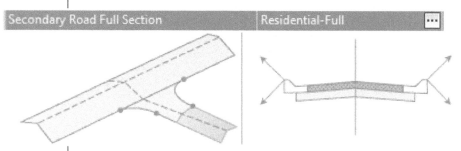

Figure 8–44

21. For the Secondary Road Half Section – Daylight Left, select
the **Residential-Half Curb LT** assembly, as shown in
Figure 8–45.

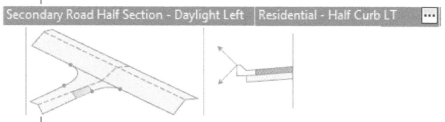

Figure 8–45

22. For the Secondary Road Half Section - Daylight Right, select
the **Residential-Half Curb RT** assembly, as shown in
Figure 8–46.

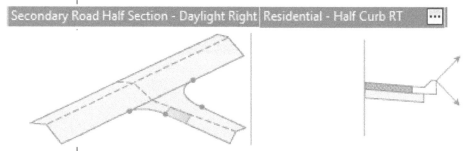

Figure 8–46

23. When finished, click on **Save as set...**, browse to *C:\Civil 3D
Projects\Ascent-Config\Assembly* Sets and save this set as
(Your Initials)-Collector-Residential-TEE.xml (shown in
Figure 8–47). Doing this will make it easier to create such
intersection types in the future.

Figure 8–47

24. Now, click **Create Intersection**. You might need to perform a **REGEN** to display the newly created Intersection Corridor.

25. In the Event Viewer, expand **Action** and select **Clear All Events**, as shown in Figure 8–48. Click the **X** to close the Event Viewer.

Figure 8–48

26. Restore the **Working** layer state by selecting it from the Layer States drop-down list, as shown in Figure 8–49.

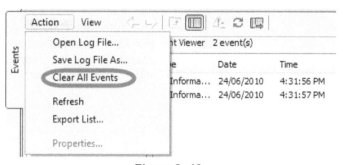

Figure 8–49

27. Save the drawing.

Task 2 - (Optional) Create another intersection.

In this optional task (time permitting), you will create another intersection and adjust the two corridors.

1. Zoom out and pan to see the entire extents of the **Jeffries Ranch Rd** corridor.

2. Select the **Jeffries Ranch Rd** corridor.

3. Expand the Modify Region panel and select **Delete Regions**. Select the region from the roundabout to the eastern end; you will have to select it twice.

4. Press <Esc> to deselect the corridor.

5. In the *View* tab>Named Views panel, select the preset view **Corr-inter-2**.

6. In the *Home* tab>Create Design panel, click ⊕ (Create Intersection).

7. The Autodesk Civil 3D software sets an **Intersection** object snap and prompts you to *Select Intersection Point*. Select the intersection of the Jeffries Ranch Rd and Driveway alignments, as shown in Figure 8–50.

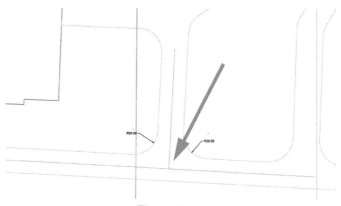

Figure 8–50

8. Position the Create Intersection wizard so that the intersection is also displayed in the drawing.

9. On the *General* page, set the following options:

- *Intersection Name:* **Intersection–(Jeffries Ranch & Driveway)**
- Accept the default *Intersection Marker Style* and *Intersection Label Style* settings
- *Intersection Corridor Type:* **Primary Road Crown Maintained**

10. Click **Next>**.

The Intersection Wizard may remember the last values you entered.

11. For this intersection, do the following:

- Set the offset parameters for the Primary Road, Jeffries Ranch Rd to **15.5'** for the right and left sides.
- For the Secondary Road, Driveway, set the offset parameters to **14.75'** for the right and left sides.
- Click **OK** to close the dialog box.

12. In the *Geometry Details* page, select the **Create curb return alignments** option and click **Curb Return Parameters**.

13. In the Intersection Curb Return Parameters dialog box, note the preview for the **NE-Quadrant** in the drawing. Set the *Curb Return Radius* to **28.0**.

14. Click **Next>>** at the top of the dialog box to switch to the **NW-Quadrant**. Note the change in the drawing. Set the *Curb Return Radius* to **28.0'**. Click **OK** to return to the *Geometry Details* page.

15. In the *Corridor Regions* page, you can create a new corridor or add this intersection to an existing corridor. Select the **Create corridors in the intersection area** option, select the **Add to an existing corridor** option, and select **Jeffries Ranch Rd** from the drop-down list, as shown in Figure 8–51.

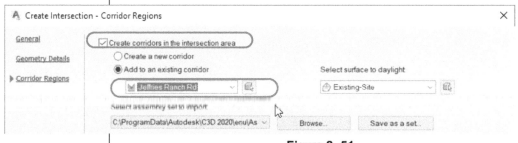

Figure 8–51

16. In the Corridor Regions dialog box, click **Browse...** and browse to the *C:\Civil 3D Projects\Ascent-Config\Assembly Sets* folder. Open the *Collector-Residential-TEE.xml* set.

17. Click **Create Intersection**. You might need to perform a **REGEN** to display the newly created intersection corridor.

18. In the Event Viewer, expand **Action** and select **Clear All Events**. Click the **X** to close the Event Viewer.

19. Zoom out a bit and select the **Jeffries Ranch Rd** corridor.

20. Select the leftmost triangular grip in the corridor region, as shown in Figure 8–52, and drag it so it is just barely before the boulevard island.

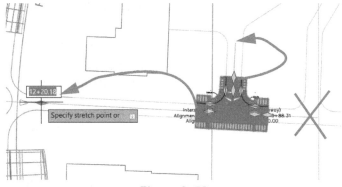

Figure 8–52

21. Repeat the process for the Driveway section, but not the right portion. You want to leave that as is, in case you want to create another intersection there.

22. Press <Esc> to deselect the corridor.

23. In the Event Viewer, expand **Action** and select **Clear All Events**. Click the **X** to close the Event Viewer.

24. Freeze the **C-ROAD-INTS-TEXT** layer.

25. Save the drawing.

8.4 Roundabouts

Roundabouts are becoming very popular everywhere. Many existing intersections are routinely being upgraded to more efficient and safer roundabout designs.

Autodesk Vehicle Tracking has a very robust set of roundabout tools and editing features. The roundabout tools within Civil 3D are a subset of the Autodesk Vehicle Tracking tools.

For more information on Autodesk Vehicle Tracking, consult the Autodesk Vehicle Tracking: Fundamentals guide (published by ASCENT).

Civil 3D has powerful features to simplify preliminary layout of roundabout geometry. Editing options are also available, and as you make changes to the layout, you will see the dynamic nature of the objects, as well as the adherence to design standards. Using the geometrically constrained roundabout objects makes it viable to explore multiple design solutions.

Roundabout Standards

All roundabouts are created in accordance with defined rules or standards. The Roundabout Standard Explorer holds a number of these standards from several countries, as shown in Figure 8–53. All standards are grouped by nationality, and custom standards can be created as well.

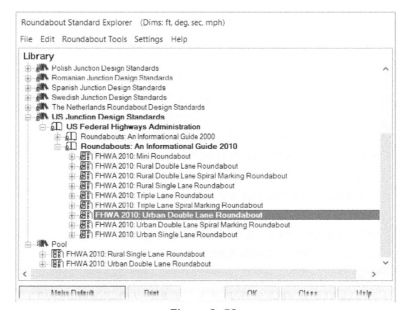

Figure 8–53

Creating Roundabouts

The **Create Roundabout** command is found on the *Home* tab> expanded Intersection panel. Before you create your roundabout, there are some elements required, such as:

- Civil 3D existing and final surfaces (optional)
  - If no surfaces are available, only a 2D roundabout will be created without any corridor segments.
- Alignments
- Profiles (optional)
  - If no profiles are available, only a 2D roundabout will be created.

When the **Create Roundabout** command is launched, the New Roundabout Details dialog box will open, as shown in Figure 8–54. Set all the appropriate settings.

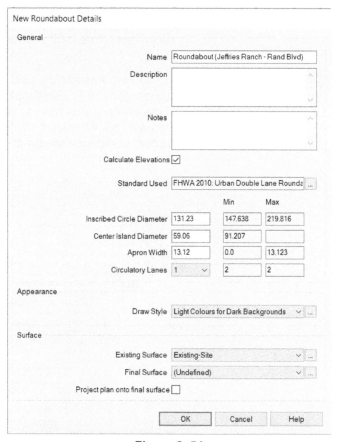

Figure 8–54

Place the center point of the roundabout in the drawing, then add the arms (or approaches) of the roundabout by clicking on (or near) the intersection of the Civil 3D alignments.

When adding each approach, the New Arm dialog box will appear, as shown in Figure 8–55. Enter a unique name for each new arm created.

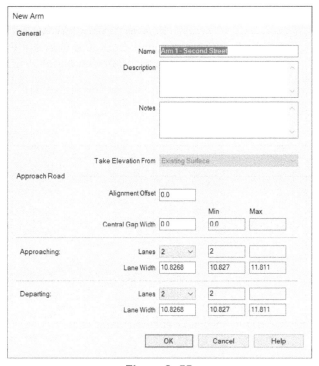

Figure 8–55

Each new approach creates the full geometry necessary for the roundabout. As the roundabout is created, either a 2D vehicle roundabout or a full 3D corridor model is created, as shown in Figure 8–56. The corridor model settings are able to be turned on at any time during the creation or editing process.

With corridor model settings turned off   *With corridor model settings turned on*

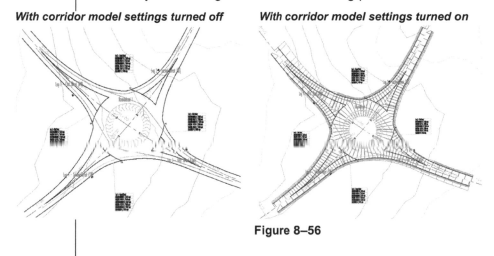

Figure 8–56

Real-time feedback is also added when the roundabout is created. A table is provided for each arm of the roundabout, providing fastest path and performance data. All tables stay up to date as the roundabout is being created and edited.

If using the corridor model creation while creating the roundabout, the Corridor Properties will populate with all of the appropriate baselines and regions, as shown in Figure 8–57.

Figure 8–57

Heads Up Display

As you create the roundabout, little boxes appear for each approach arm, as shown in Figure 8–58. This is called a Heads Up Display (HUD). HUDs show the critical design values related to each approach arm. These include radii and calculated speeds.

Figure 8–58

The data is color coded:

- Green: Values are within the limits specified in the standards.

- Amber: Values are getting close to the limiting value.

- Red: Values are outside of the limits.

The HUDs are dynamic tables. If you adjust the roundabout, the values will update. You will also notice color changes as limits are approached.

Practice 8c | Roundabout with Corridor

Learning Objectives

- Create a 3D roundabout.
- Turn off the Civil 3D corridor aspects of the roundabout for easy viewing.

In this practice, you will create a 3D roundabout using Civil 3D alignments and the existing surface. Then, upon studying the roundabout and its specifications, you will simplify the drawing by turning off the Civil 3D corridor and its surface.

To create a roundabout with proper elevations, an interim design surface named **IDG-Roundabout** has been created. The concept of *Interim Design Surfaces* is discussed in more detail in *Chapter 9: Grading*.

1. Continue working with the drawing from the previous practice or open **COR1-E.dwg** from the *C:\Civil 3D Projects\Working\ Corridors* folder.

2. Select the preset view **Corr-Round**.

*Note: If you are working in the **COR1-E.dwg**, the required surface is already referenced and you can skip Steps 3 to 5.*

3. In the Toolspace, *Prospector* tab, under the *Data Shortcuts* collection, expand the *Surfaces* collection.

4. Under the *Surfaces* collection, select the surface **IDG-Roundabout**, right-click, and select **Create Reference**.

5. Set the surface style to **_No Display** and leave all the other values as their defaults.

6. If the Roundabout Standard Explorer opens, do the following (as shown in Figure 8–59):

   - Expand *US Junction Design Standards>US Federal Highways Administration>Roundabouts: An Informational Guide 2010*.
   - Select **FHWA2010 Urban Double Lane Roundabout**.
   - Click **Make Default**, then click **Proceed**.

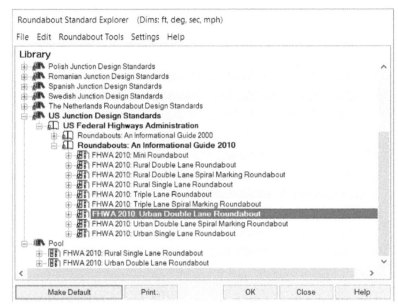

Figure 8–59

7. In the *Home* tab>Create Design panel, expand the Intersection drop-down list and select (Create Roundabout).

8. In the New Roundabout Details dialog box, set the following, as shown in Figure 8–60:

- *Name:* **Roundabout (Jeffries Ranch - Rand Blvd)**
- *Notes:* **For training purposes only**
- *Calculate Elevation:* **Checked**
- *Standards Used:* **FHWA2010 Urban Double Lane Roundabout** (as shown above in Figure 8–59)
- *Existing Surface:* **IDG-Temp** (from drop-down list)
- *Final Surface:* **(Undefined)**
- *Project plan onto final surface:* **Unchecked**

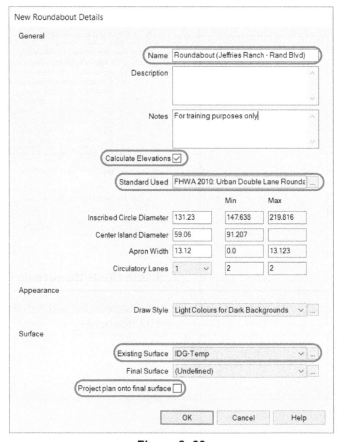

Figure 8–60

9. Click **OK** to close the New Roundabout Details dialog box. You are now prompted for *the location for the center of the roundabout*. Select a point on (or near) the intersection of the alignments, as shown in Figure 8–61.

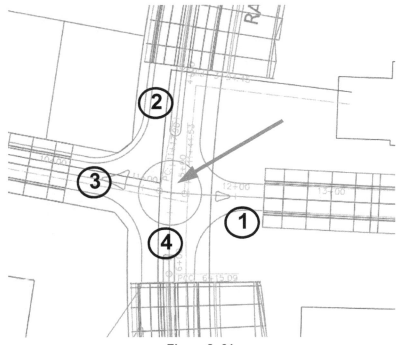

Figure 8–61

10. You are prompted for the line defining the new access road center line. Select the alignment labeled **(1)** in Figure 8–61.

11. Continue to select arms 2 through 4 and enter the following information:

	Name	Central Gap Width	Approaching and Departing Lanes
Arm 1	Arm - Jeffries Ranch Rd East	0	Lanes: 1 Lane Width: 15.5
Arm 2	Arm - Rand Boulevard - North	18	Lanes: 2 Lane Width: 11.0
Arm 3	Arm - Jeffries Ranch Rd West	0	Lanes: 1 Lane Width: 15.5
Arm 4	Arm - Rand Boulevard - South	18	Lanes: 2 Lane Width: 11.0

It can take quite a while for Civil 3D to preform the calculations, so be patient.

12. When you are finished selecting all four approaches, press <Enter>.

Corridor surfaces are covered later in this chapter.

13. The roundabout, corridor, and corridor surface are created, as shown in Figure 8–62

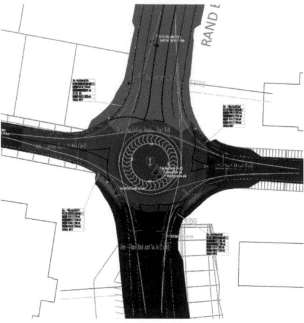

Figure 8–62

14. In the Prospector, expand the Surfaces branch and note the new surface that has been created, namely **Roundabout (Jeffries Ranch - Rand Blvd) Top**. Right-click on it and select **Surface Properties**.

15. Set the *Surface style* to **_No Display**.

16. Examine the surface statistics (on the last tab of the Surface Properties dialog box.) Click **OK** when done to close the dialog box.

17. Review the roundabout and the HUDs for each branch.

18. Restore the **Roundabout-Hide** layer state by selecting it from the Layer States drop-down list.

19. Save the drawing.

8.5 Corridor Section Review and Edit

Creating complex corridors can be greatly simplified using

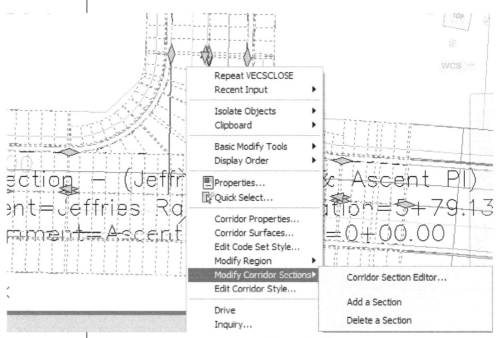 (Corridor Section Editor). It is accessed through the shortcut menu or contextual ribbon after selecting a corridor, as shown in Figure 8–63.

Figure 8–63

This command launches the *Section Editor* contextual tab, which enables you to review and edit sections interactively using the appropriate panels. The **Parameter Editor**, as shown in Figure 8–64, enables you to review and change most subassembly parameters.

Figure 8–64

The editor enables you to modify those sections that need special attention, such as different daylight slopes. The editor also enables you to add and remove some subassemblies or links directly to and from a section. These parameter changes, additions, and deletions can be done for a single section or for a range of sections. An example is shown in Figure 8–65.

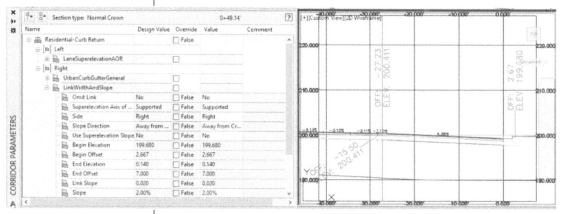

Figure 8–65

To more easily display the modifications in the corridor section, you can work in three different zoom modes in the **View/Edit Corridor Section** command:

- **Zoom To Extents:** Ensures that the full assembly is in view when you navigate to another station after zooming in.

- **Zoom to a Subassembly:** Ensures that a selected subassembly remains at the center of the view when you navigate to another station. The zoom level is also maintained.

- **Zoom to an Offset and Elevation:** Ensures that the current zoom level is maintained when you navigate to another station after a zoom.

Before launching the **Corridor Section Editor** command, you can set up multiple viewports using ▦ (Edit Viewport Configuration) for viewing the plan, profile, and section during the **Section Edit** command. Then, while in the **Corridor Section Editor** command, a Station Tracker indicates the current section (with a vertical line), in both the plan view and any associated profile views.

Hint: Project Explorer

The new Project Explorer offers alternatives to the Section Editor, providing additional flexibility and improvements. For more information, see *Appendix B: Project Explorer*.

Practice 8d | Corridor Section Editor

Practice Objectives

- Inspect a corridor with the Section Editor to review and adjust the corridor.
- Show what is happening with existing and proposed surface data at predefined intervals along an alignment using section views.

1. Continue working with the drawing from the previous practice or open **COR1-F.dwg** from the C:\Civil 3D Projects\Working\Corridors folder.

2. Select the preset view **Corr-Inter**.

3. Select the Jeffries Ranch Rd corridor.

4. Invoke the *Corridor Section Editor*, either by clicking the icon in the corridor contextual ribbon or through the right-click menu (*Modify Corridor Section>Section Editor*).

5. In the *Section Editor* tab>View Tools panel, click

    (Viewport Configuration) and set the following, as shown in Figure 8–66:

   - *Layout*: **Three Above**
   - *Horizontal Split*: **60%**
   - *Vertical Split*: **40%**
   - *Viewport 1*: **Section**
   - *Viewport 2*: **Profile**
   - *Viewport 3*: **Plan**

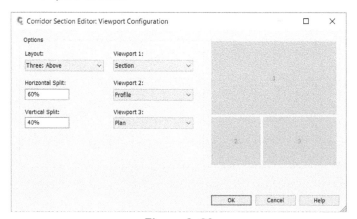

Figure 8–66

6. Click **OK**.

7. On the status bar, set your annotation scale to **1"=50'**.

8. Select station **6 + 50.00'** from the Station Drop down list in the Station Selector panel.

9. Invoke the *Parameter Editor* () from the Corridor Edit Tools panel.

10. Navigate to *Right>LaneSuperelevationAOR>Sub-base Depth* and change the Value to **2.00'** and add an appropriate comment in the Comment space. Notice as you change the value, the section updates in the section editor.

11. Uncheck the True toggle as shown in Figure 8–67 and note how the section returns to its previous state.

Pave1 Depth	0.08		False	0.08	
Pave2 Depth	0.08'		False	0.08'	
Sub-base Depth	**2.00'**	ⓘ ☑	True	2.00'	Testing different dep
Width	15.50'		False	15.50'	

Figure 8–67

12. Close out of the *Parameter Editor* by clicking on the **X** in the upper right corner.

13. Close out of the *Section Editor* by clicking on the **green checkmark** in the upper right corner.

14. On the status bar, set your annotation scale back to **1"=60'**.

15. No need to save the drawing since you didn't make any changes.

8.6 Corridor Surfaces

The *Surfaces* tab in the Corridor Properties dialog box enables you to build the proposed surfaces based on corridor geometry. You can create these surfaces from corridor links, and/or from feature lines based on marker points (point codes). As the corridor changes, its surfaces automatically update.

The two most common types of corridor surfaces are Top and Datum surfaces.

- **Top surfaces:** Follow the uppermost geometry of the corridor. These are useful for many purposes, such as in the display of finished ground contours and as a way of determining rim elevations of proposed utility structures.

- **Datum surfaces:** Generally follow the bottommost corridor geometry, where the corridor and the existing surface meet. These can be used in both Surface-to-Surface volume calculations and Section-based Earthworks calculations to determine site cut and fill totals (when compared to existing ground).

Other surfaces may be created and assigned materials for rendering purposes. You can render using the Autodesk Civil 3D software, however better results are achieved when using rendering specific programs like Autodesk® 3DS Max®, Autodesk Navisworks®, etc.

You can create Corridor Surfaces using the right-click menu of a selected corridor, the corridor's contextual ribbon, or the Corridor Properties dialog box.

Corridor surfaces: As with all Autodesk Civil 3D surfaces, these cannot contain vertical elements. Include slight offsets so that vertical curbing and similar geometry are not absolutely vertical.

Overhang Correction

In some configurations, Autodesk Civil 3D assemblies might have top or datum points, or links in locations that might lead to incorrect surfaces, such as the datum surface represented by the heavy line in Figure 8–68.

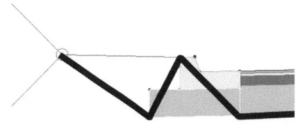

Figure 8–68

In these cases, the **Overhang Correction** option forces these surfaces to follow either the top or bottom of the corridor geometry, as shown in Figure 8–69. This setting is typically only required for Top and Datum surfaces.

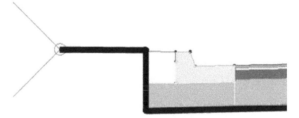

Figure 8–69

Surface Boundaries

Corridor surfaces, as with all Autodesk Civil 3D surfaces, often benefit from a boundary to remove unwanted interpolation between points. The *Boundaries* tab in the Corridor Surfaces dialog box enables you to add these boundaries in a number of ways: by selecting a closed polyline or by interactively tracing the boundary using a jig.

The best option for Top and Datum surfaces is often to *automatically* add a boundary that follows the daylight feature lines on both sides. This can be done using the new **Create Boundary from Corridor Extents** command.

For rendering specific surfaces (such as Asphalt, Concrete, etc.), you need to either trace the boundary or pick a polyline representing the boundary.

Practice 8e | Corridor Surfaces

Practice Objective

*   Create a finished ground surface from the design corridor.

Task 1 - Adjust corridor regions.

1. Continue working with the drawing from the previous practice or open **COR1-F.dwg**.

2. In the AutoCAD Model Space window, select the **Ascent Pl corridor**. Note the diamond grips on either end of the corridor. Select the end (top) grip and stretch the corridor so it reaches the beginning of the cul-de-sac. For the beginning (bottom) grip, move it until it starts at the end of the Intersection, as shown in Figure 8–70.

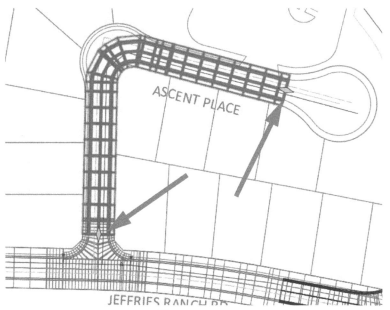

Figure 8–70

3. Select the north portion of the **Rand Boulevard** corridor and adjust where it overlaps with the roundabout by dragging the grips to the edge of the roundabout, as shown in Figure 8–71.

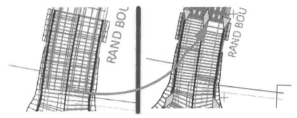

Figure 8–71

4. Press <Esc> to deselect the corridor.

5. Select the west (left) side of the **Jeffries Ranch Rd** corridor and adjust it in a similar matter, as shown in Figure 8–72.

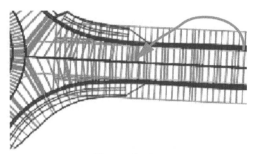

Figure 8–72

6. In the Event Viewer, expand **Action** and select **Clear All Events**. Click the **X** to close the Event Viewer.

7. Press <Esc> to deselect the corridor.

8. Select the roundabout and note the different grips. Select the triangular grip at the upper part of the eastern (right) arm. Drag it so it no longer overlaps with the Jeffries Ranch Rd corridor. Repeat for the lower part, as shown on the right side of Figure 8–73.

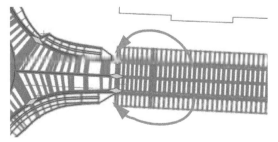

Figure 8–73

The Event Viewer tells you there is a problem at the far eastern end of **Jeffries Ranch Rd**.

9. Press <Esc> to deselect the corridor.

10. In the Event Viewer, expand **Action** and select **Clear All Events**. Click the **X** to close the Event Viewer.

11. Time permitting, adjust the other two arms in a similar matter. It can get confusing and complicated, so they have been adjusted for you in the next drawing, if needed. The final adjustments should look like Figure 8–74.

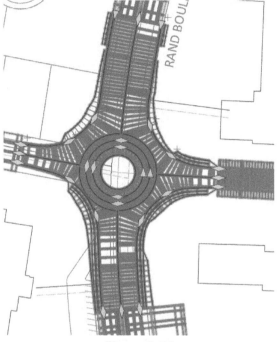

Figure 8–74

Task 2 - Create corridor surfaces.

1. Continue working with the drawing from the previous task if you successfully matched up the corridors. If you did not complete that step, open **COR1-F1.dwg**.

2. Select the **Ascent Place** corridor.

3. Click (Corridor Properties) on the *Corridor* contextual tab>Modify Corridor panel.

4. In the *Surfaces* tab, do the following, as shown in Figure 8–75:

- Click 🏠 (Create a Corridor Surface).
- The surface displays in the dialog box with the default name **Ascent PI Surface - (1)**. Rename the surface to **Ascent PI Top** by clicking on the surface name.
- The default surface style **ASC_Contours 2' and 10' (Design)** works well for this task, so leave it as the active surface style.
- In the *Add Data* area, verify that the *Data type* is set to **Links** and the *code* is set to **Top**. Click ➕ (Add Surface Item).

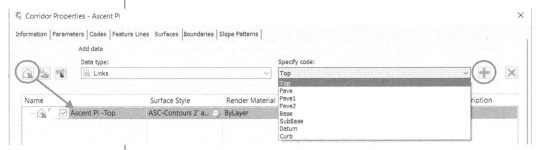

Figure 8–75

5. Set the *Overhang Correction* to **Top Links**.

6. Select the *Boundaries* tab. Right-click on the corridor surface name and select **Corridor extents as outer boundary**, as shown in Figure 8–76.

This automatically adds a boundary that follows the corridor extents (in most cases, the daylight lines) on both sides.

Figure 8–76

7. Click **OK** to close the Corridor Properties dialog box. If prompted, select **Rebuild the Corridor**.

8. In the Event Viewer, click the **X** to close the Event Viewer.

9. Repeat the same procedure for Jeffries Ranch Rd, both for a Top surface and a Datum surface. This time, select the Jeffries Ranch Rd corridor and in the contextual ribbon, pick Corridor Surfaces, as shown in Figure 8–77.

Figure 8–77

10. Name them *Jeffries Ranch Rd Top* and *Jeffries Ranch Rd Datum*, give them the appropriate **Overhang Corrections** and **Surface Styles,** as shown in Figure 8–78. You will use the Datum Surface to compute earthwork quantities.

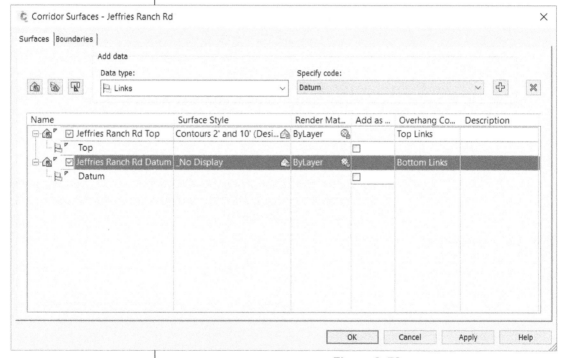

Figure 8–78

11. Remember to give boundaries to these two surfaces and apply them as **Corridor extents as outer boundary**.

12. Click **OK** to close the Corridor Properties dialog box. If prompted, select **Rebuild the Corridor**. The corridor surface has been created and displays using contours.

*The Event Viewer tells you there is a problem at the far eastern end of **Jeffries Ranch Rd**.*

13. In the Event Viewer, expand **Action** and select **Clear All Events**. Click the **X** to close the Event Viewer.

14. Save and close the drawing.

8.7 Sample Line Groups

Sample lines are objects that sample corridor elements for display in cross-sections and are used to form the basis of material lists that are used in corridor volumetric calculations. Sections are organized into groups for ease of selection and for managing common properties. A drawing can have any number of sample line groups for the same alignment.

Sample lines can be included in Data Shortcuts and referenced into your production drawings.

The **Sample Lines** command is located in the *Home* tab>Profile & Section Views panel, as shown in Figure 8–79.

Figure 8–79

Selecting this command opens the Create Sample Line Group dialog box, as shown in Figure 8–80.

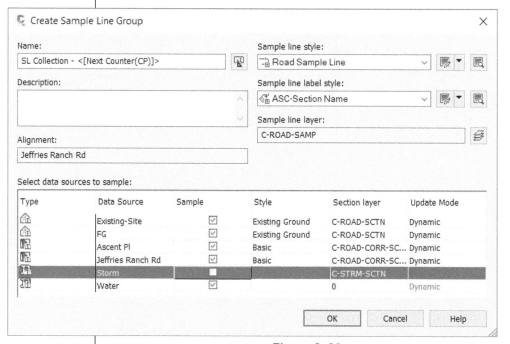

Figure 8–80

The Create Sample Line Group dialog box identifies all of the elements that might be included in the section:

-  (corridor geometry)

- (terrain surfaces)

- (corridor surfaces)

- (pipe networks).

The *Select data sources to sample* area displays:

- The object type
- Where the object comes from
- Whether or not to sample the object
- The style to use for the sections
- The preferred layers
- The update mode for the section.

After adjusting the values for the Create Sample Line dialog box and clicking **OK**, the Sample Line Tools toolbar becomes active, as shown in Figure 8–81.

Figure 8–81

The Sample Line Tools toolbar is the control center for creating sample lines. The default method is **At a Station**, as shown in Figure 8–82, which means you are able to select a specific station at which to add a sample line.

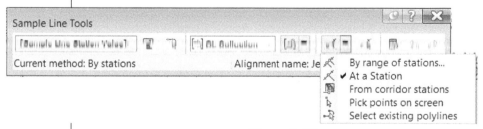

Figure 8–82

Other methods include:

- **By range of stations:** Enables you to specify a range of stations, sampling width, and other options where you want sample lines to be created. Sampling increments can be relative to an absolute station, or relative to a station range set.

- **From corridor stations:** Creates a sample line at all of the predefined corridor sections. This method also opens the Create Sample Line dialog box in which you can define the station range and swath widths for the sections.

- **Pick points on screen:** Enables you to select points in the drawing to define the path of the section. This type of section can have multiple vertices.

- **Select existing polylines:** Includes section lines based on existing polylines in the drawing. The polyline does not have to be perpendicular to the center line and can have multiple segments.

The dialog box that opens for the **By range of stations** option is shown in Figure 8–83.

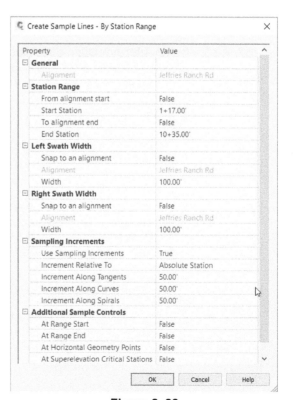

Figure 8–83

After creating the sample line group, the Toolspace, *Prospector* tab lists the individual sample lines under the sample line group's name. Each entry in the list includes all of the sampled elements for a section, as shown in Figure 8–84.

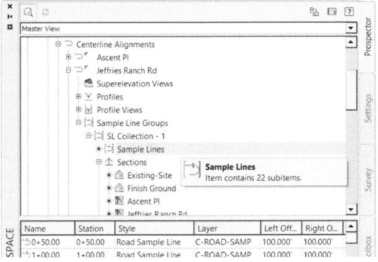

Figure 8–84

Modifying Sample Line Groups

New sample line groups can be added, existing groups can be deleted, swath widths (section sample width) can be adjusted, and new data sources can be added (such as newly created pipe networks) using the Modify drop-down list in the Sample Line Tools toolbar or the *Sample Line* contextual tab, as shown in Figure 8–85.

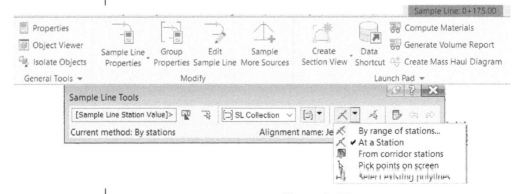

Figure 8–85

Sample line properties (such as display styles) can also be adjusted through the sample line group's properties, in the Toolspace, *Prospector* tab.

Practice 8f

Creating Sample Lines

Practice Objective

- Create sample lines and review sample line data in preparation for creating cross-section sheets.

Task 1 - Corridor Section Editor.

1. Do not continue from the previous drawing. Open **COR1-G.dwg** from the *C:\Civil 3D Projects\Working\ Corridors* folder.

2. In this drawing, the Ascent Pl corridor has also been completed with the knuckle at the bend and a bulb in the cul-de-sac. The top and datum surfaces for Rand Boulevard have also been added.

3. Change the *Annotation Scale* to **1"=30'** in the Status Bar, which is a scale more appropriate for displaying cross-sections.

4. Hover the cursor over the Data Shortcuts and review the tooltip which displays, shown in Figure 8–86. Ensure that your Data Shortcuts are set so the **Working Folder** is set to *C:\Civil 3D Projects\Data Shortcuts\Fundamentals* and the **Data Shortcuts Project Folder** to *Ascent-Development*. If required, right-click on Data Shortcuts to set the **Working Folder** and **Data Shortcuts Project Folder**.

Figure 8–86

5. Select the preset view **Corr-QTO**

6. In the *Home* tab>Profile and Section Views panel, click  (Sample Lines).

7. When prompted to select an alignment, press <Enter> and select **Jeffries Ranch Rd** from the long alignment list. Click **OK** to exit the dialog box.

The Create Sample Line Group dialog box opens, listing multiple data sources.

8. Verify that the *Sample* column is cleared for all but the following, as shown in Figure 8–87:

- **Existing-Site**
- **Jeffries Ranch Rd** (corridor)
- **Jeffries Ranch Rd Top**
- **Jeffries Ranch Rd Datum**

Leave the other settings at their defaults and click **OK**.

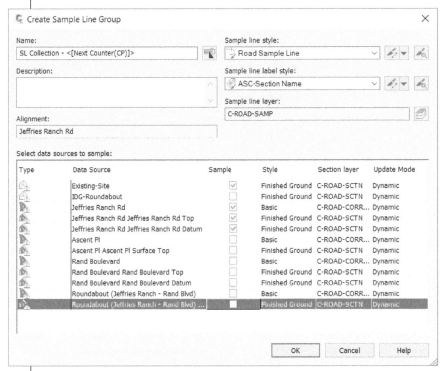

Figure 8–87

9. In the Sample Line Tools toolbar, select to create sample lines **By range of stations…**, as shown in Figure 8–88.

Figure 8–88

10. In the Create Sample Lines dialog box, do the following, as shown in Figure 8–89:

- Under *Station Range*, set *From alignment start* and *To alignment end* to **False**.
- Set the *Start Station* to **117'** and the *End Station* to **1035'**.
- Set both the Left and Right Swath Width[s] to **100'**.
- Under *Sampling Increments*, check that *Increment Along Tangents* and *Increments Along Curves* is set to **50'**.

This is because the alignment extends beyond the design ground data.

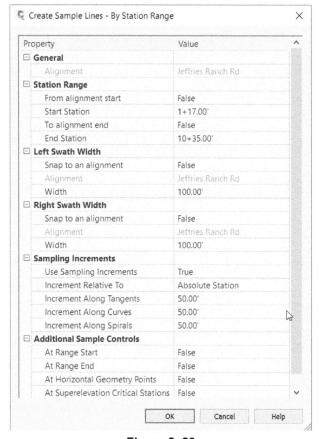

Property	Value
⊟ **General**	
Alignment	Jeffries Ranch Rd
⊟ **Station Range**	
From alignment start	False
Start Station	1+17.00'
To alignment end	False
End Station	10+35.00'
⊟ **Left Swath Width**	
Snap to an alignment	False
Alignment	Jeffries Ranch Rd
Width	100.00'
⊟ **Right Swath Width**	
Snap to an alignment	False
Alignment	Jeffries Ranch Rd
Width	100.00'
⊟ **Sampling Increments**	
Use Sampling Increments	True
Increment Relative To	Absolute Station
Increment Along Tangents	50.00'
Increment Along Curves	50.00'
Increment Along Spirals	50.00'
⊟ **Additional Sample Controls**	
At Range Start	False
At Range End	False
At Horizontal Geometry Points	False
At Superelevation Critical Stations	False

Create Sample Lines - By Station Range ×

OK   Cancel   Help

Figure 8–89

11. Click **OK** when done. The sample lines are created, but no labels are assigned yet because Civil 3D is prompting you for more locations.

12. In the Command Line, press <Enter> to finish placing sample lines and to close the dialog box. Now the sample line labels appear, as shown in Figure 8–90.

JEFFRIES RANCH RD

Figure 8–90

13. Save the drawing.

Task 2 - Review Sample Line data.

1. In the Toolspace, *Prospector* tab, expand the *Alignment* collection, expand the *Centerline Alignments* collection, expand the *Jeffries Ranch Rd* collection, expand the *Sample Line Groups* collection, and select **SL Collection-1**, as shown in Figure 8–91.

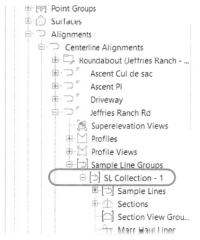

Figure 8–91

2. Right-click and select **Properties**. In the Sample Line Group Properties dialog box, in the *Sections* tab, you can re-assign styles and layers, and add new data sources.

3. Click **Sample more sources...** in the top right corner.

4. Review the Section Sources dialog box, as shown in Figure 8–92. Click **OK** to exit.

Later on when the pipe networks are created, you will need to add them to this list so they will appear in the section views.

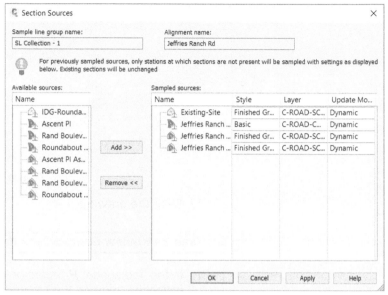

Figure 8–92

5. In the Sample Line Group Properties dialog box, the *Sample Lines* tab enables you to change the swath widths of individual sections numerically. Click **OK** to exit.

6. Save the drawing.

8.8 Section Volume Calculations

Two types of quantity takeoffs can be calculated based on sections: earthwork volumes and material volumes. Earthwork volumes represent the amount of cut (existing material above the vertical design) or fill (the vertical design above the existing material). Material volumes are the amount of materials required to build the road. Materials include asphalt pavement, concrete curbing, sub-base materials, and other materials.

Earthwork Volumes

Earthwork volumes represent an amount of displaced surface materials. The displacement represents the excavation of high areas or filling of low areas in the existing ground surface, relative to the vertical road design.

One goal road designers strive for is to balance the amount of excavated material (called cut) and the amount of material to be added (called fill). On any site, not all of the excavated material (cut) is reusable. For example, the spoil materials could be from a bog, a type of material that does not compact well, or rock debris. The reuse of cut material can be a percentage of the overall cut value and affects the overall earthwork calculation. An example is shown in Figure 8–93.

Figure 8–93

Earthworks calculations are applied between the existing ground surface and the datum surface of an assembly. Note that the Datum Link is the last link of the assembly, and thus the corridor.

The datum surface represents the roadbed on which the sub-base gravel, asphalt, and concrete materials lie. Earthwork volumes affect the revisions that occur to a roadway design. For example, excessive cut material (i.e., material needing excavation) could lead to raising the vertical design or, if possible, moving the horizontal alignment to create less cut.

The datum is basically where the underside of the proposed corridor meets the existing surface.

Mass Haul

A mass haul diagram can be generated and used as a visual representation of the cumulative cut and fill material volumes along a corridor. Contractors use mass haul diagrams as a primary tool in determining and balancing haulage costs when bidding on an earthwork job. Mass haul is the volume of excavated material multiplied by the distance it is required to be moved. When the mass haul line is above the balance line, it indicates how much cut there is going to be at that station. When the mass haul line is below the balance line, it indicates the volume to be filled. To generate a mass haul diagram, you need an alignment, a sample line group, and a materials list. The mass haul diagram calculates and displays the following:

- The distance over which cut and fill volumes balance.

- Free haul and overhaul volumes.

- Volumes offset by borrow pits and dump sites.

Construction costs can be reduced by enabling the designer to compare alternative designs, add dump sites, and borrow pits at key locations in the free haul distance, thus eliminating a portion of the overhaul volume. An example of a mass haul diagram is shown in Figure 8–94.

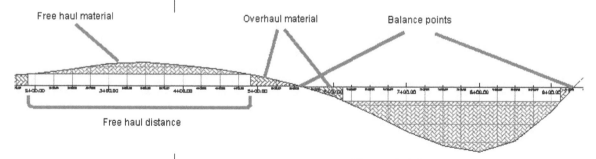

Figure 8–94

Material Volumes

Subassembly shapes represent the materials available for quantity takeoffs. These quantities come from the subassembly shapes (e.g., curb, pave, shoulder, sidewalk, etc.).

Quantity Takeoff Criteria

The Quantity Takeoff Criteria defines the surfaces and materials to be analyzed. Takeoff criteria can identify two surfaces for earthwork calculations and a list of shapes for material volumes.

The criteria style entries are generic because they are intended to be used on multiple corridors, which might contain different subassembly components. When computing section calculations, you are prompted to identify which entries correspond to the corridor shapes. The Quantity Takeoff Criteria dialog box is shown in Figure 8–95.

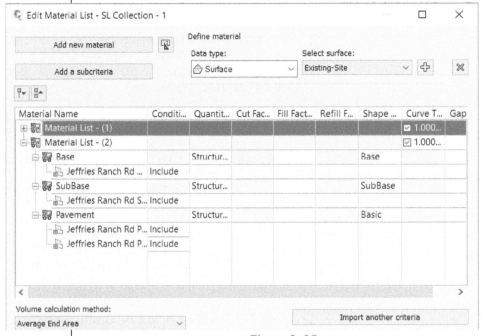

Figure 8–95

Define Materials

After defining the volume criteria, you create data from the criteria settings. In the *Analyze* tab>Volumes and Materials panel, click  (Compute Materials) to set the alignment and a sample line group to use for data extraction. The command is shown in Figure 8–96.

Figure 8–96

When the Edit Material List dialog box opens, you can associate surfaces and/or structures (subassembly shapes) to the appropriate entries. Click **OK** to exit. The Autodesk Civil 3D software then calculates the required report data.

Practice 8g

Compute Materials

Practice Objective

- Calculate quantities of a corridor and display them.

Task 1 - Generate earthworks quantities.

In this task, you will compute the site cut and fill required to create the datum surface below the corridor. You will then calculate the construction materials that will be placed above the datum (asphalt, gravel, etc.).

1. Continue with the previous drawing or open **COR1-H.dwg** from the *C:\Civil 3D Projects\Working\Corridors* folder.

2. In the *Analyze* tab>Volumes and Materials panel, click

    (Compute Materials), as shown in Figure 8–97.

Figure 8–97

3. In the Select Sample Line Group dialog box, accept the default alignment **Jeffries Rand Rd** and sample line group **SL Collection - 1**, as shown in Figure 8–98. Click **OK**.

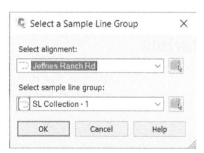

Figure 8–98

4. In the Compute Materials dialog box, select **Existing-Site** for the *EG* and **Jeffries Ranch Rd Datum** for the *DATUM*, as shown in Figure 8–99. Click **OK** when done.

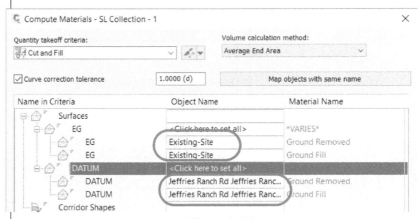

Figure 8–99

5. Generate a volume report. In the *Analyze* tab>Volumes and Materials panel, click 🖼️ (Volume Report).

6. In the Report Quantities dialog box, ensure that you select the correct XSL file. Click 📂 next to the *Select a style sheet* field, as shown on the left in Figure 8–100. Browse to and select **earthwork.xsl**, as shown on the right, and open it. Click **OK** to close the Report Quantities dialog box.

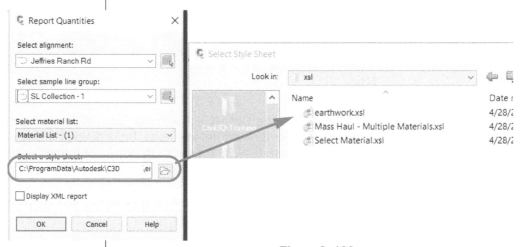

Figure 8–100

7. Internet Explorer will open when the HTML format report is created. Depending on your Internet Explorer security settings, you might be prompted to permit the script to run. Click **Yes** if this prompt displays. Your report displays similar to that shown in Figure 8–101.

Volume Report

Project: C:\Civil 3D Projects\References\DWG\Proposed\Corridor-Complete.dwg
Alignment: Jeffries Ranch Rd
Sample Line Group: SL Collection - 1
Start Sta: 1+50.000
End Sta: 10+00.000

Station	Cut Area (Sq.ft.)	Cut Volume (Cu.yd.)	Reusable Volume (Cu.yd.)	Fill Area (Sq.ft.)	Fill Volume (Cu.yd.)	Cum. Cut Vol. (Cu.yd.)	Cum. Reusable Vol. (Cu.yd.)	Cum. Fill Vol. (Cu.yd.)	Cum. Net Vol. (Cu.yd.)
1+50.000	89.56	0.00	0.00	31.28	0.00	0.00	0.00	0.00	0.00
2+00.000	145.03	217.21	217.21	16.14	43.90	217.21	217.21	43.90	173.31
2+50.000	1199.74	1160.83	1160.83	5.11	18.87	1378.05	1378.05	62.77	1315.27
3+00.000	1334.47	2346.50	2346.50	35.97	38.03	3724.54	3724.54	100.81	3623.74
3+50.000	1262.57	2404.67	2404.67	239.57	255.13	6129.21	6129.21	355.94	5773.27
4+00.000	704.95	1821.78	1821.78	564.45	744.47	7950.99	7950.99	1100.41	6850.58
4+50.000	0.37	653.07	653.07	1194.30	1628.47	8604.06	8604.06	2728.88	5875.18
5+00.000	0.00	0.35	0.35	1271.33	2282.99	8604.41	8604.41	5011.87	3592.54
5+50.000	0.00	0.00	0.00	1579.50	2639.65	8604.41	8604.41	7651.52	952.89

Figure 8–101

8. Close the HTML report.

9. Create an AutoCAD table listing earthwork volumes. In the *Analyze* tab>Volumes and Materials panel, select **Total Volume Table**, as shown in Figure 8–102.

Figure 8–102

10. Pick the *Cut and Fill with Net* Table Style, and accept the other defaults in the Create Table dialog box, as shown in Figure 8–103, and click **OK**. When prompted, click in empty space to create the table.

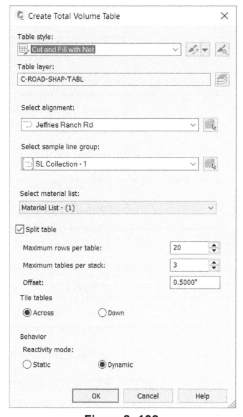

Figure 8–103

11. Select a point in Model Space to insert the table, as shown in Figure 8–104. Note that the top left of the table is the reference point.

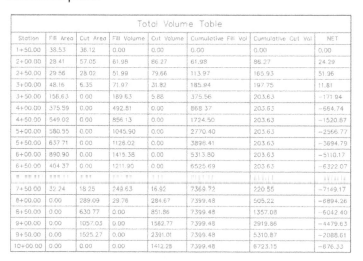

Station	Fill Area	Cut Area	Fill Volume	Cut Volume	Cumulative Fill Vol	Cumulative Cut Vol	NET
1+50.00	38.53	36.12	0.00	0.00	0.00	0.00	0.00
2+00.00	28.41	57.05	61.98	86.27	61.98	86.27	24.29
2+50.00	29.56	28.02	51.99	79.66	113.97	165.93	51.96
3+00.00	48.16	6.35	71.97	31.82	185.94	197.75	11.81
3+50.00	158.63	0.00	189.63	5.88	375.56	203.63	−171.94
4+00.00	375.59	0.00	492.81	0.00	868.37	203.63	−664.74
4+50.00	549.02	0.00	856.13	0.00	1724.50	203.63	−1520.87
5+00.00	580.55	0.00	1045.90	0.00	2770.40	203.63	−2566.77
5+50.00	637.71	0.00	1128.02	0.00	3898.41	203.63	−3694.79
6+00.00	890.90	0.00	1415.38	0.00	5313.80	203.63	−5110.17
6+50.00	404.37	0.00	1211.90	0.00	6525.69	203.63	−6322.07
8+00.00	0.00	0.00	0.00	1.11	0.00	0.00	0.00
7+50.00	32.24	18.25	249.63	16.92	7369.72	220.55	−7149.17
8+00.00	0.00	289.09	29.76	284.67	7399.48	505.22	−6894.26
8+50.00	0.00	630.77	0.00	851.86	7399.48	1357.08	−6042.40
9+00.00	0.00	1057.03	0.00	1582.77	7399.48	2919.86	−4479.63
9+50.00	0.00	1525.27	0.00	2391.01	7399.48	5310.87	−2088.61
10+00.00	0.00	0.00	0.00	1412.28	7399.48	6723.15	−676.33

Figure 8–104

12. Save the drawing.

Task 2 - Calculate material quantities.

Your assemblies include five defined shapes: Pave1 and Pave2 (the top two courses), Base, Sub-base, and Curb. The default Material List only includes one material for Pavement so you will need to adjust it. You will not calculate curb volume at this time.

1. In the *Analyze* tab>Volumes and Materials panel, click

    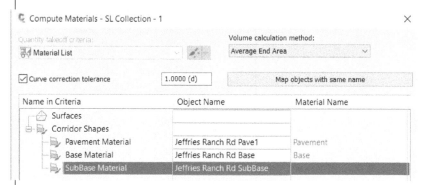 (Compute Materials).

2. In the Select Sample Line Group dialog box, accept the default alignment **Jeffries Ranch Rd** and sample line group **SL Collection - 1**, and click **OK**.

3. In the Edit Material List dialog box, click **Import another criteria**.

4. In the Select a Quantity Takeoff Criteria, select **Material List** and click **OK**.

5. In the Compute Materials dialog box, shown in Figure 8–105:

    - For *Pavement Material*, select **Jeffries Ranch Rd Pave1**.
    - For *Base Material*, select **Jeffries Ranch Rd Base**.
    - For *SubBase Material*, select **Jeffries Ranch Rd SubBase**.
    - Click **OK**.

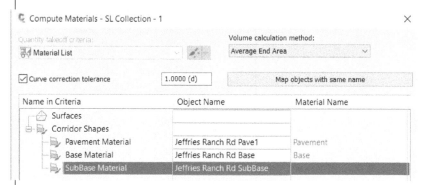

Figure 8–105

6. Click **OK** to close the dialog box and calculate the material.

7. Generate a volume report. In the *Analyze* tab>Volumes and Materials panel, select **Volume Report**.

8. In the Report Quantities dialog box, select **Material List - (2)** and ensure that you select the correct XSL file in the Select a style sheet drop-down list. Click [icon] next to the drop-down list. Browse to and select **Select Material.xsl** and open it. Click **OK** to close the Report Quantities dialog box.

9. Internet Explorer will open as the Autodesk Civil 3D software creates an HTML format report. Depending on your Internet Explorer security settings, you might be prompted to permit the script to run. Click **Yes** if this prompt displays. The report will display with the volume of Pavement 1 from your corridor, as shown in Figure 8–106.

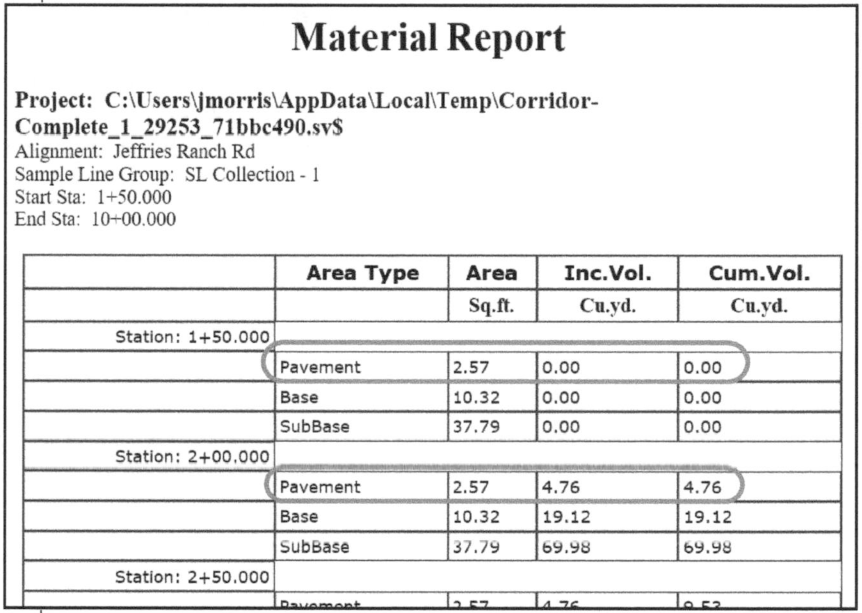

Material Report

Project: C:\Users\jmorris\AppData\Local\Temp\Corridor-Complete_1_29253_71bbc490.sv$
Alignment: Jeffries Ranch Rd
Sample Line Group: SL Collection - 1
Start Sta: 1+50.000
End Sta: 10+00.000

	Area Type	Area	Inc.Vol.	Cum.Vol.
		Sq.ft.	Cu.yd.	Cu.yd.
Station: 1+50.000				
	Pavement	2.57	0.00	0.00
	Base	10.32	0.00	0.00
	SubBase	37.79	0.00	0.00
Station: 2+00.000				
	Pavement	2.57	4.76	4.76
	Base	10.32	19.12	19.12
	SubBase	37.79	69.98	69.98
Station: 2+50.000				
	Pavement	2.57	4.76	9.53

Figure 8–106

10. Close the HTML report.

The road design, specifically the corridor assembly, has a second shape called Pave 2. This is also Pavement, but might be based on a different composition than Pave 1. You can quantify this value as a separate amount, but for demonstration purposes, you will create a total volume for Pavement.

11. In the *Analyze* tab>Volumes and Materials panel, click [icon] (Compute Materials).

12. In the Select Sample Line Group dialog box, accept the defaults and click **OK**.

13. In the Edit Material List dialog box, shown in Figure 8–107:

- In the *Name* column, select **Pavement**. Click 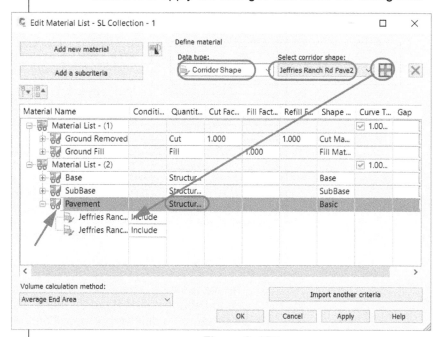 (Delete).
- Click **Add new material**.
- Click on the new material name and rename it **Pavement**.
- In the *Quantity Type* column, select **Structures**.
- In the Data type drop-down list, select **Corridor Shape**.
- In the Select corridor shape drop-down list, select **Jeffries Ranch Rd Pave 1**.
- Click ➕ to add **Jeffries Ranch Rd Pave 1** to the *Pavement* collection.
- In the Select corridor shape drop-down list, select **Jeffries Ranch Rd Pave 2**.
- Click ➕ to add **Jeffries Ranch Rd Pave 2** to the *Pavement* collection.
- Click **OK** to apply the changes and close the dialog box.

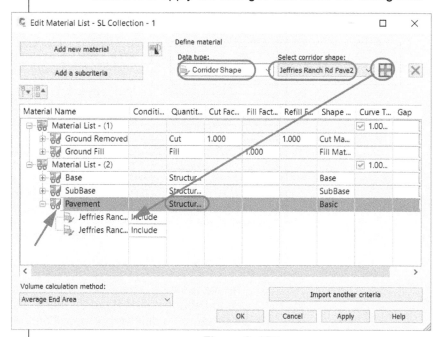

Figure 8–107

14. As in Steps 8 to 10, generate a volume report. In the *Analyze* tab>Volumes and Materials panel, select **Volume Report**.

- In the Report Quantities dialog box, ensure that you select the correct XSL file in the Select a style sheet drop-down list. Click 📂 next to the drop-down list. Browse to and select **Select Material.xsl** and open it. Click **OK** to close the Report Quantities dialog box.

- Internet Explorer will open as the Autodesk Civil 3D software creates an HTML format report. Depending on your Internet Explorer security settings, you might be prompted to permit the script to run. Click **Yes** if this prompt displays. Your report will display, as shown in Figure 8–108.

Material Report

Project: C:\Users\jmorris\AppData\Local\Temp\Corridor-Complete_1_29253_71bbc490.sv$
Alignment: Jeffries Ranch Rd
Sample Line Group: SL Collection - 1
Start Sta: 1+50.000
End Sta: 10+00.000

	Area Type	Area	Inc.Vol.	Cum.Vol.
		Sq.ft.	Cu.yd.	Cu.yd.
Station: 1+50.000				
	Base	10.32	0.00	0.00
	SubBase	37.79	0.00	0.00
	Pavement	5.15	0.00	0.00
Station: 2+00.000				
	Base	10.32	19.12	19.12
	SubBase	37.79	69.98	69.98
	Pavement	5.15	9.53	9.53
Station: 2+50.000				

Figure 8–108

15. Create drawing tables displaying this information, using the **Material Volume Table** command in the Volumes and Materials panel, for each material, as shown in Figure 8–109.

Figure 8–109

---

16. Be sure you select **Material List - (2)** and then select which material you want to create the table for, as shown in Figure 8–110.

Figure 8–110

17. Repeat these steps to create a table for each of the three materials, as shown in Figure 8–111.

Base Material Table			
Station	Area	Volume	Cumulative Volume
1+50.00	10.32	0.00	0.00
2+00.00	10.32	19.12	19.12
2+50.00	10.32	19.12	38.23
3+00.00	10.32	19.12	57.35
3+50.00	10.32	19.12	76.47
4+00.00	10.32	19.12	95.58
4+50.00	10.32	19.12	114.70
5+00.00	10.32	19.12	133.82
5+50.00	13.17	21.75	155.57

SubBase Material Table			
Station	Area	Volume	Cumulative Volume
1+50.00	37.79	0.00	0.00
2+00.00	37.79	69.98	69.98
2+50.00	37.79	69.98	139.96
3+00.00	37.79	69.98	209.94
3+50.00	37.79	69.98	279.92
4+00.00	37.79	69.98	349.90
4+50.00	37.79	69.98	419.88
5+00.00	37.79	69.98	489.86
5+50.00	47.45	78.94	568.80

Pavement Material Table			
Station	Area	Volume	Cumulative Volume
1+50.00	5.15	0.00	0.00
2+00.00	5.15	9.53	9.53
2+50.00	5.15	9.53	19.05
3+00.00	5.15	9.53	28.59
3+50.00	5.15	9.53	38.12
4+00.00	5.15	9.53	47.65
4+50.00	5.15	9.53	57.18
5+00.00	5.15	9.53	66.71
5+50.00	5.57	10.84	77.55

Figure 8–111

Task 3 - Changing code set styles.

The corridors are now designed and ready to be shared with the rest of the design team. Before you share the corridors you need to make some changes to their display, so as not to show the assemblies. You can also change the display of the assemblies. This is done with the appropriate code set styles.

1. Select all four corridors in the project.

2. In the *Properties* palette, under *Data*, click on the drop-down list for *Code Set Style* and select **ASC-All Codes - No Display**, as shown in Figure 8–112.

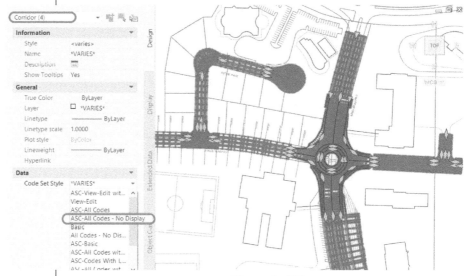

Figure 8–112

3. Note the changes in how the corridors are displayed.

4. Select the preset view **Assem-Residential**.

5. Change your drawing scale to **1"=40'**.

6. Select any one of the assemblies, and in the right-click menu, pick **Select Similar** (at the bottom of the list). This selects all assemblies in your drawing.

7. As you did above, change the *Code Set Styles* through the Properties palette. experiment with the different styles, and end up with **ASC-View-Edit**.

8. Save the drawing.

9. (Optional) Save the drawing as **<Your Initials>-Corridors-Complete.dwg** in the *C:\Civil 3D Projects\References\DWG\Proposed* folder.

10. Update the relative paths of the referenced drawings in the alert box.

11. (Optional) Add the four corridors and corridor surfaces to the project as Corridor Data Shortcuts.

Chapter Review Questions

1. Which of the following items must you have before you can create a corridor model? (Select all that apply.)

   a. Assembly

   b. Profile

   c. Survey Database

   d. Alignment or feature line

2. Which tab in the Create Intersection Wizard do you use to set the Curb Return Parameters?

   a. General

   b. Corridor Regions

   c. Geometry Details

3. Where would you go to create a surface representing the finished ground of a corridor model?

   a. Toolspace, *Prospector* tab>*Surfaces* collection

   b. *Home* tab>Create Ground Data panel

   c. *Home* tab>Create Design panel

   d. Corridor Properties

4. What does the Corridor Section Editor enable you to do?

   a. Review and edit each parameter of a subassembly.

   b. Adjust the existing ground grade at a specific station.

   c. Change the assembly being used at a specific station.

   d. Change the grid displayed behind a cross-section.

5. What does a mass haul diagram represent?

   a. The total cut and fill materials for a project site.

   b. The total weight of a corridor mass.

   c. The total weight that can be hauled on a corridor model.

   d. Cumulative cut and fill material volumes along a corridor.

6. What are sample line groups?

    a. Objects that sample corridor elements for cross-sections.

    b. Groups of lines where the surveyor sampled the soil.

    c. Lines connecting corridor points.

    d. Groups of lines that connect corridor shapes.

Command Summary

Button	Command	Location
	Compute Materials	• **Ribbon:** *Analyze* tab>Volumes and Materials panel • **Command Prompt:** ComputeMaterials
	Corridor Properties	• **Contextual Ribbon:** *Corridor* tab> Modify Corridor panel • **Command Prompt:** editcorridorproperties
	Corridor Section Editor	• **Contextual Ribbon:** *Corridor* tab> Modify Corridor Sections panel • **Command Prompt:** vieweditcorridorsection
	Create Corridor	• **Ribbon:** *Home* tab>Create Design panel • **Command Prompt:** createcorridor
	Create Intersection	• **Ribbon:** *Home* tab>Create Design panel • **Command Prompt:** createintersection
	Sample Lines	• **Ribbon:** *Home* tab>Profile & Section Views panel • **Command Prompt:** CreateSampleLines
	Select Similar Subassemblies	• **Contextual Ribbon:** *Assembly* tab> Modify Subassembly panel • **Command Prompt:** selectsimilarSA
	Subassembly Properties	• **Contextual Ribbon:** *Assembly* tab> Modify Subassembly panel • **Command Prompt:** editsubassemblyproperties
	Tool Palettes	• **Ribbon:** *Home* tab>Palettes panel • **Command Prompt:** <Ctrl>+<3>

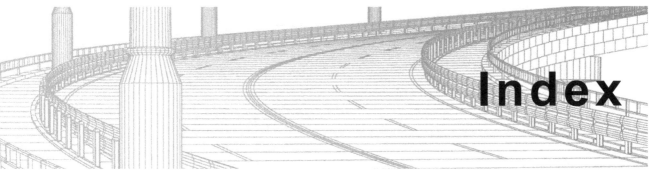

Index